THE WORLD'S GREAT
ARTILLERY
FROM THE MIDDLE AGES TO THE PRESENT DAY

THE WORLD'S GREAT
ARTILLERY
FROM THE MIDDLE AGES TO THE PRESENT DAY

HANS HALBERSTADT

Grange
BOOKS

This edition first published in 2002 for Grange Books
An imprint of Grange Books plc
The Grange
Kingsnorth Industrial Estate
Hoo, nr Rochester
Kent ME3 9ND
www.grangebooks.co.uk

ISBN 1-84013-478-X

Editorial and design by:
Amber Books Ltd
Bradley's Close
74-77 White Lion Street
London N1 9PF

Project Editor: Charles Catton
Editor: Siobhan O'Connor
Design: Graham Curd
Picture Research: Lisa Wren, Ken Botham

Printed and bound in Italy by: Eurolitho S.p.A., Cesano Boscone (MI)

Picture credits:

Aerospace Publishing: 48 (t), 51 (t), 55 (mr & br), 59 (b), 60(t), 62, 66–67 (all), 68 (b), 69 (both), 71 (b), 73 (both), 77 (b), 81 (both), 82, 85 (b), 87 (t), 89 (t), 90 (t), 92 (b),
94 (both), 97 (both), 107 (both), 110, 112 (both), 117, 145 (t), 151 (both), 153 (t), 155 (both), 159 (both), 168, 169, 172. Amber Books Ltd: 46, 121 (t), 127 (both), 142 (t),
153 (b), 161 (b), 165. John Bachelor: 8 (both), 9, 10, 11, 12, 13, 14, 15, 17 (br), 19, 20 (both), 21 (t), 23 (t), 26, 30(t), 34 (b), 38 (both), 43 (t), 52 (t), 63, 103, 121 (b), 129, 133,
136 (t), 150, 174. Mary Evans Picture Library: 28 (b), 29, 30 (b), 32, 34–35, 36, 39, 40–41 (both), 42–43 (b). Christopher F. Foss: 164. TRH Pictures: 6–7, 16–17, 18, 21
(b), 22 (both), 23 (b), 24–25 (E. Nevill), 27 (E. Nevill), 28 (t), 31 (E. Nevill), 33 (USMC), 37 (E. Nevill), 44–45, 47, 48 (b), 49 (both), 50–51 (t & br), 52–53, 53 (t), 54–55,
56–57 (both), 58–59 (t), 60–61 (b), 64–65, 68 (t) (USNA), 70–71, 72, 74–75, 76–77, 78–79, 80, 83, 84, 85 (t), 86–87, 88–89, 89 (b), 90 (b), 91, 92 (t), 93, 95, 96 (USMC),
98–99 (USMC), 100–101 (USNA). 102 (USNA), 104–105 (USNA), 106, 108, 109 (USNA), 111 (USNA), 113 (USNA), 114–115, 116, 118–119, 120, 122–123 (both),
124–125 (both), 126, 128, 130, 131, 132 (both), 134, 135, 136–137 (b) (USMC), 138–139 (LTV), 140–141 (both), 142 (b), 143, 144, 145 (b), 146 (MLRS), 147, 148–149,
152, 154–155, 156–157 (Yves Debay), 158, 160–161 (GIAT), 162–163, 166–167 (USDoD), 170–171, 173 (BAEE).

Acknowledgements

Any book on artillery worth its propellant must first and foremost acknowledge a debt to Ian V. Hogg. No other author has studied this fascinating topic
in such depth and detail. His books have been the foundation for several chapters of this volume, particularly those on European systems from World War
I to the present. Also, thanks to Will Fowler; Loren Griffen; Jim Clark; the Korean War Veterans Association; the Heavy Artillery Alliance; the Old
Comrades Association of New Zealand (the Old Comrades merit a special salute for the most extensive and interesting artillery history site on the
Internet; particularly Wally Ruffell, the group historian.); Mike Green graciously shared his extensive library and insights; and, especially, to my
commander and wife of many years, April Halberstadt, for her supporting fires and precise corrections, the biggest salute of all.

A Note on Terminology

Artillerymen have a version of the English language all their own, with some unique definitions for common words. A glossary at the end of this book
will help with some of the arcane acronyms and many of the other terms and expressions are explained in the text. Some gunners, though, will object to
my use of the term 'weapon'. These artillerymen maintain that the real 'weapon' is the projectile. The rest of the world cannot look down the bore of a
large cannon without thinking that it and all its sisters and cousins are called weapons and that the ammunition used to feed it belongs in a different
category. For the purposes of this book I have used 'weapon' to describe the delivery device rather than the shot, shell, canister, smoke, illumination,
'nuke', or any other projectile. Readers will be driven mad by the similar designations for some different weapons, particularly German and American of
the World War II era. The US has, over the years, designated dozens of weapon systems 'M1', from rifles to huge cannon, and the Germans had several
different howitzers designated, for example, FH 17. I have attempted to keep them apart as much as possible. Finally, the field of artillery is far too big to
fit between the covers of any single book. This one includes some important ones and leaves others out, and if the reader's favourite has been somehow
neglected, we apologize. It will certainly be included in any future book.

Specifications and Data

Data and specs for weapons systems often vary considerably, based on the exact variant and, to some extent, the whim of the publisher of the data. The
information in this book comes primarily from Janes Information Services and Ian Hogg's many books, particularly *Twentieth Century Artillery*, published
by Grange Books (2000).

CONTENTS

CHAPTER ONE
SIGHTING SHOTS

Artillery has come a long way since the first experiments with gunpowder, bronze or iron tubes and crudely-shaped stone shot: now it is one of the most fearsome weapons available to a commander on the battlefield.

It has been nearly 40 years since I first became acquainted with artillery, but I remember it all quite vividly. It was a memorable experience. I was a young helicopter machine-gunner with a few minutes to kill. We had flown into a very remote Vietnamese Army camp, deep in the jungle, with a supply of live pigs, fish sauce and bags of rice. The pilots were off somewhere having lunch and a section of ARVN (Army of Vietnam) were firing 105mm (4.13in) howitzers at invisible targets far away, over a ridge, their rounds being corrected by an observer in an L-19 aircraft that was occasionally visible in the distance.

The guns were firing at high angles of elevation, directly over the entire camp. I watched the crews serve their weapons for a while, then found a comfy spot on the grass about 20m (21yd) in front of the gun line. With a flak jacket for a pillow, I amused myself for a while by watching the big projectiles zooming upwards through space. You can learn to watch projectiles in flight, even machine-gun bullets, if you know where to look and if the background is uncluttered. On this day, I watched the black dots soar up and over towards the ridgeline after every shot, until they were too small to see with the naked eye, a process that lasted perhaps a second or so for each rapidly disappearing projectile.

The pattern was somewhat monotonous. The gun crew would load, then receive its fire command. Next, the gun went 'BLAM!', the shell streaked away, and after a long interval would come the distant, muted, flat crump as the projectile detonated and the sound

■**LEFT: The storming of the Heights of Alma in the Crimea by the British 1st Division, shown here overcoming a Russian gun position. The gun's crew lie dead behind their weapon.**

travelled slowly back over the mountain. Then the pattern changed. I heard the fire command, then the BLAM, and watched the round as it began its journey when it suddenly erupted in a momentary flash of orange fire, followed by a puff of black smoke that quickly dissipated. I was trying to figure it all out when, out of a clear blue sky, it began to rain. The raindrops were made of steel and had sharp edges.

Like an idiot, I forgot about my body armour (under which I might have hidden at least part of myself) and watched and listened. Fragments of metal rained down on the outpost for what seemed like half a minute, the ones thrown upwards at the detonation taking forever to come back to earth. Bits and pieces kicked up dust all around me, around the bunkers, around my helicopter and around the amazed gun crew. That one round seemed as if it had saturated the entire army compound with shell fragments.

It was what is called a 'muzzle-premature' round, and they happen occasionally. I learned a lot from that experience. One was that, despite the rain of steel, nobody was hurt and no damage was done to anything in the compound. Most of the splinters were directed away from us, and the area behind the shell is the safest, with just 10 per cent or less of the fragments in the pattern when the shell burst. Artillery, as I learnt, is complicated, interesting and possibly even dangerous when you are the one on the firing side. It all depends on how it is used.

ARTILLERY DEFINED
In ancient times, it was easy enough to know what was artillery and what it wasn't; today, things are more complex. It used to be that an artillery weapon was a simple cannon of some sort; however,

'Mad Margaret'

Calibre: 640mm (25in)
Weight: 16,400kg (36,155lb)
Length: 5.1m (5.6yd)

Barrel length: 5.1m (5.6yd)
Effective range: n/a
Elevation: none

Traverse: none
Muzzle velocity: n/a
Country of origin: Burgundy

even then, some observers would quibble with you about cannon aboard ship versus cannon ashore. Today, the debate is even more complicated.

For the purposes of this work, artillery is considered to include weapons that are ground-based, crew-served and used at least part of the time against personnel targets. That leaves out a lot of weapons that look like cannon, act like cannon or execute missions that cannon have traditionally been assigned. In this latter category are the grenade launchers, such as the US Mk 19 and M203, both of which fire projectiles that look a lot like miniature artillery rounds, but that are normally operated by one man. Tank cannon are also omitted, despite all the family resemblance and overlap of mission, as they have a specialized mission that really needs a specialized book of its own.

This book, then, is about traditional tube and rocket artillery: guns, howitzers and battlefield surface-to-surface rockets, all of which require the services of a dedicated crew of specialist gunners. That alone is a very large subject, and, as Ian Hogg has observed, you have to draw the line somewhere.

ARTILLERY BASICS

One of the first things apprentice 'cannon-cockers' learn is the distinction between cannon, howitzer and mortar, the three basic types of tube artillery.

A cannon (also sometimes called a 'gun') is typically a high-velocity weapon with a long barrel, intended primarily for direct-fire engagements. The length of the barrel on a pure cannon is typically at least 20 times the diameter of the bore. Cannon have a flat trajectory and, prior to World War II, had very limited

elevation, up to 20 degrees or so. Modern cannon are rarely found any longer in the field artillery; instead, they are used in tanks such as the Abrams and Challenger, each firing projectiles at speeds of more than 1500m/sec (5000ft/sec). That velocity and trajectory are virtues in battles with armoured vehicles, but handicaps in many other kinds of engagement.

As a result, pure cannons have been rare on the battlefield, except in the anti-tank and anti-aircraft roles, for many years. Light cannon are classified as having bore diameters smaller than 100mm (3.93in), heavy cannon have bores up to about 122mm (4.80in), and super-heavy cannon are those of 150mm (5.91in) and more.

A howitzer looks very much like a cannon, but has a shorter barrel and can be used for both direct- and indirect fire

Muhammed's Great Gun

Calibre: 762mm (30in)
Weight: 18,264kg (40,265lb)
Length: n/a

Barrel length: 5.2m (5.69yd)
Effective range: n/a
Elevation: none

Traverse: none
Muzzle velocity: n/a
Country of origin: Ottoman Empire

missions. It has lower velocity and a steeper, more arcing trajectory than the cannon. Lower and slower are not usually virtues, except in tube artillery. Unless you are in a tank or combat vehicle, it is relatively easy to hide safely from cannon fire: all it takes is a small hill or a depression in the ground. If you are out of sight, you are usually out of danger from the traditional cannon. A howitzer's arcing trajectory, in contrast, can reach around behind that hill and pound anything that is hiding.

HOWITZERS AND MORTARS
Howitzer barrel lengths are normally shorter than cannon, usually between 12 and 20 calibres. Light howitzers are normally of 100mm (3.93in) calibre and below, mediums are those up to about 150mm (5.91in), the heavies are from about this up to 200mm (7.87in), and the super-heavies are the monsters bigger than that. The tubes on howitzers can be elevated to quite high angles, about 45 degrees and sometimes greater.

Mortars are artillery pieces designed for very high-angle fire from very short barrels. These barrels are normally less than 12 calibres in length and are designed to fire at elevations of 40 degrees to about 80 degrees. Light mortars today are about 60mm (2.36in) weapons, the mediums are about 80mm (3.15in) and the heavies are more than 100mm (3.93in). Mortars are still normally muzzle-loading smoothbores, the only ones left in common use today.

All of these classifications would be simple enough, except that for many years artillery designers have been combining elements of all three types, to the point where it is sometimes difficult to tell exactly what designation to give each weapon.

The United States fields two primary tube artillery weapons today, one 105mm (4.13in) and the other 155mm (6.10in). Like other modern weapons of the same calibres, both are hybrids with characteristics that combine the traditional flat-shooting gun and high-angle howitzer, an achievement attained by varying the amount of propellant behind the projectile.

This versatility enables the gun crew to execute a very dramatic and tactically useful kind of fire mission. This exercise is called time-on-target (TOT), and it puts two rounds on a visible target at the same moment from a single gun. Using data from the fire-direction centre (FDC), the gunners point the gun tube at a high angle and fire the first round on a high, long, low-velocity trajectory.

They then quickly reload with a high-velocity charge, re-lay the gun with a lower angle for the flatter trajectory, and fire the second round at precisely the correct moment. If they have fired correctly, both projectiles detonate at the same time, saturating the target with steel and fire. When a battery of M109 self-propelled gun-howitzers – all six of them – fire a TOT mission, and twelve 155mm (6.10in) high-explosive rounds detonate over an enemy position, the effect is lethal and awesome.

Even mortar design refuses to stand still. During World War I, huge weapons that looked like breech-loading howitzers were used; however, their extremely short barrels and high angle of fire qualified them as mortars. As the modern US 60mm (2.36in) mortar gunner can put the base of the tube against a tree and 'trigger fire' rounds at very low levels of elevation, just like a howitzer, it is no wonder that novice gunners are a little confused by it all.

KING OF BATTLE
The role of the big guns is an ancient and honourable one, going back to long before the introduction of gunpowder, cannon and rockets. The job has not changed very much in more than a thousand years. Now, as then, guns are a way of putting serious combat power on the battlefield in a decisive fashion. A thousand years ago, that meant using 'tension' artillery to fling massive rocks into or over the walls of fortifications or into massed formations of infantry.

It was an efficient method of killing people and destroying things, quickly and in large quantity. That's what war is about – making things simply too difficult for the other side to operate and imposing your will upon them. Artillery does that, whether it be by using massive rocks tossed by spring-tensioned *onagers* or 203mm (8in) cannon which fire nuclear projectiles.

Big guns put heavy pressure on an enemy at long range or across a broad front. A commander who has an efficient artillery organization – one that is well supplied, equipped and trained – can 'put steel on target' many miles away, far out of the sights of the guns and their gunners, and does this at critical times and places.

Bombard (1480)

Calibre: 200mm (7.8in)
Weight: n/a
Length: n/a
Barrel length: n/a

Effective range: 200–300m
(218–328yd) (est)
Elevation: none
Traverse: none

Muzzle velocity: 100m/s
(328ft/sec) (est)
Country of origin: Italy

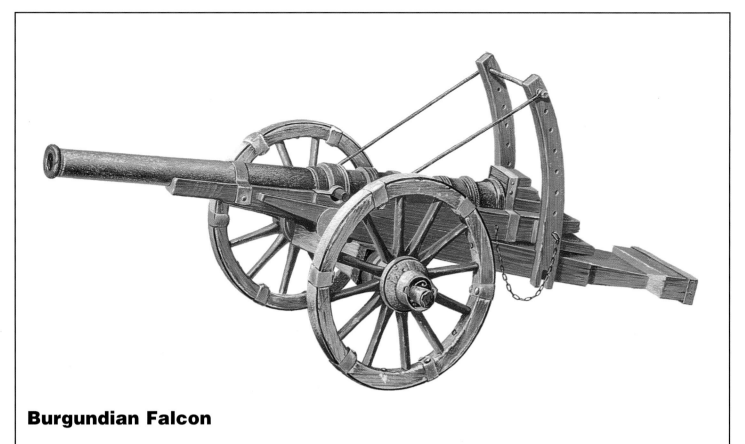

Burgundian Falcon

Calibre: 75mm (2.95in) (est)
Weight: 500kg (1100lb) (est)
Length: 3m (3.2yd) (est)

Barrel length: 2m (2.2yd) (est)
Effective range: 300m (est)
Elevation: 0° to 40° (est)

Traverse: none
Muzzle velocity: n/a
Country of origin: Burgundy

A modern multiple-launch rocket system, the MLRS, which is used by most NATO nations, can saturate a target 100m (110yd) wide and 200m (220yd) long with small, lethal submunitions. Every shot has enough capability to kill a person and destroy any vehicle which happens to be present in that large area at a maximum distance of 42km (26 miles). Each MLRS carries six rockets, ready to fire, and can fire them all in a salvo that will destroy an entire enemy battalion in an assembly area.

Combat power of that magnitude which is delivered at such great ranges, does more than kill people and wreck equipment: the killing power shocks enemy soldiers and their commanders, making them doubt their ability to survive and prevail. Simply facing the existence of such systems forces the enemy commander to keep his distance, as well as inhibiting his actions and tempering his resolve.

The failure of the enemy's resolve, the spirit that makes the difference between defeat and victory, is the real objective of any artillery attack, a principle that is as true today as it was in the American Civil War of the 1860s.

Artillery today still engages point targets, such as fortifications, vehicles, aircraft and facilities. It also engages area targets, such as assembly areas, enemy troops in the open or in prepared positions, convoys and armour units on the move or camped in hiding places. Artillery can search with fire and can suppress enemy activity by placing both direct- and indirect fire. While artillery alone does not win wars, it has been essential to every major land conflict of the past 1000 years.

THE PRE-GUNPOWDER ERA

Long before the first primitive cannon fired the first tiny cannonball, artillery was an important part of battle. Siege engines using levers and gravity, or tensioned cords, were used against both point and area targets 2000 years ago.

The simplest of these siege engines was probably the *onager*, from the Greek 'wild ass', used by the Romans to lob rocks into besieged towns and fortifications. Roman soldiers also used *ballistas* to throw 27kg (60lb) projectiles 477m (500yd). These were kinetic energy weapon with a performance which, even by today's standards, would be considered

respectable, even if it did take all day to get off a second shot.

That kind of retained energy does serious damage; back then, it would easily punch through masonry walls. A normal structure would be demolished with the first shot; a castle wall would take some time and repeated impacts, but a *ballista* was capable of making a breach through which infantry could then make their assault.

Romans also used the catapult, a large version of the crossbow and a terrifying anti-personnel weapon which was used against massed infantry at long range. This was one of the pioneer 'point target' crew-served weapons, capable of shooting hefty spears over long distances and sometimes even managing to skewer the enemy's soldiers.

The crowning glory of the pre-gunpowder era, though, was a huge and powerful device known as a *trebuchet*. These weapons could easily throw 37kg (100lb) rocks over castle walls to ranges of 457m (500yd). They were slow to load, immobile, and difficult to aim, but accepted a wide range of projectiles. Besides large rocks, *trebuchet* gunners used their huge machine to fling dead animals, live prisoners and burning objects into space and down inside besieged castles. We can do a lot with modern weapons, but none of them equals the versatility of the *trebuchet* when it comes to ammunition.

ARTILLERY DEVELOPMENT

There is some dispute about the actual origins of gunpowder and its use in guns. Conventional wisdom reports that it was a Chinese invention, and so it surely was.

The Chinese, however, may not have linked its use to guns, using it instead in fireworks until they began importing firearms from Europe during the 1400s. The English Franciscan monk Roger Bacon described a formula for gunpowder in the early 14th century:– ' … seven parts saltpetre, five of young hazlewood (charcoal), and five of sulphur … '. Other written accounts of its use in Europe are also to be found.

When this compound was ignited in a confined space, people noticed. The reason for this is that traditional gunpowder – or 'black' powder – when ignited expands to about 4000 times its volume in a very short period of time. The sudden expansion and increase in pressure must have propelled all sorts of things purely by accident until the power of the substance was put to work under controlled conditions for the first time.

Small arms (i.e., firearms used by a single soldier) were possibly in use by 1284, but there is some doubt about early references on the topic, and another suggested reference to cannon and powder at Ghent in 1313 is also suspect. There is no doubt, however, that just a few years later, in 1326, the city of Florence was paying for the construction of cannon and manufacture of gunpowder. A year later, English forces in Scotland may have used guns of some kind, and in 1331 cannon were certainly employed in Italy at the siege of Cividale.

In 1339, the first cast guns were made. Using techniques adapted from the casting of church bells, artillery weapons were cast, again with bronze, a material with a low melting point and considerable toughness. These little vaselike devices, 'pot-de-fer', were used by French raiders in an attack on Southampton, England, and again in 1339 against the English under King Edward III.

Although some of the smaller weapons of the very early years were apparently cast of bronze, most artillery tubes of the first-generation technology were built exactly like barrels and of the same materials: wooden staves supported by metal bands. This system of manufacture was good enough to field practical, if not terribly effective, weapons.

There must have been a lot of burst barrels before the gunners figured out suitable charges. The flash and bang of these devices would have been quite a surprise when first encountered, a tactic that might have been worth more than weight of metal in the plan of battle.

The thickness and length of the wooden staves increased, the bands got thicker and, within a few years, the wooden staves were replaced with iron. These guns must have leaked smoke and fire at every seam, but their effectiveness improved to the point where they were actually lethal – at least used at short range – and intimidating to every person within their sight.

Beginning about 1340, guns and gunpowder began to make a radical change in the tactics and technology of war. Cannon were used at Lucca, Italy, in 1341, and by the Muslims against the Spanish in 1342. By 1345, the English king, Edward III, had accumulated an arsenal of 100 large guns. Within just 10 years, what were once just tiny, arrow-shooting weapons became massive tubes which had the capacity to fire large iron- and stone shot.

In 1370, a cannon foundry was in operation at Augsburg, in what is now southern Germany. A few years after that, in 1375, French artillerymen were firing 37kg (100lb) stone projectiles from

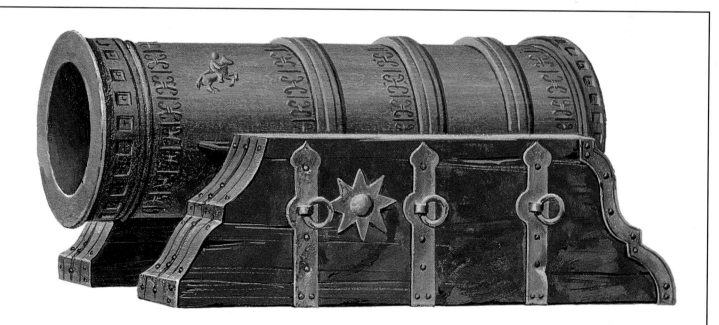

Great Gun of Moscow or Tsar Cannon (1586)

Calibre: 890mm (35in)
Weight: 40,000kg (88,185lb)
Length: n/a

Barrel length: 5.34m (5.8yd)
Effective range: n/a
Elevation: none

Traverse: none
Muzzle velocity: n/a
Country of origin: Muscovy

Falconet

Calibre: 60mm (2.36in)
Weight: 250kg (551lb) (est)
Length: 1.83m (6ft)
Barrel length: 1.83m (6ft)
Effective range: 500m (546yd) (est)

Elevation: -20° to 45° (est)
Traverse: 360°
Muzzle velocity: n/a
Country of origin: Europe

a massive battery of 32 cannon during the famous siege which took place at Saint-Saveur-de-Vicomte.

A cannon foundry opened for business in Venice the next year, and quite quickly all sorts of military organizations were equipping themselves with guns of all sizes and shapes. They were making a difference on the battlefields of Europe, too, and there were many armed forces at the time: a militia force from Bruges (in modern Belgium) was routed by forces from Ghent with the aid of small cannon.

Gunners were an odd lot, often civilian contractors or soldiers with special privileges and extra pay, no doubt compensation for their skills and for the additional risks these men incurred. They named their cannon: 'Messager', 'Godegrace', 'Gobette' and 'Neelpot' were some of the guns used by Henry V at

Agincourt, each 1642kg (4400lb) monsters with bad dispositions. Two burst during the siege of Aberystwyth, which explains some of that extra pay.

Use of cannon was as much psychological as tactical: the noise, flash and smoke did as much damage as the impact of the projectile. The utility of these weapons was obvious, however, and so the development of guns, gunpowder and gunners was in full flower from about 1350 to about 1450. Artillery was now an indispensable part of the arsenal of every major and minor political power.

THE 14TH CENTURY BOMBARD

Among the first really effective weapons was the bombard, a short, heavy weapon seen from the mid–1300s, which was a crude combination of a present-day mortar and a howitzer. Bombards had no

carriage or mount but were propped up with blocks of wood and lashed to heavy timbers driven in the ground to keep them from recoiling out of sight when they were fired.

Large stone spheres which had been roughly shaped served as projectiles, and the lack of precision employed in the manufacture of gun, projectile and propellant made crewing these weapons an adventure. Excitement was added by the proximity to the enemy and his deadly crossbows; the bombard's range was a few hundred metres at best. Gunners had to be protected by large shields during re-loading, as each round took hours to prepare.

The term 'bombard' later came to be applied to somewhat larger weapons as well as weapons of the type earlier identified as mortars. Ten to twenty men were required to serve these large weapons, and, if they knew their business, they could get off one shot about every half hour or so.

The projectiles were large – up to 99.8kg (220lb) – with effective ranges of around 275m (300yd). As the projectiles were never exactly the same size, or even perfectly round, the barrels of these bombards were often tapered to accept almost any sized ball. Such a system precluded the propellant from fully expanding on ignition, or even igniting completely, before the projectile was ejected from the weapon, but precision gunnery was not yet the fetish that it would later become.

About this time, in 1385, the first British brass cannon were being cast, at the order of the Sheriff of Cumberland. Ottoman Turks were blasting away with cannon at the Christians during the Battle of Kossovo the following year, and soon after this, England's Richard II went off to attack and subdue the Irish with 8 big guns and 200 rounds of ammunition. Large weapons were being put into action, from one side of the 'civilized' world to the other.

While small cannon were being designed, cast and hauled around for use in mobile warfare, huge siege guns were being made that were designed to be used from static mounts, primarily as defensive weapons. There were many of these monsters built during the 15th century, and some of them still survive. One of these is a giant with a 508mm (20in) bore cast from bronze, and measuring 4.11m (13ft 6in) long, which was known as 'Mons Meg'.

This huge gun weighs 6604kg (14.560lb) and may still be seen at Edinburgh Castle in Scotland. It served for 150 years before being relegated to firing the occasional salute, one of which sent a projectile the astounding distance of 3.39km (2 miles).

Until the middle of the 15th century, gunpowder really was a powder, simply a mixture of the three essential components in a dry, dusty state. This mixture tended to separate into its components during travel and therefore was a very unreliable propellant for the gun operators. Then someone had the bright idea of mixing the potassium nitrate, charcoal and sulphur with water, before drying it into a solid cake. This cake was first broken up into small flakes, then screened into bits of roughly similar size, before being loaded into the barrels of the guns.

The result was a large number of burst barrels. This mixture was not only much more reliable; the entire propellant now ignited almost instantly and was much more effective than a fine powder. A much smaller volume of propellant was found to provide much greater power and range. Gunners were soon able to calculate exactly how much powder they needed to use to achieve firing maximum effect, and as a result, they stopped splitting the guns.

Until about 1450, cannon were relatively immobile. Transported only with difficulty and installed on sturdy mounts before the battle, they were lucky to get off more than a few shots before serious difficulties arose. During the ebb and flow of the battle, infantry and cavalry could wash over the gun positions several times during a fight, and whomever won kept the guns.

Improved mobility began to be seen in the mid-15th century in great measure, because this was when Swiss forces started mounting their guns on large wheels and firing them from carriages. Mobility, firepower, range and lethal effect began to influence the battle in serious ways.

In 1450, at Formigny, two culverin cannon helped French forces break the formation of English archers during battle. Three years later, massed cannon and small firearms were a decisive factor on a battlefield for the first time, routing an English force at the Battle of Castillion. Here the guns were tactically employed from carefully prepared positions as the primary force, in an intentional and devastating way.

Bombards of this era were available in many sizes and styles. A typical example survives in the Musée de l'Armée in Paris. It is a forged, wrought-iron cannon with a huge 457mm (18in) bore diameter, a barrel about 1m (40in) long and a separate powder chamber to accept and focus the charge.

SIEGE GUN:1453
Even in those dim and distant years, so soon after the introduction of the very fundamentals of the gunner's art, artillery was quite amazingly powerful and effective. Mohammed II attacked Constantinople in April 1453 using a force of massive siege cannon of immense size. Cast in Hungary, these tubes were 5.18m (17ft) long and 17.27 tonnes (17 tons) in weight; each gun was moved into position by 60 oxen and 400 men.

Half the force of men prepared a roadway for the guns, while the others pulled on ropes to keep the huge weapons from falling over as they were moved along it. Mohammed's men took seven days to prepare the guns before they

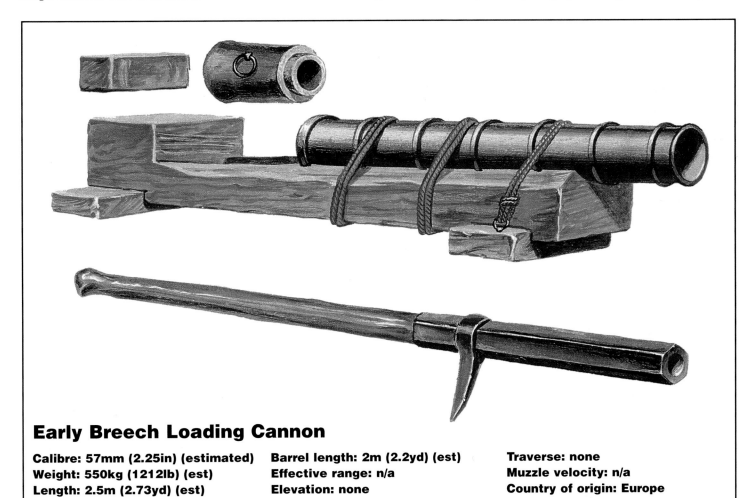

Early Breech Loading Cannon

Calibre: 57mm (2.25in) (estimated)
Weight: 550kg (1212lb) (est)
Length: 2.5m (2.73yd) (est)

Barrel length: 2m (2.2yd) (est)
Effective range: n/a
Elevation: none

Traverse: none
Muzzle velocity: n/a
Country of origin: Europe

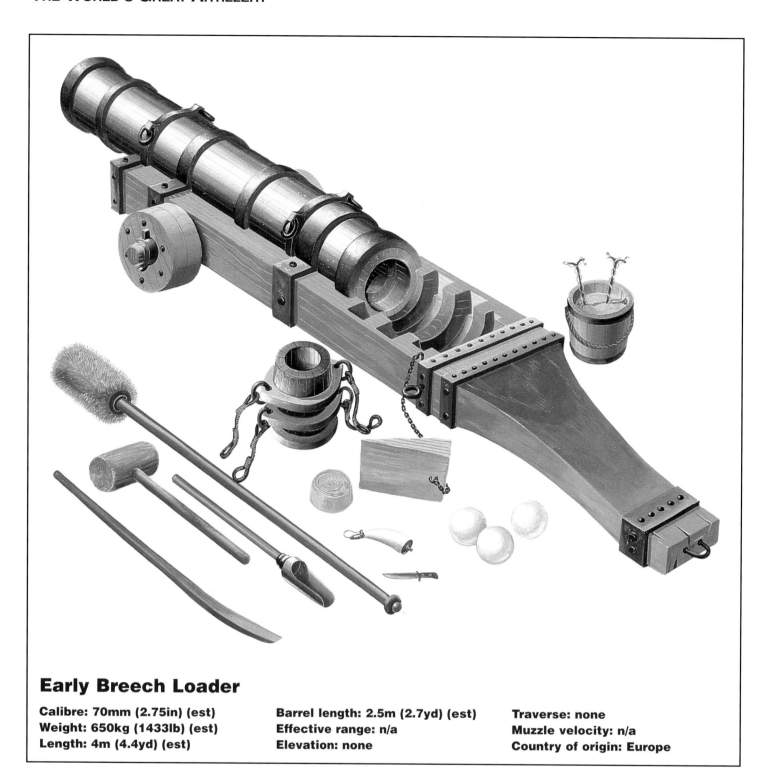

Early Breech Loader

Calibre: 70mm (2.75in) (est)	**Barrel length: 2.5m (2.7yd) (est)**	**Traverse: none**
Weight: 650kg (1433lb) (est)	**Effective range: n/a**	**Muzzle velocity: n/a**
Length: 4m (4.4yd) (est)	**Elevation: none**	**Country of origin: Europe**

opened fire. Seven times a day, each of the guns sent a 680kg (1500lb) stone projectile, 762mm (30in) in diameter, at the city walls of Constantinople. After about a month and a half, on 29 May 1453, the guns finally punched a hole through the walls, and the infantry attacked through the breach, storming the city and capturing it. Similar weapons became quite popular and were sophisticated for their time. In 1464, Sultan Muhammad Khan commissioned 42 monster cannon to guard the Dardanelles; each weighed 18.29 tonnes (18 tons) with a 762mm (30in) bore.

These huge cannon were still present for duty more than 300 years later in 1807, when an English naval force appeared. The ancient relics were filled with propellant and projectiles, then fired. Instead of exploding, they worked just as well as when they were new. One shot alone killed and wounded more than 60 crewmen on one of the British vessels. The Turks and the British finally negotiated, however, and today one of these impressive and historic weapons is on display for visitors at the Tower of London, a present from Turkey to the English monarch.

THE FIRST BREECH-LOADERS

Around 1470, the first practical breech-loading cannon were introduced. Other breech-loading cannon had been made for some time, massive weapons, the breech section of which was threaded onto the barrel. Re-loading took time and manpower to unscrew the breech, stuff it with powder and shot, then reassemble it.

The new system, called culverin or *veuglaire*, tended to be long, slender tubes open at each end, firing a shot about 102mm (4in) in diameter. The breech was a metal component about the shape and size of a large beer *stein*, with about the same capacity. This was charged with powder and ball, then installed in position at the breech. Wedges secured this crude breechblock in place and thereby prevented it from flying loose after each discharge.

Propellant gas, of course, leaked past the joints with a vengeance, but the gunners of the time were not too demanding about such things. The long bore allowed the propellant to develop its energy fully, which offset the leakage somewhat, and it also made the weapon easier to aim.

ENGLISH CAST-IRON CANNON

Until the mid–1500s, the fabrication of cast guns and cannonballs was a highly imperfect art. Brass and bronze weapons were costly and comparatively rare. Iron was difficult to smelt and cast, until one English foundry operator, William Hogge, began large-scale production in 1543. Hogge's foundry obtained an order for 120 guns in addition to a huge order of cast-iron shot.

It was a period of high tension, as both French and Scottish forces threatened England during 1545. Hogge first constructed a furnace twice the size of those then in common use and began selling excellent cannon to the Office of Ordnance. Sakers, falconets, demi-culverins and guns of all sizes became available, and they were all on the market with shot to match.

Queen Elizabeth granted Hogge the right to sell his surplus production to friendly nations – Denmark, Sweden and Holland, among others – but not to France. For a time, Hogge had a monopoly on the production of good cast-iron guns. They were highly regarded all over Europe, and other foundry operators tried hard to discover the secret of English guns. Two Belgian foundrymen solved the puzzle in 1620, and soon excellent cannon were being cast, first in Liege and then later in Sweden. The English monopoly was lost, but excellent English guns would continue to make their mark on history.

By the time 17-year-old Gustavus Adolphus II ascended the throne of Sweden in 1611, artillery had long been considered as an essential element in the combat forces of Europe. There were a multitude of those forces, and warring factions marched back and forth all across the continent, shooting and hacking each other during a nearly continuous series of conflicts. At the time, Sweden was one of the dominant European powers, and this young king was just the man to expand his nation's influence and control. Gustavus Adolphus II accomplished this with a revolutionary use of all his forces, particularly artillery, in ways still used today.

Like other commanders of the time, Gustavus used all kinds of cannon: naval, siege and field. Gustavus's emphasis, however, was on an agile force. He wanted one that could move quickly around the battlefield and apply decisive combat power where it was likely to have the maximum effect.

Unlike other commanders of the time, he avoided static sieges in favour of pitched battle, and that meant a developing a specialized arsenal. Instead of monster guns which fired huge projectiles at long and predictable intervals, he bought and employed small, light, mobile guns that could be quickly moved to a critical location and fired into a wall of moving enemy soldiers. And to do that, his artillery commander developed and produced a special gun for these new Swedish tactics.

Bronze Cannon

Calibre: 51mm (2in) (est)
Weight: 450kg (992lb) (est)
Length: 2.5m (2.73yd) (est)

Barrel length: 1.25m (1.4yd) (est)
Effective range: n/a
Elevation: none

Traverse: none
Muzzle velocity: n/a
Country of origin: Europe

Gustavus's artillery commander was one Colonel General Lennart Torstenson, an imaginative and experienced professional gunner with perfect understanding of the implications of mobile tactics. While enemy forces were still using heavy, comparatively static weapons, Torstenson came up with two strong, light, cast-iron cannon. One of these cannon fired a 1.81kg (4lb) shot, while the other cannon could fire a projectile weighing 4.08kg (9lb).

Both of these guns were mounted on a simple carriage with two large wheels and a single trail, quite similar to that used centuries later in the American Civil War. Just two horses could quickly transport these light guns. Their gunners were trained to move rapidly into a firing position and get off a shot, then collect their weapon and move out.

'FIXED ROUND' CARTRIDGE

One of the many revolutionary things introduced by Gustavus's Swedish gunners was the first use of 'fixed rounds' or prepared ammunition as standard procedure. While other gunners were scooping up loose gunpowder out of a barrel for every shot they wanted to fire, the Swedes were simply popping a complete cartridge down the bore of their cannon and firing.

This cartridge contained a combination of pre-measured propellant and shot, and it came in one, nearly foolproof, package. The result was that individual gun crews could get off three rounds during the height of battle for every one which their enemies managed to fire.

These same Swedish gunners used a canister of anti-personnel rounds, rather than a single, solid shot, and the combined effect of these projectiles with the rapid rate of fire was just one more way in which the Swedish forces dominated their battlefields.

Gustavus and Torstenson attached two light, horse-drawn guns to each 1000-man infantry and cavalry regiment, a novel use of artillery at the time. These cannon moved with the soldiers and were under the control of their immediate commanders. That meant the commanders could put steel downrange where and when it would do the most good, firing at the critical moment,

LEFT: 'Le Combatant', a French 16-pounder cast in 1674, capable of firing a 7.25kg (16lb) projectile with good accuracy and terminal effect to about 1000m (914 yd).

infantry. Musketeers could fire a volley, then retreat to the protection of the square while they reloaded.

All European armies of the time used this successful field formation, except for Sweden. Instead, the Swedes deployed their forces on a line, only six men deep, with their musketeers, artillery and pikemen working together as a mobile combined-arms team.

A FAMILY OF WEAPONS

Between 1756 and 1763, after the defeats of the Seven Years' War, Frenchman Jean-Baptiste Vaquette de Gribeauval developed a new system of artillery that would have a profound influence on armies for many decades. This system was an attempt first to simplify the equipment of the French Army's artillery, then to reorganize it internally, and

finally to integrate artillery into the system of battle in what we call today a 'combined arms team'.

Gribeauval's system, developed and promoted in 1765, simplified artillery by introducing a family of three cannons of 1.81kg (4lb), 3.63kg (8lb) and 5.44kg (12lb), and one howitzer, a 152mm (6.0in) design. These new guns had standardized mounts, limbers and wheels that were lighter and easier to repair on the march or on the battlefield. At the time, there were three types of caisson for each gun, and the guns had to be shifted from their travelling position on the carriage to a firing position before combat.

Napoleon had been a gunner early in his career and established a committee to take Gribeauval's system and refine it. This process had begun in 1802. From the committee's recommendations came additional proposals for simplification, and French artillery consequently adopted a 6pdr (2.72kg) intended to replace both the 4pdr (1.81kg) and 8pdr (3.63kg) cannons which were based on the Gribeauval pattern.

without sending some liaison officer to beg for cannon support from another unit perhaps miles away. This tactic of rapid response was part of a new kind of battle plan, something that would quickly become standard procedure.

When the Swedish Army and its lightweight artillery rolled off to war in 1630, it was fighting against opposing forces which used tactics based fundamentally on infantry with the 'Spanish Square'. In this formation, soldiers with 5.49m (18ft) long pikes massed together in squares; in each square soldiers stood in ranks up to 50 men deep. The long pikes turned this formation into a massive porcupine equipped with sharp quills, unapproachable by enemy cavalry or

Bronze Mortar

Calibre: 127mm (5in) (est)
Weight: 450kg (992lb) (est)
Length: 1m (1.09yd) (est)
Barrel length: 0.5m (0.55yd) (est)
Effective range: n/a

Elevation: 20° to 60° (est)
Traverse: none
Muzzle velocity: n/a
Country of origin: European

Along with the new gun came a new carriage, limber and caissons, as well as a new howitzer, the 24pdr (10.89kg). Napoleon demanded 4 cannon for each 1000 men in infantry or cavalry regiments, and insisted that they fight near those other units, and that they fight in a coordinated way.

At the same time, the entire role of artillery in French service was reformed. Its part in French battle doctrine was likewise reformed, and made the equal of the infantry and cavalry. The emphasis was on mobility and the capability to achieve massed gunfire focused on the place where it would do the most good. Previously, artillery batteries duelled with the enemy's batteries; now, they were generally to ignore counterbattery fire and support the attack by blowing away enemy infantry.

French artillery could do this under Napoleon as its commanders were, at last, general officers who had participated in the planning of operations, understood what we call today 'commander's intent' and knew what was required of the guns as the fight evolved. Napoleon insisted that his guns had enough ammunition at all times to fight two battles, about 300 rounds, and he also insisted that ammunition be used carefully and only on targets that made a difference to the big picture. His army pioneered the role of a chief of artillery and ensured that every corps had its own indigenous artillery commander.

This combination of reforms was extremely successful. The fledgling United States Army adopted the 6pdr (2.72kg) as its own, and would keep it in service until the late 18th century, 70 years after it was designed. The United States also adopted the whole Gribeauval system, along with French influences that would endure until nearly 1900.

ROCKET ARTILLERY
Rockets have been used to inflict mischief and mayhem for many centuries, all the way back to AD 1258, when the Mongols captured Baghdad, and perhaps before. Some were used against French forces in 1268, and by the French against the British in 1429. By 1650, the German

■ABOVE: 'Belliqueux', a French 16pdr cannon from 1738. The design and production of such guns was considered an art and most weapons of the era were extensively embellished .

Christopher Fredrich von Geissler was producing huge rockets for military uses weighing up to 54kg (120lb), and British expeditionary forces were attacked with rockets during campaigns in India.

All this primed William Congreve, an English attorney and son of an artilleryman, to attempt in 1799 to develop a superior rocket for military use. The result was a family of weapons introduced in 1804, from tiny, ineffectual 9pdr (4.08kg) rockets to massive missiles weighing 136kg (300lb). The smallest ones were too small to do any good, while the biggest ones were simply too large to manage. The 11kg (24lb) and 15kg (32lb) rockets, however, became an excellent alternative to the guns of that time, just at the beginning of the Napoleonic Wars, and were used extensively for many years in many conflicts.

They were sturdy little constructions, made of sheet iron, with a choice of two types of warhead, one incendiary and the other explosive. The incendiary version had a sharp point and was supposed to impale itself in the woodwork of enemy vessels. Holes in the pointed cap allowed the warhead to spread fire both fore and aft, setting fire to the ship. A long stick provided a small measure of guidance and kept the missile headed in approximately the intended direction.

Another version used an explosive charge in a solid iron warhead. A powder train that functioned as a time fuse detonated the charge. The rocket motor served as the first portion of this delay mechanism; as it burned out, a small train of fine gunpowder was initiated, and detonated the main charge after an interval. Oddly enough, this worked as well as other weapons on the battlefield.

British naval forces used these rockets extensively, and Americans are still frequently reminded of one particular failed rocket assault: that made on Baltimore's Fort McHenry during the War of 1812. Francis Scott Key was a prisoner aboard a British warship during that attack in 1814, and he watched the assembled British rocket ships pour their fires on the American fort. Key later commemorated the event in a poem subsequently put to music and adopted as the national anthem. The song includes the stirring refrain:

And the rockets' red glare,
the bombs bursting in air,
Gave proof through the night
that our flag was still there.

Land Service Mortar (1769)

Calibre: 140mm (5.5in)
Weight: 450kg (992lb) (est)
Length: 0.75m (29in) (est)
Barrel length: 0.5m (19.6in) (est)
Effective range: 686m (750yd)

Elevation: 20° to 80° (est)
Traverse: none
Muzzle velocity: n/a
Country of origin: Great Britain

Rockets proved more effective in other battles, however, and were used often and with good effect against French vessels. Rockets of the Congreve pattern, in 10.89kg (24lb), 14.51kg (32lb), and 19.05kg (42lb) sizes, were accepted for use in the Royal Artillery and were used frequently until 1850. By that time, tube artillery had become much more accurate and could deliver a larger projectile across a greater distance.

HALE'S MILITARY ROCKETS
William Hale substantially improved military rockets in 1844. He eliminated the guidestick in favour of fin stabilization, a development that produced weapons that were very much like those issued today.

He also developed a better way to load powder into the rockets. Congreve's method used fine gunpowder which was packed firmly into the body of the rocket under pressure of a large weight that essentially hammered the propellant as it was loaded. This would form a dense block of material.

This method of packing the rocket motor resulted in irregular densities and consequent inaccuracy when fired. It also produced occasional sparks during loading, which produced explosions. Hale used a system of hydraulic pressure for loading, with better results.

Both the Hale and Congreve rockets had a range of 3700m (4000yd) or so, and delivered an effective warhead. Although not very accurate, they were considered practical enough to be part of the inventory of the armies of many nations; Russia, France, Sweden, Switzerland, the United States as well as many others, were the owners of rocket forces.

Although rockets retained the capability of being packed by man or animal into locations where large guns could not go, they gradually lost favour. A very few rockets would be used during the American Civil War, but their time would come again, during World War II.

Until the middle of the 19th century, muzzle-loading smoothbore cannon had been all that any commander required for hundreds of years. Smoothbore weapons

18th Century Cannon and Limber

Calibre: 93mm (3.67in)
Weight: 270kg (595lb) (est)
Length: 3.25m (3.55yd) (est)

Barrel length: 1.37m (1.5yd)
Effective range: 1000m (1093yd)
Elevation: 0° to 3°

Traverse: none
Muzzle velocity: n/a
Country of origin: n/a

were accurate only to a few hundred metres; their projectiles were smaller than the bores in order to facilitate rapid loading, and the round shot rattled down the barrel when fired. That gap, too, permitted the escape of much of the propellant gas, reducing the shot's range and velocity. These inadequacies did not present a problem, as long as the infantry was banging away with similar weapons and engagement distances were close. That all changed when European infantry began using soft lead, hollow-base Minie bullets in rifled muskets around 1850. These bullets were demonstrated to be effective at much longer ranges, up to 550m (600yd) and more. All of a sudden, potential enemy infantry had a stand-off weapon that could engage an artillery battery in comparative safety.

The Prussian Army then began issuing the Dreyse 'needle gun'. The Master General of the Ordnance requested that

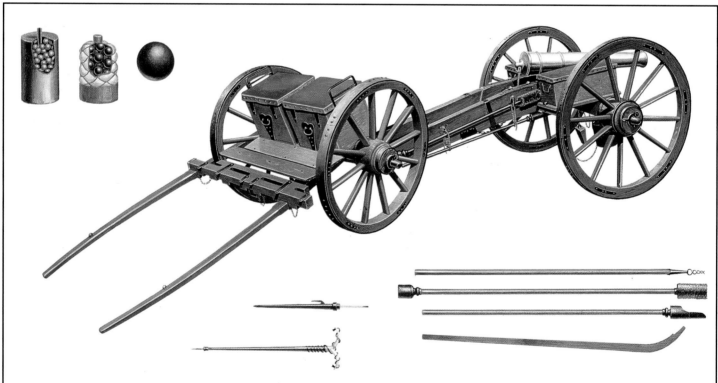

Light 6-pounder (1776)

Calibre: 93mm (3.67in)
Weight: 262kg (578lb)
Length: 3m (3.28yd) (est)

Barrel length: 1.37m (1.5yd)
Effective range: 1050m (1150yd)
Elevation: 0° to 3°

Traverse: none
Muzzle velocity: n/a
Country of origin: Great Britain

British industry develop new weapons that could possibly incorporate these features, and three inventors produced serious designs: Armstrong, Whitworth and Lancaster. All the designs were innovative and radical departures from the existing technology. All these designs had major teething problems, too.

The Special Board on Rifled Guns, convened in 1858, selected Armstrong's design. After seeing its excellent accuracy and tremendous range, which were far superior to the existing smoothbore, the Armstrong gun was chosen. Six weapons, ranging from a 6pdr (2.72kg) to a 110pdr (49.90kg), were accepted for use by British forces and put into manufacture.

Armstrong's breech-loading design was hardly perfect, but its introduction marked the end of the smoothbore muzzle-loader for most weapons and the foundation of the designs used in cannon today. The transition to breech-loaders took 30 years, and is in some ways not quite complete, as there are still many smoothbore muzzle-loaders in front-line service today.

As issued, Armstrong's guns were constructed of forged wrought-iron tubes built up in layers that made for an exceptionally strong gun for the time. The breech was the tricky part, and it remained the tricky part for many years to come. Armstrong's design used a two-part system: a vertically sliding block held in place by a massive screw. The screw portion of the assembly was not solid, but a heavy tube with an inside diameter large enough to allow the shell or bolt to be passed straight through to

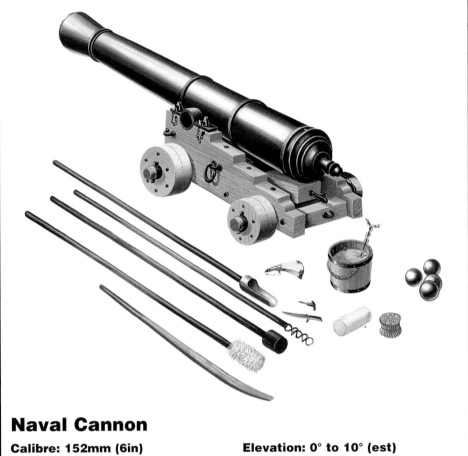

Naval Cannon

Calibre: 152mm (6in)
Weight: 1200kg (2645lb) (est)
Length: 5m (5.46yd) (est)
Barrel length: 4.5m (4.92yd) (est)
Effective range: n/a

Elevation: 0° to 10° (est)
Traverse: none
Muzzle velocity: n/a
Country of origin: Europe

the chamber, followed by a separate powder bag. A heavy block of iron that could be lifted out by hand – once the screw pressure against its rear face was removed – sealed the breech. After the

■BELOW: A selection of French 16-pounders from the 17th and 18th centuries on display outside Les Invalides in Paris, demonstrating the similarity in gun design of the period.

■LEFT: A 228mm (9in) French cannon of 1810. By this time, most cannon had lost the ornate embellishments of earlier models in favour of stronger construction and simplified design.

bands on the projectile (a lead jacket over the iron) and an obturation system that actually worked. With a better projectile seal to prevent gas escaping, much less powder was needed – exactly half in the 4.08kg (9lb) version – while still providing much longer range. The whole package was lighter by 227kg (500lb), offered 550m (600yd) more range, and was about 12 times more accurate than the previous standard.

There were problems, however, as there are with any new weapon, particularly with any radical new weapon. The breechblock occasionally blew out when it had not been properly installed, the copper seals leaked and eroded when poorly maintained, and the lead layer on the projectile peeled off until an alternative form of manufacture was tried. The guns were expensive and unfamiliar. In 1865, another Ordnance committee recommended going back to muzzle-loaders, but this time with rifling. The report was accepted.

chamber had been loaded, the block was replaced and the screw tightened. Ignition was with a T-shaped friction primer inserted in the vent.

Armstrong not only rifled the bore in a way very similar to current practice, he also reduced the diameter slightly near the muzzle, ensuring that the projectile was centred. Squeeze-bore weapons using the same idea became very common in World War II and were thought revolutionary at the time. There were other innovations: the first mechanical traverse system on the carriage, driving

MUZZLE-LOADING'S LAST SHOT
One of the great arguments in favour of the muzzle-loader was its apparent safety, and it was certainly true that solid cannon did not come apart as easily as Armstrong's weapons. The Royal Artillery and Royal Navy both reverted to muzzle-loading, and would perhaps still be feeding their cannon from the front except for an incident that converted even the sceptics to breech-loading.

It happened on 2 January 1870, aboard HMS *Thunderer*. The ship's main guns, a pair of power-operated 38.6 tonne (38 ton) 305mm (12in) cannons, had been loaded and apparently fired. In fact, only one charge had ignited and the other misfired but as both guns normally fired

■LEFT: This 1806 French mortar is made of cast bronze, an expensive metal that is also prone to erosion. Its elevation is fixed at about 45° so its range is altered by the amount of powder used.

■RIGHT: This is a good example of a mid-19th century cannon used in the siege of Lucknow, India, that began in May 1857 and concluded in March 1858, during the Indian Mutiny.

together, the misfire was undetected. When both guns were re-loaded, another 39kg (85lb) bag of powder and another 363kg (800lb) projectile were placed on top of the first; at the next shot, the double-shotted cannon came apart. The two stubby guns were both enclosed with their crews in a tight, round armoured turret that concentrated the blast. All the men serving the guns in the turret were killed, as were many on deck.

The *Thunderer* incident could not have occurred with a breech-loading weapon, and the advocates of the Armstrong gun were not shy about saying so. At the same time, Prussian artillerymen in Europe were using breech-loaders exclusively and proving the system's practicality on the battlefield, adding weight to the arguments of the Armstrong gun's proponents.

KRUPP WORKS' SLIDING BREECH

The latter quarter of the 19th century was a busy one in the Krupp Works in Essen, Germany, and in France, too. These were both places where artillery technology was rapidly evolving due to the increasing pressure of war.

Two improved breech assemblies were invented and tested by firing at each other during the Franco–Prussian War of 1870–71. One was Krupp's sliding block system, which was similar to Armstrong's, except that the block moved laterally. Nordenfelt's used a rotary block to seal the breech. Both of these systems relied on metallic cartridges to provide the gas seal, and fortunately both of them worked quite well.

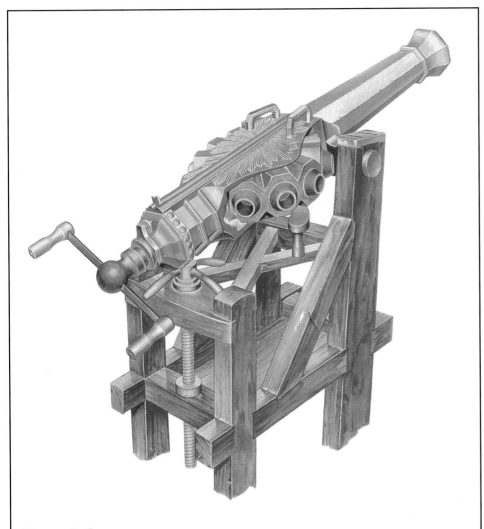

Revolving cannon

Calibre: 76mm (3in) (est)
Weight: 600kg (1323lb) (est)
Length: 2.5m (2.73yd) (est)
Barrel length: 2m (2.2yd) (est)
Effective range: n/a

Elevation: 0° to 20° (est)
Traverse: none
Muzzle velocity: n/a
Country of origin: France

CHAPTER TWO
THE AMERICAN CIVIL WAR

From the bombardment of Fort Sumter to the final surrender of the Confederate forces, artillery played a key role on both sides of the American Civil War, the bloodiest conflict in that nation's history.

The small town of Gettysburg, Pennsylvania was, and still is, a quiet rural crossroads surrounded by rolling countryside, fields and wooded hills. Twelve roads still intersect there, just as they did in late June 1863, when the Confederate Army of Northern Virginia clashed in battle with the massed forces of the Union.

On 24 June 1863, Confederate General Robert E. Lee brought his superb Army of Northern Virginia north, into Maryland and Pennsylvania, on a massive sweep. This threatened not just the Union capital of Washington and the important city of Philadelphia, but also the confidence of the Union Army and Union population. Lee and the Southern forces had, for two terrible years, seemed always to be the master of the battlefield.

As reports of Lee's rampage into Pennsylvania filtered to the White House, President Abraham Lincoln sacked his inept army commander, General Hooker, and replaced him with George Gordon Meade. General Meade took the Army of the Potomac north, hunting for the Confederate Army. He found them, pretty much by accident, on 1 July, north of the town of Gettysburg.

The first day of battle involved probes, skirmishes and forced marches, as the two massive armies converged on the little community of 2500 souls. Union forces were pushed through the town, onto the high ground running south and east, even then known as Cemetery Ridge. Lee ordered one of his

■ **LEFT: 12-pounder Napoleons, the standard cannon in the American Civil War. It combined good accuracy, a wide selection of effective projectiles and reasonable mobility.**

commanders, Richard Ewell, to pursue the Federals. This he duly did, until he discovered a Union artillery position on the hill and commanding its western approaches. Ewell paused to consolidate his forces and his plan, and what could have been a moderately bloody Confederate victory became a mutual blood-letting of epic proportions, and a crucial Confederate defeat.

Meade drove his divisions, brigades, regiments and batteries towards the town and the high ground, where the survivors of the first day gathered, sheltered and dug in. Cemetery Ridge is very rocky ground, steep in places and wooded on its eastern slope, but mostly open on the west. It is excellent defensive terrain. While the tired gun crews kept the Rebel infantry at bay, Meade's Army of the Potomac flooded into Gettysburg from the south and the east. All night, after epic forced marches, the regiments arrived and were positioned by Meade's staff.

All along the crest of the ridge, and behind it, the artillery batteries set up shop. The ammunition wagons sheltered on the reverse slope, under the trees, while the guns and limbers were positioned behind hastily positioned rock walls. First light revealed the massed Confederate Army in battle array on parallel high ground about 2.75km (1.5 miles) to the west, Seminary Ridge. The blood-letting was about to begin.

The American Civil War lasted four years, from April 1861 until April 1865, and was easily the bloodiest conflict in United States history. During those four years, more than half a million men died in battle, from wounds or from disease. Not even World War II produced similar casualties. From the war's beginning until its the end, artillery played an

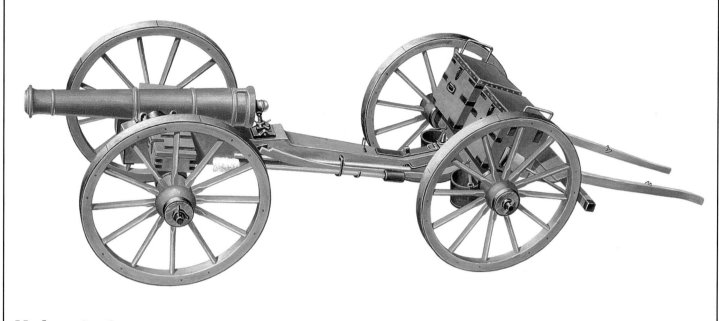

Union 6pdr

Calibre: 93mm (3.67in)
Weight: 398kg (884lb)
Length: 3m (3.28yd) (est)

Barrel length: 1.52m (60in)
Effective range: 1392m (1523yd)
Elevation: 0° to 5°

Traverse: none
Muzzle velocity: n/a
Country of origin: USA

essential role in the battles. The opening shots in 1861 were fired by heavy seacoast guns at Fort Sumter, North Carolina, and a barrage by a field artillery battery near Appomattox Court House, Virginia, helped to force the final surrender in 1865.

In many ways, the American Civil War was the apogee of the long muzzle-loading technology era. During this long, brutal war, many kinds of weapons, projectiles and tactical methods of employment were designed, tested and refined in battle.

M1857 'NAPOLEON' 12PDR

The artillery weapon of choice for both sides of the conflict was a simple bronze smoothbore called the 'Napoleon'. Named after Napoleon III, Emperor of France, this weapon was mobile, powerful, simple to build and use, and effective.

Cast of bronze instead of iron, the Napoleon was a tough, sturdy cannon that could take a heavy powder charge or a double charge of case and not rupture. Its 117mm (4.62in) bore accommodated a solid iron shot that weighed 5.44kg (12lb), a very hefty projectile. When backed with a standard charge of 1.13kg (2.5lb) of powder, the Napoleon would accurately throw that heavy shot almost a mile (1480m/1619yd), with five-degree elevation. Despite the smoothbore, it was a precision weapon for the time, quite

able to engage an enemy gun in a duel at 1000m (9144yd) or more, and put it out of action with a few shots. With 10-degree elevation, the M1857 put its 5.44kg (12lb) of steel on targets at 1911m (2090yd). Union and Confederate weapons both used the same name, but there were differences. The Union version, designated the M1857 12pdr Field Gun, used a bronze tube 1.68m (66in) long and weighing 556.56kg (1227lb).

Like most artillery of the time, the Napoleon fired solid shot, shell, shrapnel and case projectiles. The popularity and success of the weapon were based partly on its bore size – directly related to the utility of its projectiles – and the weapon's comparatively light weight, strength and mobility.

Gunners fired solid shot at long range, against enemy artillery positions, massed troops and similar larger targets. One of these solid shot would slice a swath through a formation of infantry, taking off heads, arms and legs, and smashing torsos to a mangled pulp. It was common for Civil War soldiers to see these 5.44kg (12lb) balls of iron bouncing along the battlefield like oversized baseballs, almost slow enough to catch. The impression was deceptive, though, and a soldier who failed to dodge one of these nearly spent projectiles could easily suffer a fatal injury from the heavy oncoming ball.

Napoleons fired huge numbers of shells, too. Typically weighing around 4.3kg (9.5lb), these spherical projectiles were filled with about 900g (2lb) of black powder bursting charge which was initiated with a fuse.

The M1857 12pdr in all its variants was tremendously important to both contending armies. Of the 360 Federal tubes and 272 Confederate guns in action at the Battle of Gettysburg, about 40 per cent were Napoleons. A fairly wide variety of ammunition was used in these cannons – shell, canister, case and solid shot – weighing from 4.3kg (9.5lb) to almost 6.8kg (15lb). Muzzle velocity for most of these projectiles was in the region of 457m/sec (1500ft/sec).

A good crew could deliver precision fire at the rate of about two rounds per minute. When the enemy infantry was swarming up the hill and closing on the battery position from 368m (400yd) or less, they could deliver four rounds of canister per minute, till one side or the other turned and ran, or died.

As good as the Napoleon was, it had one important problem: its weight. These cannon were strong and sturdy, but only because their bronze bores were thick and heavy. That made mobility a problem, and when practical wrought-iron, and later steel, rifles were introduced with tube weights far lower, the Napoleons began to disappear.

PARROTT FIELD RIFLES

Parrott rifled cannon were fairly common during the American Civil War, but not quite so highly regarded as the Napoleon or 76.2mm (3in) Ordnance Rifle. They were manufactured with a process which was invented in 1861 by Captain Robert Parker Parrott at the West Point (New York) Foundry.

His method involved slipping a welded reinforcing band of iron over the breech section of a cannon, providing reinforcement of this critical part of the gun. Other manufacturers were reinforced at the breech, but Parrott's method was different. Iron expands considerably when it is hot, so Parrott expanded the band by heating it to red-hot in a forge. He then slipped it over the cast tube, chilled by pumping water down the bore. Once in proper position, the band was allowed to cool and shrink, so that it gripped the tube tightly.

Parrott's design was not unique, and other American and British cannon foundries made weapons with similar

reinforcement; however, Parrott's was the most common of the type during the Civil War. The technique worked well enough for the portion of the tube that it covered, but Parrott rifles tended to burst just in front of the band, sometimes after only a very few rounds. Even so, many were produced and used in the war. They were easy and inexpensive to make, economical to fire and accurate at long range. Their habit of coming apart at the seams occasionally was considered a minor sin under the circumstances.

About 600 10pdr Parrott Rifles were issued during the Civil War, in two variants, models 1861 and 1863. The first of these had a 73mm (2.9in) bore. Both were light, agile weapons of about 405kg (900lb), 2m (78in) long and effective out to 1800m (2000yd). In 1863, the weapon was modified to use the standard 76.2mm (3in) ammunition of other army cannon, with the old weapons removed from service to be rebored and new Parrotts made with a 76.2mm bore. The 10pdr's charge was just 454g (1lb) of powder.

Also popular was the 20pdr Parrott. This weapon was a scaled-up version, 453.36kg (1000lb) heavier and with a bore 93mm (3.67in) in diameter. With a standard 0.907g (2lb) propellant charge and 15-degree elevation, this weapon would accurately deliver an 8.4kg (18.75lb) shell 3960m (4400yd).

Despite their flaws, the Parrott field guns were good enough to be copied by the Confederates. Many manufacturers produced shells designed for their use. It was one of the more successful artillery weapons of the war.

As well as the lighter field artillery, the West Point Foundry produced much heavier weapons for seacoast and naval use. Among these was the only Civil War cannon to achieve much immortality, a 203mm (8in) heavy rifle called the

■BELOW: The simple carriage on which the cannon was transported was, by 1860, a sturdy but well-engineered design that helped make the Napoleon and its ilk such effective weapons.

Swamp Angel. This Parrott cannon was carefully emplaced on a platform built in a swamp outside Charlestown, South Carolina, and, at 01:30 hours on 22 August 1863, proceeded to lob its massive 79kg (175lb) projectiles approximately 7200m (8000yd) into the Confederate city. The city itself was invisible from the emplacement, so the battery commander, Lieutenant Charles Sellmer, used a compass bearing to orient the weapon – a battlefield first.

Although the commander of the firing battery had sent a message to the town demanding its evacuation, he had not signed it and so it was dismissed and ignored. When the first shells came crashing down, the civilian populace of

the town was panic-stricken. Sixteen incendiary shells were fired before first light. After a brief delay, the bombardment continued while the defenders provided accurate but ineffective counterbattery fire with their heavy mortars, the shells of which detonated in the mud without damaging anything. In grand Parrott tradition, the cannon ruptured on the 36th round and was abandoned where it stood.

M1841 6PDR FIELD GUN
Just before the Civil War was declared in April 1861, large quantities of United States Army cannon and ammunition were appropriated by secessionists, and many of the weapons they took were old

■ABOVE: Parrott rifles, like these 30pdrs, were nearly as common as Napoleons. They were accurate, inexpensive and strong. The enlarged breech could cause a burst barrel.

M1841 bronze 6pdr cannon. These small, ancient guns were quite inadequate for the duties required of them, and many were quickly melted down or bored out. Their projectiles were too small – at just 93mm (3.67in) and 2.72kg (6lb) for solid shot – to do much damage, and they were easily outranged by Napoleons and other 12pdr weapons. Even so, they made a notable contribution during the early battles of the American Civil War, and at least they had taught the gunners the drill of firing their weapon.

While the M1857 12pdr Napoleon might have been the workhorse of the Civil War artillery, the sleek racehorse – and sniper rifle – of the conflict was the elegant 76.2mm (3in) Ordnance Rifle. This weapon's rifled bore restricted the types of ammunition it could fire to primarily shell and solid iron bolts, but it delivered both ammunition types with exceptional precision of up to 1.5km (1 mile) and even to distances beyond.

■LEFT: Rail communication was critical during the American Civil War, and both sides took measures to arm trains. Artillery mounted on flatcars, with and without armour, was a common sight.

■RIGHT: The Battle of Shiloh in 1862 was one of the most memorable, partly because of the carnage inflicted by the Napoleons. A single round could make casualties of dozens of enemy soldiers.

24pdr Naval Cannon

Calibre: 148mm (5.83in)	Barrel length: 2.4m (2.62yd)	Traverse: none
Weight: 272kg (600lb)	Effective range: 915m (1000yd)	Muzzle velocity: n/a
Length: 3m (3.28yd)	Elevation: 0° to 5°	Country of origin: USA

Fabricated from wrought-iron strips heated white-hot and then hammer-welded around a 76.2mm (3in) core, the 3in Ordnance Rifle proved to be strong and light, as well as accurate and powerful. Its smooth, slender tube was 1.9m (73in) long and weighed only 370kg (816lb). The basic charge for this weapon was only 454g (1lb) of cannon powder, which was enough to throw a 3.6kg (8lb) shell about 33700m (4000yd).

Tests conducted on cannon early on in the Civil War revealed that the bands and rings which were manufactured on conventional contemporary weapons were stress points, and that these stress points were subject to failure. As a result of these conclusions, the 3in Ordnance Rifle was thereafter manufactured with a smooth, sleek contour.

One problem with the bronze cannons, including the Napoleons, was rapid bore erosion. Serious wear was detected in some of these weapons after firing just 500 rounds. The 76.2mm (3in) rifle and its wrought iron were subjected to similar tests of proof loads without eroding. More of these fine guns – 146 of them, or a total of 41 per cent of the tubes in action – fought on the Union side at Gettysburg than any other gun model.

Surprisingly enough, you can still buy and shoot a 3in Ordnance Rifle. They are manufactured for Civil War re-enactors to use, some of whom fire the weapons occasionally. They are still accurate at long range, but it is not currently considered good form to use real

■RIGHT: Swarms of Confederates attack Federals during the Battle of Gaines Mill in 1862. Muzzle-loading artillery had one principal vice: every gun needed a large crew to function.

projectiles during these re-enactments of the Civil War.

14PDR JAMES RIFLE
The 14pdr James Rifle is one example of the many slightly oddball weapons of dubious design that somehow managed to be sold to the fighting forces. Invented by a senior Rhode Island militia commander, this weapon was cast from bronze. While bronze is a strong material that can tolerate high pressures, it is somewhat soft and subject to erosion. It is simply not a good material for a rifled cannon barrel. At the very beginning of the Civil War, however, all of that did not matter too much. They needed weapons fast.

Bronze was available, and so it was ordered. The design used a specialized projectile patented by its inventor which was manufactured during 1861 and 1862 before being discarded. With a 340g (12oz) charge and 5 degrees elevation, the James Rifle's range was rated at about 1600m (1700yd).

An example of a specialized larger field gun, the 114mm (4.5in) Siege Rifle fired a 13.61kg (30lb) Hotchkiss or Shenkl shell with great accuracy and to long ranges. It was a massive weapon, though, with a tube that weighed 1565kg (3450lb), which made it difficult to move. Made of cast (instead of wrought) iron, this cannon had the same sleek

appearance as the much more common 3in Ordnance Rifle. Its shells ranged to 1900m (2100yd), with a standard charge of 1.6kg (3.5lb) of powder and an elevation of 5 degrees.

24PDR COEHORN MORTAR

The mortar had been a standard weapon for centuries before the American Civil War and had not changed very much in all that time. They were (and are) very simple weapons, not especially accurate, economical to operate and an excellent way to deliver plunging fire on an entrenched enemy.

All of these were remarkably simple devices. During the Civil War era, they were essentially very short barrelled howitzers with extremely thick barrels and designed for huge projectiles. The trunnions were at the extreme base of the tube. Cast from bronze or iron, smaller mortars such as the Coehorn were typically mounted on a thick, flat slab of wood that dispersed recoil forces directly to the ground. When the mortar needed to be manoeuvred into a new firing position, a strong gun crew could (if there were enough of them) lift the weapon and carry it a short distance.

The 24pdr (10.89kg) fired a spherical cast-iron shell weighing 7.71kg (17lb) without fuse or filling, and 144mm (5.68in) in diameter. These shells had to be loaded carefully to ensure that the fuse was orientated directly towards the mouth of the tube; a special tool called a 'shell hook' fit small recesses in the shell to facilitate placement in the weapon before firing.

Coehorn mortars in this small size were cast from bronze and weighed just 74.39kg (164lb) without their base. The bore of these mortars was only slightly more than 406mm (16in) long, not much room for the propellant to ignite fully before the projectile was ejected from the muzzle. With 2.27kg (5lb) of cannon powder and a barrel elevation of 45 degrees, the fizzing shell would be lobbed far up into the sky before it fell, 1100m (1200yd) downrange.

Defenders of fortifications bombarded by mortars such as the 24pdr Coehorn were sometimes quite contemptuous of their fire and would pause, especially at night, to enjoy the spectacle of the shell, its fuse sputtering fire, arcing up into the sky. These soldiers quickly learned to predict with some precision where the

■ABOVE: **The limber was an essential part of the gun's equipment, supporting the trail of the carriage while on the move, and supplying ammunition while in action. It was served by two men.**

shell would come back to earth. If it were not likely to be very close, they would take their time finding cover.

Any soldier in the vicinity of the impact area, however, quickly found a hole. Often these shells would have fuses cut for delayed action. They would hit and then roll around the ground, fuse sputtering and squirting sparks, like a demonic bowling ball, before exploding. As they could easily roll down into a 'bomb-proof' area while bouncing around, they could be exceptionally dangerous. As much as anything else, they were certainly dangerous to the morale of the defending soldiers.

Too large for conventional field artillery uses, the M1861 Seacoast Mortar fired an immense 330mm (13in) shell to 4000m (4325yd). Every round required 9.07kg (20lb) of powder, and the 7740kg (17.120lb) tube made moving the weapon around quite a chore. Even so, Union artillery units employed them at

Yorktown and especially at Petersburg, Virginia. The M1861 mortar's ability to throw a huge, 90kg (200lb) shell more than 3.25km (2 miles) into a defensive position was as much a psychological mission as a tactical one.

These massive weapons used a wrought-iron mount attached to a wooden bed. A ratchet device allowed elevation adjustments, but there were no sights of any kind on this or any other Civil War mortar. The time of flight for full-charge projectiles was extremely long – 40 seconds for this particular weapon at maximum range – so fuses for the projectiles were issued that were much longer than those which were used for conventional cannon, and they were calibrated up to 50 seconds.

During the siege of Petersburg, Virginia, by the Union Army in July 1864, one of these huge weapons was placed on a specially built small railroad flatcar and began helping to hammer the defences. Between July and September,

this mortar, christened the 'Dictator' by its cannoneers, fired into the Confederate positions 218 times, before being withdrawn in favour of smaller mortars. During that time, the Dictator's sheer weight of metal suppressed the enfilading fire from a Confederate artillery battery on Union forces along the entire right of the line.

32PDR SEACOAST GUN

Although they were originally intended for coastal defence, the heavy and super-heavy cannon often went into fortifications around Washington DC and other major cities during the war. They were emplaced around cities in order to defend against land assault by large enemy forces. This made sense: like the monster Parrotts and Columbiads, these weapons were far too big and heavy to move with tactical units. They could easily destroy almost any bridge without firing a shot, simply by being hauled across it.

■ABOVE: McAllister's Battery in action, 1862. Since the weapons of the Civil War had no recoil control systems, each had to be carefully, laboriously, re-laid before firing.

The 32pdr (14.52kg) was one such gun. A simple cast-iron gun without reinforcement, it boasted a 160mm (6.4in) bore and 3.13m (125in) tube. The tube alone weighed 3265.87kg (7200lb). Five degrees of elevation and 3.63kg (8lb) of powder would throw a standard shell out to 1749km (1922yd).

Monster cannon were part of America's and other nation's essential defences for 50 years prior to the Civil War. Such weapons were required to defend cities against naval assault and were designed to throw huge projectiles at besieging warships. Columbiads were among the very biggest of these, and many of them were installed in fortresses along the American coastline, all around Europe and near any seacoast city that could afford them. Columbiads first appeared in America in 1811, just in time to defend against the British Navy during the largely maritime War of 1812. By 1844, 203mm (8in) and 254mm (10in) versions were being cast and sometimes rifled.

Among the best of these were cast by a technique invented by Thomas Rodman, who was at that time a young United States Army Ordnance lieutenant. Rodman cast cannon around a chilled core, a method that produced tubes of exceptional toughness. The lines of his weapons were smooth, without bands or other stress points, another reason for their combat reliability. These weapons are distinctive for their notched breech faces, a feature fitted in order to aid in elevating the weapon.

Columbiads of the Civil War were issued in 203mm (8in), 254mm (10in) and 381mm (15in) models. The 203mm version had a 3.15m (124in) tube weighing 4177.59kg (9210lb). With five degrees of elevation, the Columbiad fired a 29.48kg (65lb) projectile to 1646m (1800yd) with 4.54kg (10lb) of propellant.

The 254mm model used an 8.16kg (18lb) charge to launch a 58.06kg (128lb) shot, also to 1646m (1800yd) with an elevation of 5 degrees.

The largest Columbiads in regular service during the Civil War were the Model 1861 'Rodman' 381mm (15in) smoothbore cannon. The tube for these huge, sleek weapons weighed 22,680kg (50,000lb) and needed 18.14kg (40lb) of coarse cannon powder for propellant. When all that powder was initiated, it propelled a 194.14kg (428lb) cast-iron shot for about 1820m (2000yd). With the weapon fully elevated to 25 degrees and charged with 22.68kg (50lb) of powder, these monster cannon could engage a ship all the way out to 4280m (4680yd). Any contemporary vessel unfortunate enough to find itself beneath the trajectory of such a shot would have had a serious problem in recovering.

Although none of the American weapons was ever fired at an enemy, they accomplished their military mission by discouraging assaults that might have been made without their emplacement.

Columbiads by the hundreds armed fortresses on both the east and west coasts of the United States during the Civil War. The successful attack on Fort Sumter, on 12 April 1861, involved the use of these weapons on both sides. Many variants on this massive theme were made, but Federal forces issued mostly three models, the M1844 in 203mm (8in) and 254mm (10in) calibres, the M1858 in the same bore sizes, and the M1861 in 203mm (8in), 254mm (10in) and 381mm (15in) calibres.

Although primarily a Union weapon, Columbiads were used by Confederate forces as well, in both captured and copied forms. The design was so successful that in 1864 one 508mm (20in) version was cast and tested. It proved to be too heavy for practical use, however, and no others were made.

■BELOW: Heavy seacoast artillery like this 136kg (300lb) Parrott rifle were tremendously powerful and inhibited assault from the sea. Three Parrott sizes were used during the Civil War.

GUN CREW PROCEDURES

A Civil War light field artillery battery going into action was a memorable spectacle. The size of a battery varied widely, even before combat losses. Federal batteries were normally authorized six guns, but often functioned with four. Confederate field artillery batteries were based on six guns. Each Union six-gun battery had about 50 men on the gun line, and about 110 horses, and all of them moved into their position on the line at a run. The entire unit, however, could be made up of 170 men when support troops were included.

The battery fought in several ways. The most common was in support of an infantry brigade. In that case, the infantry commander, a brigadier, gave his orders to the battery commander, a captain, directly or through a staff officer. The battery could also be under the operational control ('OPCON', as we call it today) of a higher headquarters, perhaps through the division chief of artillery or through the battery commander's direct superior, the artillery battalion commander. In this case, the unit fought as part of what was then called the 'artillery reserve'. Rather than

■ RIGHT: This vast congregation of Union people and horses in Fair Oaks, Virginia, is just one artillery battery, a good illustration of the support needed to keep Civil War guns in action.

be held in reserve, though, these units were reserved for the control of the overall commander. At Gettysburg, General Meade had an artillery reserve of 21 batteries with 110 guns that could be moved and used wherever needed, quite independent of the desires of division commanders. This reserve artillery held the line on the second day at Gettysburg, standing fast when the III Corps broke and ran at the Peach Orchard and Wheat Field, covering the withdrawal and providing time for the Union forces to re-form behind them, up on Cemetery Ridge.

Battery Commander

Regardless of whom the battery commander worked for, he was told where to be and when, and the 'commander's intent' for the battle. From then on, the battery commander was pretty much on his own. Normally without much interference, he selected

Boat Carriage Gun

Calibre: 86mm (3.4in)
Weight: 397kg (876lb)
Length: n/a
Barrel length: n/a
Effective range: 1618m (1770yd)

Elevation: 0° to 8° (est)
Traverse: none
Muzzle velocity: n/a
Country of origin: USA

his targets and controlled the way the battery engaged them. That was just as well, as an artillery battery was a complex organization and therefore difficult to manage.

Gun Section Commanders

Subordinate to the battery commander were three section chiefs, all lieutenants, each commanding a gun section. These

sections included 2 guns and all their personnel and equipment, about 40 men, 2 limbers, 4 caissons and between 20 and 30 horses. On the march, these section chiefs kept control of the order of march. In battle, they controlled the sections from horseback, for better visibility and mobility. Section chiefs designated the targets for the gunners, monitored the effectiveness of the fire and controlled

ammunition consumption and supply, all of this achieved under the direction of the battery commander.

'Chief of the Piece' and Gun Crews
Eight men served a fully-crewed field cannon such as the Napoleon, all under the control of the gunner, a sergeant, also known as the 'chief of the piece'. As well as the gun on its carriage, the gunner

controlled another vehicle, the limber, parked 20 paces behind the gun line.

All eight men had very specific primary duties in action and drilled long and hard until they could perform them automatically under the most difficult circumstances. When they could carry out their primary duties well, each was cross-trained in the duties of every other position. The gun crew was expected to

still function if only two men were left to serve it; in some cases, such as the action that resulted in a Medal of Honor for Corporal Samuel Churchill, cannon were effectively served by just one valiant soldier. Four of the men actually loaded and fired the gun under the supervision of the gunner. Three others prepared and carried the ammunition from the limber and brought it forwards. This is a basic description of how it operated.

The commander ordered, 'Forward into battery, MARCH!' The battery galloped into the position designated, the drivers steering the horses in a kind of fishhook manoeuvre and bringing them to a halt with the guns facing generally towards the target area. The crews either rode or ran alongside, quickly unhooking the guns from the limbers and rolling them into a line indicated by the battery commander with his extended sword. Normally, each gun was positioned 12.8m (14yd) from the next on the gun line, dispersing the battery and making each gun a little harder to hit when the inevitable counterbattery fire began.

While the guns were positioned, the drivers moved forwards a few yards, then dismounted and unharnessed the horses from the limber, another well-practised manoeuvre that took only seconds. The horses were led to cover, if any were

available, as they would be a prime target for enemy infantry or artillery. Without the horses, the guns were immobile and easily captured. From long practice, the limbers were rolled into their proper location, then each man moved to his assigned position, three at the limber and four beside the gun. Behind the gun, to the left of the trail, stood the gunner waiting for his orders.

The battery commander then ordered, 'Commence firing!' Number One stood to the right of the muzzle with his rammer and sponge. Number Two stood to the left, ready to receive the projectile and cartridge. Number Three's position was at the breech, on the right side; his primary job was to cover the vent of the cannon while it was being swabbed during the process of re-loading.

Number Four stood beside the breech on the left, ready to punch a hole in the cartridge through the vent, once it had been loaded and rammed, then to insert the friction primer and attach the lanyard; on the gunner's command, he pulled the lanyard and fired the weapon. Back at the limber, the Number Five man (the 'powder monkey') stood by while the cartridge was prepared by Number Six or Number Seven, both of whom would be busy in battle cutting fuses and inserting these fuses into the shells.

ABOVE: A neat and tidy emplacement of Union Parrott heavy rifles prepare to fire upon the much-abused Fort Sumter in July 1863. Despite some virtues, all Parrotts had a reputation for bursting.

At the command to commence firing, the gunner ordered 'Load', specified the kind of round he wanted and called out the range to the target. Immediately, Number Six or Number Seven back at the limber consulted a table on the lid of the limber that specified the proper elevation in degrees for the selected projectile, charge and range. This table also specified the time of flight for that combination. He sounded off with the required elevation.

The gunner then elevated the cannon, using his quadrant, and aligned it with the sight, using whatever profanity necessary to get Three and Four, using a handspike at the trail of the gun, to get the cannon properly aligned, making whatever corrections for wind he thought appropriate. While he did this, Six or Seven cut the fuse for the proper delay, pulled the shipping plug and stuffed it into the hole in the shell, tapping it into place.When he was ready, Number Five placed the cartridge in a special bag called a 'gunner's haversack' and carried it to the gunner for his approval. The gunner inspected the round to ensure that it was fused, that it was the projectile called for and that the cartridge was not leaking powder or otherwise damaged. He ordered 'Proceed!' and Number Five would move briskly towards the muzzle, where he delivered the round into the hands of Number Two.

Like clockwork, the round was placed in the muzzle by Two and rammed by Three, while Four covered the vent. The rammer was quickly withdrawn. One and Two stepped outside the wheels, facing in. Three steps back and Four took a friction primer and inserted it in the vent before hooking the lanyard to the primer. He then stepped away from the gun, faced away from the weapon (to keep the hook from hitting him in the face), took up the slack on the lanyard and waited for the command, 'Fire!' That command could come from the battery commander, the section chief or the gunner; in the heat and noise and smoke of battle, it could be very difficult to know exactly when to fire.

Once the piece had fired, it was essential to evaluate the fall of the shot properly. But for the smoke and confusion, that would have been a simple enough task, as a projectile in flight is easy enough to watch, even at 1417m/sec (1500ft/sec). The gunner had to

determine just where his shot went, then make corrections. While he was watching the target, the gun crew rolled the cannon back into position. The gunner called for another cartridge, realigned the cannon – probably with corrections for elevation and perhaps fuse delay – and the whole process was repeated until the order 'Cease fire!' came from one of the officers.

With training, a good gun crew could fire two or three rounds per minute. Much of that time was spent relaying the gun and getting it sighted again. In combat, with the enemy closing on the gun line, the gunner called for canister, then double canister, and refinements such as swabbing the bore and aiming the gun were dispensed with in favour of putting rounds downrange.

The infantry commander typically positioned the battery, normally in response to a local tactical situation. It was then up to the battery commander – in the absence of specific orders – to determine his targets and the method of engaging them.

CIVIL WAR AMMUNITION

Civil War artillery fired projectiles the utility and effectiveness of which had been perfected in many European wars over preceding centuries. The principal projectiles were solid shot and explosive

shell, although canister, case and grapeshot were all employed. A standard Federal field artillery battery went into action with about 200 rounds for each of the six guns, a mix in the limber chest attached to the gun and the rest in two chests on the caisson.

Shot

Solid shot was the Civil War version of a kinetic weapon, a compact, heavy projectile that did its work by simple brute force. Although solid shot was a simple projectile, its tactical use was a bit more sophisticated. At some ranges and under certain battlefield conditions, it was almost guaranteed to score if the gunners aimed in front of the target and skipped the shot along the ground. As long as the alignment of the tube on the target was correct and the range was a little short, the shot was likely to connect. Its usual target was an enemy artillery battery, an infantry company on line, a concentration of supply wagons, a group of staff officers or any other massed group. When this simple projectile struck

■ BELOW: A Model 1861 10-pounder (4.5kg) Parrott Rifle, designed for light field artillery. This cannon could deliver a 76.2mm (3in) projectile to a distance of about 2000m (2187yd).

Coehorn Mortar

Calibre: 24pdr (143mm (5.63in))
Weight: 72kg (160lb)
Length: 41cm (16.3in)
Barrel length: 457mm (18in)
Effective range: 1097m (1200yd)

Elevation: 20° to 70° (est)
Traverse: none
Muzzle velocity: n/a
Country of origin: USA

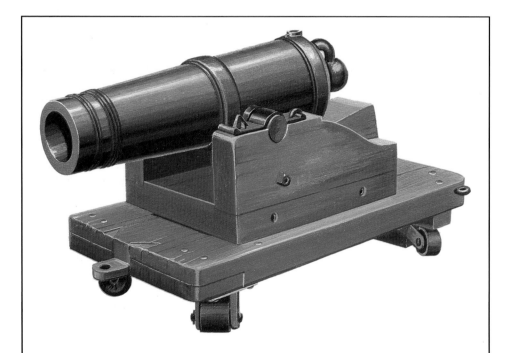

Carronade

Calibre: 32pdr
Weight: 900kg (2000lb)
Length: 1.22m (4ft)
Barrel Length: 760mm (30in) (est)
Effective range: 400m (436yd)

Elevation: 0° to 5°
Traverse: none
Muzzle velocity: n/a
Country of origin: USA

a gun carriage, for example, at any normal engagement range, the impact would likely smash the carriage and probably injure some of the eight men standing around it. If the shot struck the limber and hit any of the ammunition, the result was likely to be a massive explosion, with fragments of the limber becoming lethal projectiles.

At close ranges, a 5.44kg (12lb) solid shot travelling at approximately 305m/s (1000ft/s) would carve its way through an entire company of infantry, front to back. As it travelled, it would take off heads, arms and legs, cut torsos in half and splatter blood and tissue across a wide swath. One of the essential elements of a combat commander's plan is the use of shock, and there is nothing quite so shocking to an attacking unit as being under fire from a well-tended gun which is accurately firing solid shot, aimed right into the heart of a dense formation of oncoming soldiers.

Bolt

Rifled cannon needed elongated projectiles and some sort of driving band to seal the propellant gases and to engage the rifling of the gun. Without this seal, much of the gas would leak past the projectile without effect. Many kinds of bolt projectiles were designed and used in Civil War rifled cannon, the most distinctive of which were the elegant blocks of iron used in the Whitworth guns, a British import used by both sides.

Whitworth bolts had both a unique shape, designed for the weapon's hexagonal bore, and a unique sound in flight. All bolts seemed to have a sound all their own as they flew downrange, but the Whitworths were memorable to both the men who fired them and those on the receiving end. The quality of these projectiles varied enormously. Confederate arsenals typically produced bolts that were rough castings, with minimal machining and very simple sabots or driving bands to mate with rifled bores.

Shell

The 'basic load' for a Civil War cannon varied with time, place and model, but most contained a large proportion of shells. These projectiles could be either spherical (for smoothbore weapons) or elongated (for rifles). The most simple had walls of equal thickness, while more sophisticated shells, such as the Hotchkiss, were artfully designed for

controlled fragmentation and contained submunitions of fiendish design.

Case

Case projectiles have iron or lead balls added to the inside of a shell, along with a bursting charge, to cause casualties and damage. Sometimes also called 'shrapnel' after its British inventor, Henry Shrapnel, these rounds are designed for primarily anti-personnel use. Time fuses were often used exclusively when the gunners who fired them were trying for air bursts about 15m (50ft) over the heads of the enemy. That was a tricky accomplishment, given the fuses of the era; however, when everything worked, it was a highly effective process.

The Hotchkiss version of case shot was extremely sophisticated. At its base, a cup moved forwards at firing, expanding a driving ring that engaged the rifling of the gun and sealing the bore. Inside the shell itself was a fairly small bursting charge inside a well-designed cavity, in front of which was an iron plate; in front

of the iron plate were iron balls. When the shell detonated, these submunitions were sprayed in a controlled fan, rather than in all directions, making each shot more lethal than a conventional case round or shell. Simpler case rounds used impact or time fuses and sprayed their fragments everywhere.

All case rounds, by definition, use some kind of internal pellets – lead or iron. These are normally held in some sort of matrix that keeps them in position during firing and flight; if they were free to roll around, the centre of gravity of the projectile would shift and the accuracy of the shot would be degraded. Sulphur, coal tar and pitch were used for this matrix, each fracturing more or less reliably when the bursting charge fired.

Canister

Canister was, and still is, the round of choice when the infidels were coming over the barricades. During the Civil War, every field artillery limber had at least a few canister rounds plainly marked and

■ **ABOVE: Federal siege guns, Battery Sherman, in Mississippi. One of the soldiers is pretending to lay the piece by himself, an impossible task, while a sentry snickers in the background.**

carefully stored, ready for an emergency. These rounds are inaccurate by design, and they are intended to spray a large volume of lethal subprojectiles over a broad swath of ground; within their short range, they are murderous.

Basically, a canister round was a simple thing, no more than a tin container sized to fit the bore within which were lead or iron balls, with no fuse or bursting charge required. The standard 12pdr Napoleon's canister round contained 27 of these balls, each 12.7mm (0.5in) in diameter and packed in sawdust. A 5.44kg (12lb) howitzer used a larger projectile which contained 48 balls. The rounds were easy to manufacture and could include common musket balls and even large stones, in a real emergency.

the fuse recess of suitable projectiles. Instead of cutting the fuse to length, the fuse was prepared by simply punching a small hole in the thin metal covering a circular powder train. This disk was marked for delays of from one to five seconds. The hole allowed the powder train to be ignited anywhere along its length, a significant improvement on the tapered paper and wood designs.

Impact fuses were another European import. These devices fired the shell on impact and, by the time of the Civil War, had become fairly reliable; they typically used a sliding hammer to strike an

When fired, the flimsy container ruptured and fell away at the muzzle, and the balls spread out in a cloud of metal. Without the mass of the larger full-sized shot, these smaller subprojectiles were not very effective beyond 366m (400yd). Within that range, however, they took down attacking infantry in wholesale quantities.

At 183m (200yd) and below, they swept assault elements from the battlefield. A battery on line, firing canister at these ranges, killed hundreds of men with every fire. It was common to hear a loud, collective groan from the men in the assault after one of these massed fires as their units were struck this terrible blow.

Canister rounds were also issued for the artillery rifles, but were less effective in them than in smoothbores, as the spin imparted by the rifling spread the balls in a wider pattern.

Grape Shot

True grape shot was seldom used by land forces during the Civil War, it being a primarily naval projectile, but some of these rounds – like some naval cannon as well – were fired by field and heavy artillery units on both sides. Grape is somewhat similar to canister, but on a larger scale.

The balls were invariably cast iron, 38mm (1.5in) in diameter and, during the Civil War's later months, mounted between plates secured by a bolt running from one end to the other. These heavier projectiles carried farther, but there were few of them, only nine in a standard round for a 5.44kg (12lb) gun.

Fuse

By the time the American Civil War had begun, muzzle-loading fuse technology had been tried and tested for many years and in many wars in Europe. The lessons of these wars were applied in several kinds of fuses, some of which were quite sophisticated for their time.

These fuses all used a powder train as a delay device, normally a small amount of gunpowder in some sort of tube. When ignited, this powder train burned at a somewhat predictable rate. The outside of the plug was calibrated in seconds, allowing the gun crew to cut the fuse to a desired delay. When the gun fired, propellant gases invariably leaked past the projectile as it moved up the bore towards the muzzle. These hot gases ignited the fuse and started the sequence that detonated the shell.

The most simple and least consistent fuse was a tapered wooden plug, drilled out and packed with very finely ground gunpowder. Packing these fuses in a consistent way was always a problem, so the Union ordnance officers determined that, beginning in October 1862, all of them would be made at the Frankford arsenal. Getting these fuses consistently packed remained a problem, so another variety was used, made from paper and rolled around the powder. This provided better consistency, but remained somewhat unreliable nonetheless.

The most sophisticated and reliable fuse was a European import, the Bormann design. This Belgian device used a small threaded disk instead of a tapered plug, and it was threaded into

internal primer. On impact, the hammer moved forwards to impact the primer, the flash of which detonated the main bursting charge.

Prepared Cartridges

Gunners had learnt long before the Civil War that there was not much time during battle for measuring powder and loading cannon one element at a time. Instead, field guns were almost invariably loaded with prepared cartridges of powder and projectile, all in one neat package. This was particularly important with the use of shells; if the fuse happened to face the

■BELOW: Seen here at Fort Hamilton, the biggest of the coastal defence cannon were the gigantic Columbiads, the result of casting iron into a mold with a water-chilled bore.

breech and powder instead of the muzzle, the propellant gases would detonate the shell in the bore of the gun, rupturing the tube and injuring the gun crew.

To preclude this, shells were mounted on wooden or metal discs, retained by straps that kept the fuse pointed towards the muzzle. A bag of propellant powder was tied to this disc, making for a complete round. The round needed a small amount of preparation before firing, but having the powder already secured to the projectile made the loading sequence much faster than if loose components were used.

As an example of what a field artillery unit requisitioned, during July, August and September 1863, Battery G, 2nd Illinois Light Artillery was issued 566 Hotchkiss shells for its 20pdr Parrotts and 12pdr Wiard guns, 80 canister

rounds, 746 cartridge bags for their 6pdr, 566 paper fuses and 895 primers.

THE EARLY BREECH-LOADERS

The most accurate long-range weapons in common use during the Civil War were British imports to the Confederacy, and both were the product of Joseph Whitworth. Rebel sharpshooters routinely dropped Union soldiers with Whitworth rifles at ranges of up to 1.6km (1 mile). Rebel artillerymen routinely chopped Union artillery batteries to pieces with Whitworth 70mm (2.75in) cannon.

Whitworth's system replaced the system of small bands and grooves used in conventional rifling with a bore of hexagonal cross-section and projectiles to match, a variation on the idea of pre-cutting rifling used by other systems. The difference was his system worked.

This innovative bore and projectile system was part of a weapon with other innovations. Breech-loaders had been tried for centuries before the Civil War, but Whitworth's rifle was the first modern pattern to get a serious trial. It was found wanting; its breech was weak and complicated, and it leaked gases at firing. It also often broke. Whitworth gun crews sometimes wired the breech shut and fed the gun from the muzzle. It could not tolerate pressures high enough to exploit fully the accuracy of the projectile.

Whitworth's rifle was, however, clearly the way of the future. Even the Yankees who were on the receiving end – and who were forced to listening to the loud, distinctive whine of the gun's projectiles as they flew over the battlefield – knew that the days of the muzzle-loader were just about over.

The 12pdr Whitworth's tube was made of iron and steel, was 2.64m (104in) long and weighed 495.32kg (1092lb). With 794g (1.75lb) of powder and 5 degrees of elevation, the weapon delivered its steel bolt to a very respectable 2560m (2800yd). With 35 degrees, the projectile flew out to a distance of about 9144m (10,000yd), nearly 6 miles.

LATER COASTAL ARTILLERY

When the final ceasefire order was given in 1865, the art and science of muzzle-loading artillery were at their zenith. Millions of rounds of shot and shell, canister and case had been fired by both sides, at a tremendous cost in blood and treasure. Soon, the cast-iron and bronze smoothbore cannons would be replaced by lighter, stronger weapons that were more economical and had better range.

The cannon of the Civil War were heavy and needed large crews to fire. Still, the war demonstrated what organic and independent artillery units could do, and it was often decisive. The United States Army would keep its 3in Ordnance Rifles in service for another 30 years, but they and their ilk were obsolete for this entire time. The age of the lightweight, agile and accurate breech-loading steel rifle, which could be operated by a small gun crew, had finally dawned.

The Case of the Disappearing Gun

At the same time, an age of much larger guns developed. These were the heavy coastal defence guns that experience in the Crimean War, the American Civil War and, later in the century, Japan's war with Russia, proved to be essential. It was a time of conversion for the naval forces of the world, from the wooden ships and short-range muzzle-loading guns, to the breech-loading naval rifles of

■BELOW: This 381mm (15in) Rodman is defending Washington, D.C. The tube weighed 22,679kg (50,000lb). The shot weighed 194kg (428lb), and could travel 5000m (5468yd).

large calibre and tremendous reach which were transported under heavy armour and at high speed.

These new mobile weapons served to elevate the threat to every port facility and so this threat had to be countered. At the same time, many years of various conflicts which hd ripped through and across Europe suggested that the Franco–Prussian war of 1870–71 could begin again, and that this could happen at any time.

As a result, during the last two decades of the 19th century, a tremendous building boom occurred all around Europe. It also took off on both coasts of the United States as well as in many other places around the world. Because a new age of fortification had commenced, a tremendous amount of imagination, money and cast iron and steel was invested in these countries as well as being invested in the guns that would protect them.

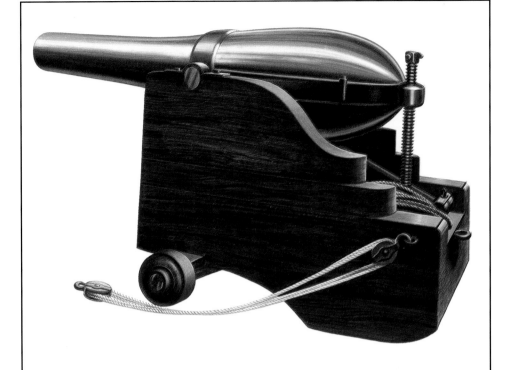

Dahlgren Naval Gun

Calibre: 30pdr (111mm (4.4in))
Weight: 1440kg (3200lb)
Length: 2.4m (95in)
Barrel length: 2.4m (95in)
Effective range: 2000m (2180yd)

Elevation: 0° to 5°
Traverse: none
Muzzle velocity: n/a
Country of origin: USA

A whole new family of guns and textbooks on how to use them evolved. Britain began producing the 152mm (6in) Mk 7 in large numbers and installing them on barbette mounts and in concrete emplacements all around the globe. These excellent guns could fire a 45kg (99lb) shell 11.43km (7.1 miles) and offered 360-degree traverse. Such was their effectiveness that they would stay in service for 70 years, until the 1950s.

M1900 12in Gun and M1901 Mount

In the United States, a tremendous variety of guns and mounts were being developed for coastal defence. Among these was the M1900 12in (305mm) Gun on its M1901 mount.

Installed in a carefully designed and constructed embrasure, this cannon used counterweights in a well situated below the gun, hydraulic buffers and massive cast-iron arms to expose the piece only momentarily just before firing. Recoil forces were partially countered by the hydraulic buffer and partially by the counterweight, which today would be called a 'recuperator'. The weapon's gigantic barrel and breech assembly 'ran out' to the rear.

The gun was supported by two sets of arms, both on trunnions, in an arrangement that allowed the whole tube to swing back and down about 3m (10ft). At the end of this travel, instead of returning to battery as normal guns do today, a latch system stopped the gun and held it in this lower position, out of sight and ready for loading.

Through a complex system of rods and cams, the gun layers were still able to aim the piece from their stations on a platform alongside the gun's firing position and orient the gun to fire on targets up to about 16km (10 miles) away. Only when ready to actually fire was the counterweight released, allowing the ordnance to return to battery, perfectly aligned for firing.

There were several variations on this theme which were used by the US Coastal Artillery for guns from 152mm (6in) to 406mm (16in), right up to and throughout World War II. By World War I, however, these guns were becoming obsolete and they were no match for the might of aerial bombing, which quickly proved that such weapons were now vulnerable dinosaurs and comparatively easy targets to find and destroy.

CHAPTER THREE
STORM OF STEEL 1900–1935

World War I was the conflict that saw the artillery piece claim the battlefield as its own. Thousands of guns were deployed on either side of the Western Front, ranging from light field pieces to giant howitzers shelling Paris.

By the turn of the 20th century, a tremendous revolution in gunnery was well underway. The long era of simple, muzzle-loading black powder cannon on simple carriages used for simple, direct-fire missions was over. Conversion to a much more complex set of technologies and missions was rapidly evolving. At the cusp of the new century and the new era, a French gun, the M1897 75mm (2.95in), pushed the revolution along by combining features from other guns into one remarkably efficient design. It was quickly imitated by German, British, and Italian gun-makers, and was soon improved by all.

Europe had experienced an entire century of brittle encounters between all the major powers and most of the minor ones, too. European nations were heavily fortified and heavily armed, ready for mobilization. In 1900, the manufacture of weapons was a growth industry.

Although Europe was prepared for war, the United States was not. Located far from the constant bickering of the European nations, the United States tried to keep from overseas involvement. The nation attempted to avoid participation in World War I, for many practical and political reasons, but the torpedo attack on the liner *Lusitania* in 1915, followed by the German declaration of unrestricted submarine warfare in early 1917, changed American minds. War was declared in April 1917, and a very poorly trained and equipped US expeditionary force was sent to France.

■LEFT: A highly-polished Ordnance Quick-Firing 13-pounder seen during the Trooping of the Colour ceremony. The gun signalled the beginning of modern artillery in British service.

The appearance of the French Quick-firing 75mm (2.95in) gun generated a lot of interest in the American artillery community. Development of a US field gun with the same characteristics was undertaken in 76.2mm (3in), 120mm (4.7in) and 203mm (8in) calibres, but none was approved for production before World War I. As a result, when participation in the war became politically unavoidable, US artillery systems and practices were woefully out of date. No suitable domestic weapon was available for the use of the American Expeditionary Force (AEF), other than small numbers of the US Model 1916.

US artillery units were mostly issued French and British weapons for use overseas. In addition, British- and French-designed cannons were produced in large numbers by US factories: the French M1897 75mm (2.95in) field gun; the French 155mm (6.10in) GPF long-range gun; another French 155mm system, the Schneider howitzer; and the British 75mm M1917, which was chambered to accept the French 75mm round. All three French guns would have a strong and lasting influence on US artillery system design; the last examples of this breed of guns have only just recently been retired from service.

A wide spectrum of artillery weapons had been developed or issued during the years leading up to World War I. There were for example light, very portable but not especially effective guns, designed for the horse artillery and light infantry. As a result of lessons learnt during battles between the Russians and the Japanese, the Russians and the Turks, the British and the Boers, and the French and everybody, the whole notion of field artillery was changing. In the first decade

Canone de 75mm *Mle* 1897

Calibre: 75mm (2.95in)
Weight: 1160kg (2557lb)
Length: 2.7m (106in)

Barrel length: 36 calibres
Effective range: 8500m (9295yd)
Elevation: -11° to 18°

Traverse: 6°
Muzzle velocity: 529m/s (1735ft/s)
Country of origin: France

of the 1900s, it became apparent that a successful combat organization needed quick-firing direct-fire cannon of at least 75mm (2.95in), plus accurate indirect-fire howitzers of at least 100mm (3.94in). It was obvious there was also a need for men who understood how to use them.

As a result of many wars, big and small, most nations had developed huge breech-loading guns for coastal defence and emplaced them by the hundreds in static defences. At the same time, German arms companies were working to adapt these huge weapons to mobile land operations. Germany was also working on monstrous breech-loading mortars, which would be capable of defeating the supposedly impregnable defences of potential enemies. British and Italian experience produced small modular cannon designed for mountain operations, light, compact and easily disassembled for transport on men or mules, with very high elevation for engagements over hill and dale.

At the turn of the century, breech-loading weapons were standard issue, but had not been in service long enough for all the defects to be worked out of their increasingly complex mechanisms. Some cannon still had only 'carriage recoil' and rolled backwards and out of position after

every shot, while German and French guns, with hydro-spring or hydro-pneumatic 'recuperators', could fire accurately and as fast as they could be re-loaded. It was a time of curiously free-market tendencies. Krupp could, and did, sell weapons to anybody who could pay for them, including those who were potential enemies of Germany. By the end of the 19th century, European design and engineering dominated cannon and mortar design, with weapons that were then modified and improved upon by their various customers.

AMMUNITION AND PROJECTILES

The years between the end of the American Civil War and the beginning of World War I had seen a tremendous evolution in many aspects of the art and science of artillery. Yet the basic projectile employed was still an anti-personnel fragmentation type, not too different from the shells used four decades previously. That would change rapidly.

One thing that had changed was the type of propellants and bursting charges. Nitrocellulose explosives were first developed in the mid–19th century and perfected about 1884 by a French ordnance officer, Paul Vieille. These blasting agents had the virtue of

increased '*brisance*', a term for the speed and power of an explosive reaction, and produced less visible smoke. Despite the fact that they were called 'smokeless' powders, they were neither powders nor without smoke. The manufacturing process extruded the damp material in strands resembling pasta or small ropes, inspiring a new name for the material, 'cordite'.

The old canister rounds of the Civil War era were improved by replacing the tin container for the balls with a steel shell, a projectile invented by artillery officer Henry Shrapnel. At the base of the shell was a bursting charge, then a large number of steel or lead pellets, while a fuse was placed at the top. A tube communicated the effects of the fuse with the bursting charge; when the projectile detonated, ideally about 9m (30ft) above the heads of an enemy force, the effect was like that of a huge shotgun. Canister rounds had the same effect, but only within a few hundred metres. Shrapnel could be fired to the maximum range of the gun with equal effect, not only at point-blank distances.

These projectiles were made even more effective by the addition of an explosive filling and an impact fuse. Ordinary shrapnel used a time fuse that, if properly calculated and fired, could be quite effective. Getting the fuse right, however, was not easily accomplished. During the war, fuses for these rounds were developed that could initiate the bursting charge at the moment of impact, if the timed part of the fuse had not already functioned. Instead of the inert filler that had been used with the original shells, molten picric acid was poured in as a filling. This tricky explosive was difficult to employ in such an application, but it was made to work. TNT was later also used as a filling, presenting its own set of problems.

Another technological evolution to come to fruition during World War I was the perfection of high explosives and their employment in artillery projectiles. High explosives had been used for many years before the war, but the blasting agents then available, such as nitroglycerine and pure guncotton, were too sensitive to shock to be used in shells. The shock of firing them could easily detonate these materials within the barrel, something that often happened during testing.

TNT, or trinitrotoluene, is an extremely powerful but stable blasting agent that is actually rather difficult to

initiate. It has the virtue of being comparatively safe to handle; it can be melted and poured into containers such as shells, making manufacture quite practical. Discovering methods to get such materials to explode reliably on cue was just one of the accomplishments of scientists during the war.

Poison gas was another technological accomplishment which appeared around the time of World War I. It was a deadly, effective weapon and a moral failure. Tear gas had been employed several times during the first months of the war; however, in April of 1915, Germany used poison gas for the first time at the Battle of Ypres in France. Very soon, both sides were using such materials, and they were delivered by conventional and specialized artillery systems. This lethal weapon has now been outlawed from the arsenals of all nations.

Artillery fuses developed during the war, evolving from very primitive powder train designs, identical to those used 50 years before, to complex clockwork designs. The introduction of high explosives required specialized powder trains within fuse mechanisms and elaborate mechanical safety devices to prevent premature detonation.

WORLD WAR I FIELD ARTILLERY

Field artillery during World War I was, at the outset, primarily light guns of small (approximately 75mm/2.95in) calibre, designed for mobility and direct fire at visible enemy positions no more than a very few kilometres away. France, in particular, based its battlefield tactics around the rapid, high-velocity fire of its new and revolutionary Quick-firing 75mm M1897 cannon.

By 1914 and the opening shots of the war, however, the war-winning qualities of the design had already been assimilated by the designs of excellent guns of British, German, Austrian and Italian manufacture, and even the United States was working on its own designs.

As the war evolved into a stalemate, heavier and more powerful guns replaced the lighter and more mobile cannon. The standard 75mm (2.95in) projectile was woefully inadequate, except when fired against a visible target, such as an enemy vehicle or machine-gun position or

■BELOW: This French gun, the *Grand Puissance, Filloux* (GPF) designed in 1917 and seen on display in Maryland, is one of the pioneer examples of mobile heavy artillery.

155mm Rimailho Howitzer Model 1904TR

Calibre: 155mm (6.1in)
Weight: 3200kg (6028lb)
Length: 2.4m (7ft 8in)
Barrel length: 15.5 calibres
Effective range: 6000m (6560yd)
Elevation: 0° to 41°
Traverse: 6°
Muzzle velocity: 320m/s (1050ft/s)
Country of origin: France

aircraft, but for the dug-in, dispersed infantry in their muddy holes, it was nothing more than an annoyance. As a result, larger and larger guns began to serve with the field artillery regiments, and they, along with the heavy artillery, began to churn the French and Belgian countryside into a moonscape,

slaughtering many thousands of soldiers from all sides in the process.

French M1897 75mm

World War I produced many important weapons and even some very famous ones, but only one inspired a cocktail, the M1897 French 75mm (2.95in). Developed at the end of the 19th century, this cannon was the ultimate secret weapon of its day. If World War I had begun in 1900 instead of 1914, its innovations might have been war-winners. The French 75 included all of the components we use today in what was, for its moment, a radical weapon.

The M1897 75mm (2.95in) combined several innovations into one revolutionary package, the first so-called 'quick-firing' gun. The key to the design was a hydro-pneumatic cylinder that absorbed recoil forces during firing, then smoothly returned the gun to battery. Prior to its introduction, all cannon shifted position at each shot and had to be repositioned and re-aimed before another round could be fired. That changed with the French 75mm.

The cylinder helped control the recoil, as did a spade on the trail and special wheel brakes. Two men aimed the weapon, while another loaded. One or two

men back at the ammunition limber used a mechanical device to set the mechanical time fuses quickly and automatically. The gun-layers stayed at their sights during every shot instead of getting out of the way as they had with previous weapons. Two gun-layers instead of one aimed the piece, the first adjusting elevation and the second azimuth, and this was a factor which also helped to speed up the weapon's rate of fire.

So the M1897 French 75mm (2.95in) combined several ideas – hydro-pneumatic recoil cylinder, trail spade, wheel brakes, fuse-setter and dual sights – into one well-designed and tested package. The result was that it fired up to 25 aimed shots per minute, a fantastic rate at the time. It changed the way in which the French Army fought, and, as its secret became known, it changed the way every army used artillery.

Had it been used sooner, it might have been decisive; however, by the time the real shooting started, German gunners had weapons at least as good, if not better. Even so, its technology was such a closely held secret that for many years members of the public were prevented from inspecting it. The weapon was guarded day and night, and, even when US forces were issued the weapon during World War I, long after its first introduction, French officials refused to permit its American gunners to know how to maintain it.

The weapon fired a 5.44kg (12lb) high-explosive projectile out to 6858m (7500yd) with an initial velocity of more than 610m/sec (2000ft/sec). The first ones had a trail that restricted elevation of the muzzle to 19 degrees positive angle, 10 degrees down angle. Although the gun could fire one round about every two seconds for short periods, its normal sustained rate of fire was six rounds per minute. In addition to the high-explosive projectile, a heavier 7.26kg (16lb) shrapnel round was also commonly fired from this weapon.

One of the other elements of the gun's success was its rotary Nordenfelt eccentric screw breechblock. A simple movement turned the block 120 degrees, ejecting the spent case from the chamber; a fresh round was seated and the breech closed, and the gun was ready to fire. Re-loading by a skilled crew took about one second. Each gun was supplied from a limber containing a ready supply of 72 high-explosive or anti-personnel fixed rounds. The French had developed sophisticated time fuses, and the mechanical device for setting the fuses was also part of the limber equipment. One or two of the gun crew used this device to prepare the ammunition, two rounds at a time, and one or more of the crew carried the rounds from the limber to the breech.

Future president of the United States Harry Truman commanded a US Army National Guard artillery unit equipped with the M1897, Battery D, 129th Field

Artillery Regiment, 35th Division, Kansas and Missouri National Guard. Battery D went into action at 04:20 hours on 26 September 1918, in support of the Argonne offensive. It fired about 30 rounds per minute until the guns became so hot that they were draped with wet blankets to cool them off.

French 75s were made and sold in huge numbers and used by many nations, including the United States, well into World War II and beyond. When Britain and France went to war against Germany in 1939, the United States was almost completely unprepared to participate in any serious shooting match. The now-elderly French 75s were still in the inventory and engaged Japanese forces in

the Philippines before US forces were quickly overwhelmed. The M1897 was grafted on half-tracks as mobile artillery and anti-tank to become the 75mm (2.95in) Gun Motor Carriage M3 and landed in the deserts of North Africa in 1942, where it was mildly successful against enemy armour, but did better against soft targets.

More than 17,000 of the weapons were manufactured, very few of which remain. Over the years, its small projectile and limited range restricted the gun's utility. They were so common, though – partly because of the legend France had enveloped them in – that they served long after much better designs became available. M1897s were still being used for training in the United States into the 1950s and by combat forces of small nations into the 1970s.

You can still buy one, though. After World War I, inspired by the powerful, smooth action of the weapon, Americans popularized a drink called the French 75 – a concoction of gin, lemon juice, sugar and champagne, so named perhaps because just one or two rounds would easily knock you flat.

German 77mm M96n/A
Like the French, German soldiers marched off to war in 1914 expecting to return home swiftly, just as they had in the war of 1871. They took with them a quick-firing gun not too different from the French 75mm (2.95in), a 77mm (3.03in) officially designated 7.7cm *Feldkanone* 96 n/A ('new type'). This gun was an adaptation of an old design, the model of 1896, which had been modified to accept a long recoil system.

■ABOVE: **This Austrian crew pause for the photographer before positioning their obsolete gun during training exercises before the outbreak of World War I. The gun is a breechloader.**

The 1896 gun used separate-loading rounds, smokeless propellant and a strange recoil control system that employed a length of rope wound around the carriage axle. It had a fine quick-acting sliding block-breech system, and its shells were filled with *Granatfuellung* 88. This was the German version of picric acid explosive, a material about 20 times more powerful than the black powder it had so recently replaced. The German cannon should have had a long recoil system installed from the beginning; if it had, the French 75mm M1897 would not have been quite so famous.

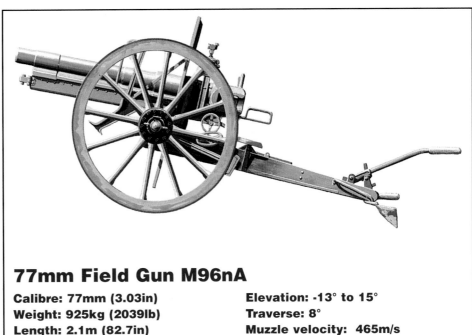

77mm Field Gun M96nA

Calibre: 77mm (3.03in)
Weight: 925kg (2039lb)
Length: 2.1m (82.7in)
Barrel length: 27.3 calibres
Effective range: 7800m (8530yd)

Elevation: -13° to 15°
Traverse: 8°
Muzzle velocity: 465m/s
(1525ft/s)
Country of origin: Germany

weapon, complete with most of the features of the French system, but as a private venture by a new company. One innovation was the addition of a shield to protect the crew; another was conversion to fixed ammunition, and the barrel was cut down in a lathe to make it lighter. The shield of the M96 n/A was helpful in two ways. It actually did protect the gunners when they were in active engagements, and attached to each side was a seat allowing two of the crew to ride on the gun while in transit. All this was done by a new armament company called Rheinmetall, which began the work

in 1895 and demonstrated the new gun only two years later. Rheinmetall's design was secretly purchased by the British during the Boer War and was soon in production, becoming England's first quick-firing gun.

Its weight ready for action was 925kg (2039lb), with a turned-down barrel 2.04m (6.7ft) long. Unlike many other guns seen then or now, it could depress as low as minus 13 degrees, as well as elevate to 15 degrees. That limited elevation did waste some potential range, a factor German gunners tried to correct by digging pits under the trail.

In fact, the French hydro-recoil system that was the foundation of the M1897 was invented and patented by a German, Konrad Haussner, in 1881, in both Germany and France. When the long recoil system was demonstrated after much development in 1894, it was soundly rejected. Around about the same time, the French noticed both the idea and the patents, and put them both to work in their new gun.

The introduction of the French M1897 startled the German artillery community, and the 77mm (3.03in) FK 96 was converted to become an almost useful

■RIGHT: Turkey has a long, colourful history in the field of artillery as an early adopter of improved technologies, like these excellent quick-firing guns captured in Palestine.

105mm M1917

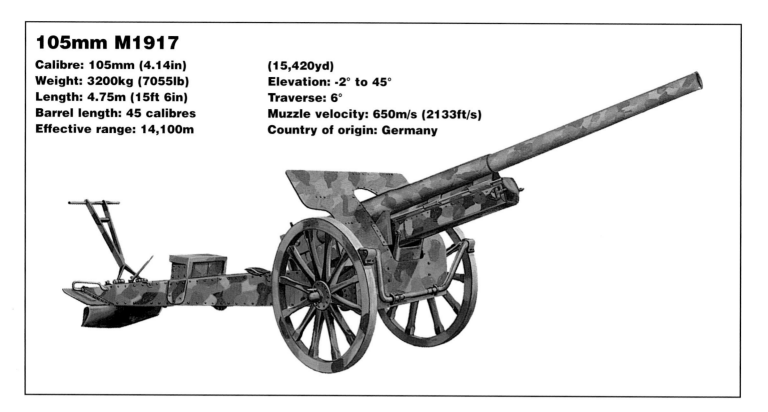

Calibre: 105mm (4.14in)
Weight: 3200kg (7055lb)
Length: 4.75m (15ft 6in)
Barrel length: 45 calibres
Effective range: 14,100m

(15,420yd)
Elevation: -2° to 45°
Traverse: 6°
Muzzle velocity: 650m/s (2133ft/s)
Country of origin: Germany

The French 75mm (2.95in) gave away range in the same way, with the cartridge being capable of 8km (5 miles), but the carriage, sights and firing tables limiting the gun's range to 6.8km (4.2 miles). Although it may seem a little odd to throw away some of the utility of a weapon, it did make some sense at the time. When both these guns were designed, it was expected that they would only be fired at visible targets and with corrections from an officer standing very close to the gun line. Their designers had not anticipated the use of field telephones and forward observers correcting fire from remote locations.

Despite its limitations, the high-velocity 77mm (3.03in) round was an essential player in German infantry operations. More 77mm shells would be fired by German artillerymen during the conflict than any other type, over 157,000,000 rounds.

German 100mm M1917 Gun

More than a dozen light field gun designs were issued to the artillery regiments, from 77mm (3.03in) to 100mm (3.94in), nearly all of them made by Krupp. The 100mm was easily the most popular of these medium guns, and the M1917 is a pretty good example of the breed.

Krupp had a long interest in 100mm (3.94in) guns and was making a breech-loading carriage recoil model in 1899. By 1902, however, Krupp was offering the same cannon with a long recoil system,

and Rheinmetall was offering its twin about the same time. This was a time of rapid technological development, as Germany and other nations scurried to develop quick-firing guns of their own, applying the lessons learnt from the French with their own improvements and modifications. In Germany, this produced a long sequence of 100mm and 105mm (4.13in) designs: for example, Krupp's 100mm *Kanone* 04 and then the 04/12 with its steel shield, firing platform, box trail and spade. Rheinmetall produced a similar gun, the *Kanone* L/35 M1913, and it was used extensively against aircraft during the war.

The M1917 was one of a series of new designs based on the old guns that appeared during the war, first the 100mm (3.94in) *Kanone* 14, with a 35 calibre length tube and maximum range of 13.2km (8.2 miles), then the 100mm *Kanone* 17. With a long, 45 calibre barrel 4.73m (15.53ft) in length, this gun had the muzzle velocity to engage targets at extreme range, more than 14km (8.7 miles). There was a penalty, however, and that was that the weight of the barrel required it to be moved as a separate load from the carriage. Both assembled and ready to fire weighed 3200kg

■RIGHT: British soldiers struggle to extract a captured German 150mm (6in) FH17 howitzer from the mud. Prolonged counterbattery fire has plowed up the soil all around the gun.

■LEFT: Various captured German field pieces on public display as spoils of war in Brussels, Belgium, after the Armistice. In the background can be seen Prince Albert's Palace.

(7040lb). Able to elevate to 45 degrees and deliver plunging fire, and with superior range over the French competition, this was a good system for the campaign against the trenches and against enemy artillery batteries. Altogether, 724 of the 1914 variant and 192 of the *Kanone* 17 were manufactured and issued, some of which were to continue in service for other nations after the war had ended.

German Light Field Howitzers

One of the most important German designs which appeared during the World War I years was Krupp's 105mm (4.13in) FH 98/09, the first German field howitzer to have a hydro-spring recoil control

system. A conversion of the 1898 howitzer, this design used a box trail and spade, a short barrel only 1.6m (63in) long and a large shield for the gunners. The design was quite successful, both as a technology and as a calibre of weapon. About 1200 of the type were produced during the war, and some of them saw export success, being ordered by Turkey, the Netherlands and Romania, as well as Bulgaria.

Despite its recoil system, the leFH 98/09 and its stubby little tube could not reach very far. Krupp developed a somewhat improved weapon, the leFH 17, for the Swiss Army. It featured an additional 420mm (16.4in) of barrel, stronger carriage, 136.5m/sec (448ft/sec) higher muzzle velocity and a tremendous improvement in range – up from 6km (3.7miles) for the 98/09 to 10km (6.2 miles) for the leFH 17.

This new gun started to combine the qualities of a cannon with those of a howitzer, but despite these improvements, only about 300 were manufactured before the end of the war.

■BELOW: March 1918, the last German offensive is launched. This crew pauses for a break amid the rubble with their 150mm (6in) howitzer laid for a fire mission against a nearby target.

Concurrently, Krupp's rival Rheinmetall designed a very successful light howitzer, the leFH 16, incorporating many of the features of these pioneering designs with some of its own. The design was presented to the German Artillery Examining Board in 1914 and tested two years later. Rheinmetall used the same ammunition and carriage of the 98/09 under the pressures of war – all somewhat obsolete, but still in the

production pipeline – and came up with an expedient design that could be produced quickly. The board selected this Rheinmetall 105mm (4.13in) howitzer to replace the Krupp 98/09 completely, and it became a very important weapon for the rest of the war, and after.

Although it had a slightly longer tube than the Krupp design, its maximum range was slightly less. The total weight was 120kg (266lb) less than the Krupp, however, improving mobility. Its deficiencies were balanced by excellent ballistics for that time, and by the end of the war a total of more than 3000 leFH 16 105mm (4.13in) howitzers had been manufactured by Rheinmetall.

It remained the standard German division support howitzer for years, until the leFH 18 appeared in 1937. The leFH 16 was produced by the hundreds after World War I and was used extensively until the end of World War II.

German 150mm Field Howitzer

Medium guns played an important role in German doctrine and, during the course of the war, guns of 100mm (3.94in) to 120mm (4.72in) evolved considerably. The 105mm (4.13in) calibre, in particular, played an important role; German gunners would fire more than 67,000,000 rounds before the armistice of 1918. Still, the heavier 150mm (5.90in) systems,

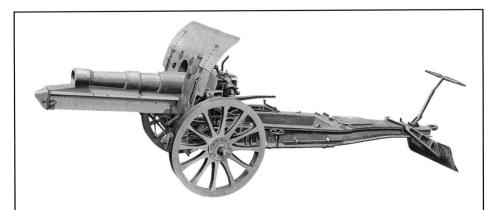

150mm Field Howitzer FH17

Calibre: 149mm (5.87in)
Weight: 2200kg (850lb)
Length: 2.1m (82in)
Barrel length: 14 calibres
Effective range: 8500m (9295yd)

Elevation: -11° to 43°
Traverse: 1°
Muzzle velocity: 365m/s (1197ft/s)
Country of origin: Germany

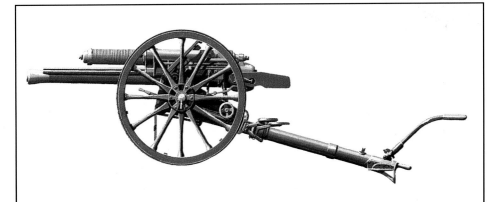

Ordnance QF 18-pounder Gun

Calibre: 84mm (3.3in)
Weight: 1284kg (2831lb)
Length: 2.5m (97in)
Barrel length: 29.4 calibres
Effective range: 8700m (9515yd)

Elevation: -5° to 16°
Traverse: 8°
Muzzle velocity: 492m/s (1614ft/s)
Country of origin: Great Britain

During the Boer War, British forces were confronted with an enemy equipped with modern German quick-firing cannon from Krupp that easily delivered a high volume of effective fire. At the same time, British artillerymen were returning fire with simple breech-loading 12pdrs (5.44kg) with a primitive and not very effective spade-and-spring recoil system that moderated, but did not eliminate, movement of the carriage.

These guns had a slow rate of fire, as each discharge required that the gun be repositioned and the shell was too small to be very effective. In 1900, General Sir Henry Backenbury quickly and secretly purchased the British Army's first quick-firing guns to counter this threat, 108 15pdr (6.80kg) guns from another German firm, Ehrhardt.

Shortly after the war, a Royal Artillery panel addressed these tactical defects. Specifications were drawn up for a new

■ABOVE: July, 1916, and the firing is hot and heavy during the Battle of Poziers Ridge. This crew is serving a British 18-pounder. The gun pit is well organized with prepared ammunition.

although firing fewer rounds – a total of 42,000,000 during the war – had much more of an impact.

There were many designs sharing this calibre in the German arsenals, including Krupp's 150mm (5.90in) FH 17. About 200 of these were built and issued, the first in 1913, with a modified version appearing in 1917. They delivered a useful 42kg (92lb) shell to 8.5km (5.3 miles), a range that seemed generous at the beginning of the war, but was considered to be less so at the end.

In common with some similar Krupp short-barrelled guns of that era, the FH 17 can depress far below modern guns, down to minus 11 degrees. At the time as they were developed, similar weapons were used in fortifications where they were often emplaced in elevated positions, and they had to be able to fire well below the horizon.

British Artillery and the 18pdr
Among the most stalwart gun designs of the World War I period must be counted the British Quick-firing 18pdr Gun, a system that, with modifications, lasted well into World War II. An evolution of lessons learned in South Africa and the Boer War, this 83.8mm (3.3in) gun fired a shrapnel shell to 8700m (9515yd).

gun to equip British field and horse artillery regiments. The new design was, from the time it was introduced in 1904 until the beginning of World War I, the most powerful and dominant field gun anywhere. This set of requirements incorporated lessons learnt from the Armstrong breech system, recent Royal Carriage Department designs, and work which had been done by Vickers on a hydro-spring recoil system.

The QF 18pdr used a hydro-spring recoil system, interrupted-screw breech and wire-wound barrel. The trail was a lightweight steel tube with a large spade attached and with two small seats on brackets, one for each of the two gun-

■BELOW: The men of J Battery, Royal Horse Artillery, are giving their lightweight 13-pounders a workout, in 1914. In combat their caps would be exchanged for tin helmets.

layers. The tube trail of the Mk 1 version of the carriage restricted the elevation of the gun to just 16 degrees, but that was corrected during World War I. The whole cradle and trail could be moved across the axle, which was a fairly primitive traverse design that allowed very limited movement of only four degrees from centreline. Again, this was something that was later corrected.

Two men aimed the QF 18pdr (83.8mm/3.3in). The man on the left aligned the gun laterally, peering through his sight through a small aperture in the protective shield. The gun was equipped with sights for both direct- and indirect-fire missions. On the right of the breech, another man elevated the gun as required by the range of the target. In front of both, attached to the shield, was a large slide rule used to set the fuses for each round. QF 18pdrs quickly became the standard gun for Royal Artillery field

batteries. Well over 1000 were made for British use before World War I began, plus another 99 built in India. Another 9444 were made in Britain and the United States during the war.

As excellent as the QF18 was for its time, the stress of wartime operations revealed some problems. The pole trail prevented the gun elevating more than 16 degrees, and that limited its range. The springs in the recoil system worked reasonably well until they broke, which they did fairly often under the pressure of sustained firing.

The QF18 was a fairly light weapon, just 1284kg (2831lb) with the Mk 1 carriage, and that made it quite manoeuvrable. The carriage and recoil system were re-designed during the war, first with a hydro-pneumatic recoil system, then with a box trail that allowed 30-degree elevation, a new version of the gun designated the QF18 Mk IV. With

more elevation, the gun could now engage targets at ranges up to 8230m (9000yd), and a better breech design improved rate of fire. The normal round during World War I was an 8.39kg (18.5lb) anti-personnel shrapnel shell containing 375 lead pellets; however, star shells, high-explosive and smoke rounds could also be fired. A good gun crew firing the Mk IV could put out 30 rounds per minute, quite a feat considering the size of the big, heavy cartridges, each of which weighed about 10kg (22lb).

The QF18 was such a sound design that it would soldier on for a 40-year career, getting pneumatic tyres in the 1930s and even a bigger barrel to eventually become the QF25.

British Quick-Firing 13pdr

At the same time as the Quick-firing 18pdr was developed, a similar gun was designed for use by the Horse Artillery.

This was the Ordnance Quick-firing 13pdr, a 76.2mm (3in) breech-loader of similar design and with the same pole trail, but even lighter and more mobile than the 18pdr.

This gun had a short barrel (24 calibres or 1.86m/73in), very limited elevation and traverse, and delivered a small, 5.67kg (12.5lb) shrapnel shell to only 5395m (5900yd). Normally moved by a six-horse team, the 13pdr weighed just 1014kg (2235lb), but it turned out to be too light in every way, ineffective in its intended combat role because of its diminutive projectile. It was, however, just right for an expedient anti-aircraft weapon, and in that capacity achieved some success.

British 3.7in Pack Howitzer

Combat operations in mountainous terrain have always imposed special conditions on men, equipment and

tactics. That was especially true for British colonial troops operating in India before World War I, lessons which were applied to battles after 1914 with this compact little howitzer.

Pack howitzers are designed to be disassembled into loads small enough for transport on mules or horses. They also tend to have extreme elevation, necessary to lob their projectiles over ridges and intervening terrain. The British 94mm (3.7in) Pack Howitzer evolved from smaller guns – a 10pdr and a 70mm (2.75in) gun – and was issued in the middle of World War I. Its barrel split into two sections, the breech and chase, connected by a massive clamp.

It was the first British gun to have a split trail, each leg of which could be broken down into two sections. The tube elevated from minus 5 to 45 degrees, and it could fire a 9kg (20lb) shell to 5395m (5900yd). Traverse was extreme by current standards: 20 degrees left or right. The whole thing weighed only 730kg (1610lb) when assembled, and it broke down into six components for transport by mule.

Another novel feature of the 70mm (3.7in) Pack Howitzer was the carriage suspension which permitted adjustment of the wheel height, independent of each other. This allowed the howitzer to be firmly supported at all points of contact with the ground on uneven terrain and was one reason for its accurate fire. The 70mm Pack Howitzer had its wooden wheels replaced by rubber tyres and steel rims during the 1930s, then served throughout World War II and was only

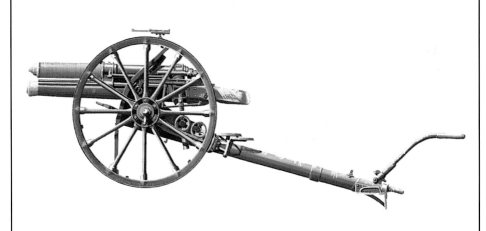

Ordnance QF 13-pounder

Calibre: 76mm (3in)
Weight: 1014kg (2235lb)
Length: 1.9m (73in)
Barrel length: 24 calibres
Effective range: 5395m (5900yd)

Elevation: -5° to 16°
Traverse: 8°
Muzzle velocity: 510m/s (2673ft/s)
Country of origin: Great Britain

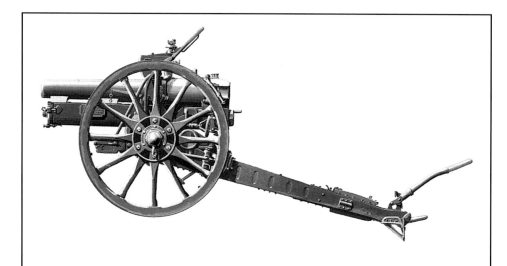

Ordnance QF 4.5in Howitzer

Calibre: 114mm (4.5in)
Weight: 1370kg (3020lb)
Length: 1.6m (64in)
Barrel length: 14.3 calibres
Effective range: 6400m (7000yd)

Elevation: -5° to 45°
Traverse: 6°
Muzzle velocity: 313m/s (1026ft/s)
Country of origin: Great Britain

trails and other modern conveniences. The fundamentals were good, however, and the calibre would become the standard for division support guns for many years.

HEAVY ARTILLERY

Heavy artillery became one of the hallmarks of the entire war. Heavy guns not only opened the war, but also fought much of it. At the end of four years, the technology had evolved tremendously. Howitzers of all shapes and sizes, from 150mm (5.91in) to 305mm (12in) and beyond, were built and laboriously put into position where they could deliver crushing blows to enemy lines and critical assets such as command bunkers and ammunition depots many miles away. Germany had been developing such weapons long before the war, while France and Britain had extensive experience with similar systems designed for naval and coastal defence.

retired in 1960, some 44 years after its introduction into service.

British 4.5in Howitzer

In addition to the useful and rapid direct fire provided by the Quick-firing 18pdr, the Royal Artillery needed something with a heavier punch and a trajectory more suited to indirect engagements. The Boers had made quite an impact on British forces, in several ways, with another Krupp design, a 120mm (4.7in) Krupp howitzer. Again, specifications were drawn up and published. Four designs were tested before the winner was selected in 1905. The winning 117mm (4.5in) howitzer came from a consortium which went by the name of the Coventry Ordnance Works.

This gun used a short-barrelled 13 calibre cannon on a box trail carriage with enough clearance for the breech to elevate from minus 5 to 45 degrees. A very useful 15.88kg (35lb) shell could be fired to 6675m (7300yd). A large shield protected the gunners from small-arms fire and some artillery fragments. Recoil was controlled by a hydro-spring mechanism, but this time the springs proved to be more robust than on the Quick-firing 18pdr, and the gun remained in service throughout World War I and most of World War II, just as first issued in 1908. Pneumatic tyres were added in the 1930s. By the outset of hostilities, only 192 had been manufactured; 3177 more were built during the war.

French Schneider Model 1913

This excellent World War I cannon introduced a design still used on modern weapons today: the hinged interrupted screw breech, an arrangement that made loading faster and more secure. The M1913 was, for its time, compact, light and sturdy. It was even more compact when a latch on the cradle was turned, releasing the tube and allowing it to be retracted and secured for travel, a concept that was soon applied to dozens of other gun systems. Schneider made many of the best guns of World War I, and many of those designs were adapted for service in World War II, particularly seeing service with US forces.

This gun was introduced in 1913 with the same basic quick-firing features included in the M1897, but with a more effective shell and a more effective cartridge. It was fairly light for its day and weighed only 2300kg (5070lb), with a 28-calibre (2.98m/117.3in) barrel. It fired a 16kg (35.27lb) shell to 12,700m (13,890yd). Compared to the 75mm (2.95in) M1897, this was a highly superior performance. Elevation was much better, too, up to 37 degrees, with a 6-degree traverse.

More than 1000 were manufactured during the war, and the M1913 continued to serve after the Armistice. It was the standard artillery piece of the French Army when World War II began, by which time it was quite obsolete, even though some had been modernized with spilt

German 210mm Howitzer/Mortar

At the outset of the war, Krupp had orders for 216 heavy, high-angle pieces of 210mm (8.27in) calibre. At the time, German military doctrine still anticipated fairly short-range engagements at visible targets and with firing corrections furnished by an observer on the gun line. By 1916, the 210mm (8.27in) projectile was even more in demand, but by now it needed to be delivered to longer ranges.

Krupp extended the tube of the original 12-calibre length barrel to 14.6 calibres, and it was re-christened the *Langer* 210mm *Morser* M16. This added less than 1km (0.6 miles) to its range – now out to 10.2km (6.3 miles) and up from 9.6km (5.9 miles) – for the 91kg (200lb) projectile. Springs were added for faster movement behind tractors instead of horses for some of these howitzers, while others retained the narrow, unsprung carriage suspension.

Although officially called a mortar, it could depress to minus 6 degrees, and that really is howitzer territory. The M16 could elevate to 70 degrees, too, and traverse slightly, two degrees left or right. It weighed 6665kg (14,696lb), not bad for such a powerful system. Besides a high-explosive projectile, a 210mm (8.27in) base-fused version was available for use against enemy fortifications.

German Mortars of World War I

Before the war, German infantrymen acquired their own organic indirect-fire support weapons through a small bit of subterfuge. These were very short, squat, simple devices called *Minenwerfer*, or 'mine throwers', and authorized to be used by the infantry's engineers. They were issued in calibres from 76mm (2.99in) to 380mm (14.96in), and, as the war deteriorated to static trenches and defensive lines, they all became quite useful. The Allies, without an equivalent at first, copied a captured version before the excellent Stokes mortar was introduced in 1915.

The 78.5mm (3.09in) version was the smallest mortar used during the war. It employed a crew of five, had a short tube and a recoil system, and it fired a small 4.53kg (10lb) shell to 1300m (1422yd). It evolved during the war into a very small howitzer, complete with trail and spade, and capable of direct-fire engagements. Wooden wheels made it mobile; however, instead of horses, the gunners put on harnesses and pulled.

A larger example was the 245mm (9.65in) Austrian Trench Mortar that could fire a high-explosive or poison gas shell weighing about 61kg (134.5lb) to

■BELOW: The men of the Royal Garrison Artillery's London Heavy Battery serve their 119mm (4.7in) gun during the Battle of the Somme in 1916, loading the shell into the breech.

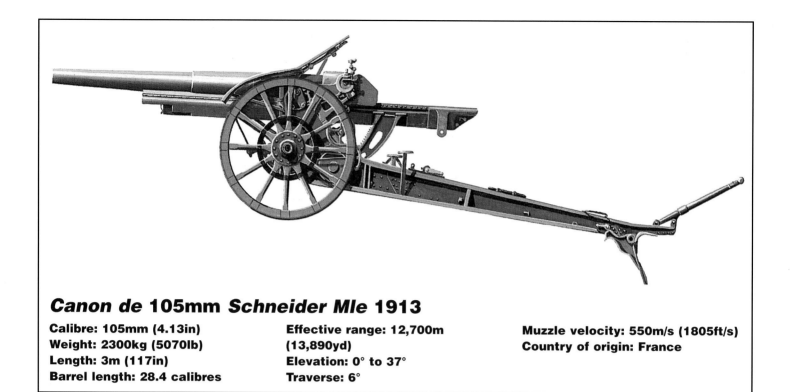

Canon de 105mm Schneider Mle 1913

Calibre: 105mm (4.13in)
Weight: 2300kg (5070lb)
Length: 3m (117in)
Barrel length: 28.4 calibres

Effective range: 12,700m (13,890yd)
Elevation: 0° to 37°
Traverse: 6°

Muzzle velocity: 550m/s (1805ft/s)
Country of origin: France

about 1km (0.6 miles). It was loaded from the muzzle in two steps: first the bagged propellant, then the projectile. These projectiles had their driving bands pre-cut to fit the rifling and were relatively huge compared to the mortar itself. This mortar also fired from a ground plate and used a hydro-spring recoil mechanism. It could elevate to 85 degrees, but that would put the projectile almost right back on the firing position. The whole package weighed 6187kg (13,640lb), a bit more than even the most sturdy German gun crew could haul around by themselves.

During the war, the German Army artillery committee took control of mortar development and production from the engineers and began to produce them in great numbers as economical alternatives to conventional field and medium artillery. The plunging fire of the mortars was found to be about twice as effective as the same calibre shell delivered from a direct-fire cannon. Mortars were also much simpler to make and cheaper; they weighed less for the same calibre and they could be manufactured much faster than guns or howitzers.

The largest of the engineer and infantry mortars was a mammoth 380mm (14.96in) model, the 380mm *Sehr Schwerer* (Very Large) *Minenwerfer*. This weapon fired a colossal 400kg (880lb) shell from an ingenious steel platform permitting all-around fire, to ranges between 365m (1200ft) and 1370m (4500ft). It required a crane for loading

the shell, which was nearly as large as the tube itself. By the end of the war, Germany had produced 12,329 light, 2361 medium, and 1234 heavy mortars.

British BL 6in 30cwt Howitzer

As an example of the difficulties confronting British gunners during the formative years of the breech-loading era, consider the 1896 design designated the Breech-loading 6in (152mm) 30cwt Howitzer. It was a stubby little creature with a very early recoil system. Besides the usual howitzer missions that could be accomplished with 35 degrees of elevation, this gun was expected to provide high-angle fire against entrenched targets; the BL 6in could be elevated to 70 degrees by dismounting the cradle and tube, and mounting them on a special wood and steel platform. Once in place, it could be easily rotated on a pivot, but this was not something that could be done quickly or with a small detachment.

Even so, this system could deliver an effective shrapnel shell weighing 53.75kg (118.5lb) to 4755m (5200yd). With its regular carriage, it was a heavy package weighing 3508kg (7733lb). Soon enough, 120mm (4.72in) howitzers would double that range, and later triple it, on lighter carriages with much better recoil control. The BL 6in was on the leading edge of the British breech-loading learning curve, however, and good enough to be made in large numbers and used extensively.

British BL 8in Howitzer

As World War I began, it was painfully apparent to all parties that heavy field artillery would be an essential part of winning the battle. The Germans were well prepared in this regard, but the British had almost nothing in the way of heavy guns. The Breech-loading 8in (203mm) Howitzer was the first system produced to fill this need. Although it proved to be a good interim design, with a massive shell and good range, it had a very inadequate recoil system.

Putting nearly 9.14 tonnes (9 tons) of iron and steel on two thin wheels and then trying to tow this package across muddy France was asking for mobility problems, and these guns were mired to the hubs, early and often. But they could throw a huge 90.72kg (200lb) high-explosive projectile more than 11km (6.84 miles), or 11362m (12,305yd). The Mk 7 version could elevate to 45 degrees and deliver plunging fire, making life even more miserable for German infantry in their uncomfortable warrens.

The recoil forces of such a large and powerful gun were more than the poor Breech-loading 8in could really cope with, and the entire carriage rolled back several metres with every shot. The gun crew placed portable ramps behind each wheel; after each shot, the gun would roll backwards, up the ramp, then come down again, sometimes on the wrong side of the ramp. It was a primitive way of doing business, but effective, and some of these howitzers were fitted with new barrels and used again during World War II.

British 12in Howitzer Mark II

Two years of warfare suggested to British artillery commanders that bigger was better, and a series of larger, longer and heavier guns was the result. The Elswick Ordnance Company concocted an even larger howitzer, a 305mm (12in) siege gun that fired from either a railway car or siege platform. Only eight of these systems were made, all in 1916, and despite their size they were soon in action in France. Two variants of the design were used: the Mark I as a railway gun and the Mark II as a siege gun firing from the ground. Both could elevate to 70 degrees and used 16.33kg (36lb) of propellant to throw a 340.19kg (750lb) shell to 10,369m (11,340yd).

The 305mm (12in) Howitzer really looked like a short-barrelled naval gun, complete with massive iron box trail mount and two cranes and a trolley for transporting the huge shells into the breech. Platforms attached to the side of the trails were necessary for the gun crew to operate its oversized controls. The gun was far too big to move by road in one piece and was instead disassembled into six subassemblies, each with its own wagon and team or tractor.

Bringing such a weapon into action took a lot of men and a lot of time. As with other siege-type guns, the 305mm (12in) Mark II mounting began by digging in a large steel beam with a pivot for the carriage, stabilized by an iron box laboriously filled with 20.32 tonnes (20 tons) of earth. The carriage was mated to this, then the cradle to the carriage, and at last the barrel mated to the cradle. The whole business could traverse only 60 degrees, so it was a good idea to make sure it was pointed in the right direction at the outset. The total weight of the gun and its mount, not including the 20-plus tonnes of dirt, was 34,019kg (75,000lb).

Its baptism of fire occurred in May 1916, at the bloody Battle of Ypres, and 22 of these systems would see combat in France. They were specialized pieces with specialized missions, and they took time and manpower to fire. The muzzle had to be depressed after every shot before re-loading, and ramming was strictly manual. An improved version with power-assisted ramming, the Mark IV, was produced, and a few were still used as coastal defence guns during World War II. The tube and breech alone weighed 9271kg (20,440lb), and the barrel was 17.3 calibres or about 5.64m (18.5ft) long. Inside were 60 grooves with a right-hand twist at a 1:15 rate. When fired, the 305mm (12in) Mark IV recoiled 1.25m (50in) as the enormous shell departed at almost 450m/sec (1500ft/sec). The Mark IV, with its longer barrel, had a maximum range of 13,122m (14,350yd).

French 155mm Guns

The 155mm (6.10in) calibre, an almost universal world standard for breech-loading systems today, seems to have its ancestry in a series of French guns going all the way back to 1877. That first one, the M1877, without any recoil system and very simple breech design, was reliable, effective and safe enough to stay in French issue for 37 years, until the beginning of World War I, when some were modernized with hydro-pneumatic recoil systems plus better breeches and carriages. The rest were still good enough, like very old soldiers, to be

M1902 76mm Gun

Calibre: 76mm (2.9in)
Weight: 1040kg (2288lb)
Length: 2.28m (89.6in)

Barrel length: 30 calibres
Effective range: 6400m (6976yd)
Elevation: -10° to 30° (est)

Traverse: 2° (est)
Muzzle velocity: 593m/s (1945ft/s)
Country of origin: Russia

mobilized and to creak off to battle just as they were, and some of those fought on throughout the war.

French science, however, had built something much more interesting around the same calibre, the *Canon de courte Mle* 155mm (TR). The TR stood for *Tir Rapide*, or 'quick firing', and this howitzer could indeed put some serious steel downrange. It was nearly a semi-automatic weapon and could fire up to 15 rounds per minute, one every four seconds, something even the most contemporary of 155mm (6.10in) designs cannot approach. An ingenious ordnance officer, Colonel Emile Rimailho, one of the three inventors of the revolutionary M1897, accomplished all this.

The M1904 used recoil forces to essentially 'cock' the mechanism of the gun, something like the way a machine gun fires from an open breech works.

After each shot, the barrel of this weapon returned to battery, while the breechblock remained open and retracted. The gun detachment placed the shell and propellant cartridge on the tray. Latches retained both components, permitting loading at all elevations, and only when the lever tripped did the round feed into the chamber and the breechblock close. This action rammed the shell and cartridge in the process, and the M1904

small, powerful weapon with a range of nearly 10km (6.2 miles), excellent for a short-barrelled gun of that era. This basic design was adapted as the *Canon de 155mm court Mle* 1915 that went to war in 1917, now delivering fire to 11.5km (7.1 miles). Once Schneider converted the gun to use bagged charges instead of brass propellant cases, this design became France's standard-issue medium howitzer, known as the M1917. These remained a mainstay until they were captured by the Germans in 1940, who continued to use them until they were worn out or recaptured.

In 1917, a new Schneider 155mm (6.10in) long-barrelled cannon appeared with proportions and features that would strongly influence artillery design, particularly in the United States, for the next 50 years. This was the *Canon de 155mm Longue* M1917, a gun-howitzer that outranged the old M1904 by 10km (6.2 miles), to 15,947m (17,440yd), using the same shell.

French 155mm Mle 1917 GPF

That same year, a French artillery officer at the Peteaux State Arsenal designed another influential 155mm (6.10in) gun, the *Canon de 155mm Longue Mle* 1917 *Grand Puissance, Filloux* (GPF). With a very long barrel, split trail and extreme on-carriage traverse for its day of 30 degrees left and right, this was a radical weapon when it appeared in 1917. It was destined for a long life in French and, with modifications, US service. The M1917 GPF included 35 degrees of elevation and that, plus the long tube, produced a maximum range of more than 16km (9.9miles).

This was an exceptionally influential design during World War I and after. It was produced in both France and the United States, and more than 700 were made before the end of the war. American artillerymen liked it so well that the Westervelt Board recommended that its design be essentially retained, with some modifications, and it went on to shoot at Germans again during World War II. At the outset of World War II, France still had about 450 in service, soon to be captured by the Germans.

French 194mm Gun GPF

The 155mm (6.10in) *Grand Puissance Filloux* (GPF) was quite successful, and Colonel Filloux developed a larger version that would work with the same carriage, a 194mm (7.63in) gun that

was ready to be fired again. It was an amazing bit of engineering. Even more amazingly, it worked well and reliably. It delivered a high-explosive 43kg (94.6lb) shell and, with elevation of 41 degrees, could put a very substantial amount of metal and explosive on anything within range. That range, however, was only 5.95km (3.7 miles), and, by the middle of the war, that was just not far enough to defeat the enemy.

■ABOVE: Vimy Ridge, April, 1917, and still the Allies lack good heavy artillery. This 152mm (6in) gun is a converted naval rifle; its only recoil system is a set of ramps behind the wheels.

Many of the best cannon designs of the war came from the inventive shops of the French firm of Schneider & Company. Among its designs was another 152mm (6in) gun, the 152mm Howitzer M09, a

210mm Howitzer

Calibre: 211mm (8.3in)
Weight: 6680kg (13140lb)
Length: 2.3m (90.36in)
Barrel length: 11 calibres
Effective range: 11,100m

(12,140yd)
Elevation: -6° to 70°
Traverse: 4°
Muzzle velocity: 393m/s (1290ft/s)
Country of origin: Germany

could reach more than 16km (10 miles), to 18,242m (19,950yd), with a shell weight nearly double that of the earlier gun, 80kg (176lb). This system, however, weighed more than 15.24 tonnes (15 tons) ready for action and had to be moved in two parts, carriage and barrel. A tracked vehicle that made movement over soft ground possible carried the barrel.

French *Canon de* 240mm

Both French and US naval and coastal guns were somewhat hastily adapted to mobile ground operations, and this is an early example of the type. French strategy for war with Germany anticipated the use of light, agile infantry forces supported with Quick-firing 75mm (2.95in) guns and machine guns in a war of rapid movement. Within months, a stalemate developed, and the little 75mm was nearly useless. Guns such as the 240mm (9.45in) M1884 had the power and reach to destroy rail junctions, artillery batteries and similar high-priority targets that would otherwise be safe from attack.

The M1884 was the heaviest French system moved by road during that war – more than 30.48 tonnes (30 tons) – and it was carried in two loads. The gun was nearly 6.7m (22ft) long, could elevate to 38 degrees and traverse 10 degrees total, launching a 140kg (308lb) projectile to a maximum range of 17,300m (18,920yd).

Despite its size, 60 were built and used for the duration of the war with enough success that they were preserved in service afterwards and would fire at the Germans once again in 1939.

German 420mm Howitzer

Those visionaries at the Krupp Works in Essen, Germany, decided late in the 1890s that the market was ripe for a really heavy howitzer that could defeat virtually any existing or planned fortification. Work commenced in 1900 on a technology demonstrator, a 350mm (13.78in) very short-barrelled howitzer capable of firing a 363kg (800lb) shell more than 9144m (10,000yd). This weapon was really a glorified mortar, with a mortar's virtue – a very high angle of plunging fire that attacked the most vulnerable part of any defended location, its top. At the same time, it had a large howitzer's ability to take massive amounts of propellant and fire a large shell a long distance.

As usual, even gigantic was not large enough. So, in 1912, Krupp produced an even bigger weapon along the same lines, this one 420mm (16.4in) with a 953kg (2100lb) shell and 14,630km (16,000yd) range. The weapon was far too big to be hauled along the dirt roads of Europe; it could only be moved by rail and then only in five flatcar loads. The idea was that it would be moved to its firing position by

rail, then assembled on-site. Krupp was commissioned to make a lighter version that could be moved by road, and that modification was finished in 1914, just in time for an attack on the Belgian forts which were outside Liege.

The new howitzer weighed just 43.69 tonnes (43 tons), less than half of the original. With a crew of 200 men and moved by a fleet of tractors, the components were delivered to a firing position outside the ring of Belgian forts. Two 'Berthas' (as they were known) and several Austrian Skoda 320mm (12.6in) guns formed a powerful battery and, on 12 August 1914, they were ready to fire. Inside the forts, the Belgian defenders felt relatively secure. The forts were very strongly constructed and were thought able to take just about anything. They were well stocked with ammunition, water, food and everything that was required to survive a long siege.

The first target was Fort Pontisse, to the south and east of the city, and the first round went downrange at 1740 hours. The German commander of one of the guns ran his communication wires back from an observation post where he served as the spotter. The gun crew noted the odd noises from the huge shell as it climbed up into the sky on its long journey, then waited breathlessly for a minute, expecting it to return to earth.

It must have taken only one round for the defenders to question the whole idea of the fort. They could hear the shell in its flight, getting louder and louder until it was a deafening roar that concluded with a clap of thunder as the projectile exploded. The very earth shook, dirt flew high into the sky in tremendous fountains and, when the gunners got the range, the concrete fortifications were shattered. The pressure wave from the exploding shells was like a hammer on every man in the place. In three days, every single one of the 12 'impregnable' forts had surrendered.

RAILWAY ARTILLERY

The monster guns that were used so frequently during World War I made a lot of sense at the time, for combatants on both sides. European nations had developed a thick network of rails that covered the Continent. Few places were out of the reach of the big guns of the era, and the only way to move them around was by rail; roads were far too muddy and undeveloped for such heavy loads. This, too, was the age of the battleship, and the massive naval rifles that armed the fleets had become a well-developed and effective technology.

The first serious combination of artillery and cannon seems to have been taken place during the American Civil War, when both Confederate and Union forces attached simple armour shields to small railcars and fired muzzle-loading guns or mortars through an aperture in the tinwork. This was followed soon enough by British and French trials on a somewhat grander scale, and the French in particular began to develop the idea seriously after the Franco–Prussian unpleasantness of 1870–71.

At first, railroad gun systems involved small, special-purpose track of 600mm (23.62in) gauge, intended only to move heavy guns from one fortification to another and up to firing positions near the German border, a programme developed by Colonel Peigne and employing 120mm (4.72in) guns. Around 1903, this programme began to adapt a 293mm (11.54in) mortar to fire from both this special 600mm (23.6in) gauge and the normal French railway gauge.

German Rail Guns

While German forces had some excellent big guns in 1914, and even some huge

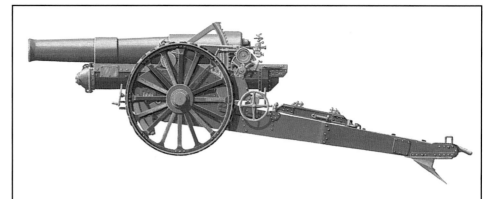

Breech-Loading 8in Howitzer Mk 7

Calibre: 203mm (8in)	(12,305yd)
Weight: 8890kg (17,500lb)	**Elevation:** 0° to 45°
Length: 3.7m (148in)	**Traverse:** 8°
Barrel length: 18.5 calibres	**Muzzle velocity:** 457m/s (2460ft/s)
Effective range: 11,250m	**Country of origin:** Great Britain

ones, none was capable of long range plus rapid mobility. That did not appear to be a critical need until the tremendous carnage of August and September 1914 produced a stalemate and static defences that seemed to be invulnerable to conventional attack. Europe was covered with a network of rail lines that came close to almost every hamlet and village. Since moving the big mortars and cannons had been accomplished more

efficiently by train than road, it was natural that the German High Command investigated putting really large cannons on railcars.

Mounting cannon on railcars is exactly what Krupp did in September 1914, adapting a 380mm (14.96in) naval cannon to a mount that allowed movement by rail to a firing site, where the gun was unloaded and installed on a prepared position. Other models followed in calibres which ranged from 150mm (5.91in) to 355mm (13.98in), and these too proved quite valuable.

With experience, a crew could emplace one of them in a night, preparing a bedding mount with pivot next to the rail line, then jacking up the whole thing – which could weigh up to 272 tonnes (268 tons) – and installing it, ready to fire. The gun detachments could be as big as the guns, with up to 3 officers, 10 sergeants and 160 soldiers assigned to one gun. Such numbers were needed to carry ammunition and for the dirty work of getting the gun emplaced. The large crew was not actually operating the gun during these missions.

The biggest of all of these was produced in 1917, the 380mm (14.96in) *Schiffskanone* 'Max' *Eisenbahn und bettungs Gerust*, or 'Max E'. This gun could fire from its special railway car or from a ground mount, engaging targets up to 47.5km (29.52 miles) away with a 400kg (882lb) high-explosive shell. Max E could depress to minus 5 degrees and elevate to 55 degrees on the ground, but only to an elevation of 18.5 degrees on the rails, as residual recoil forces would damage the track at higher elevations.

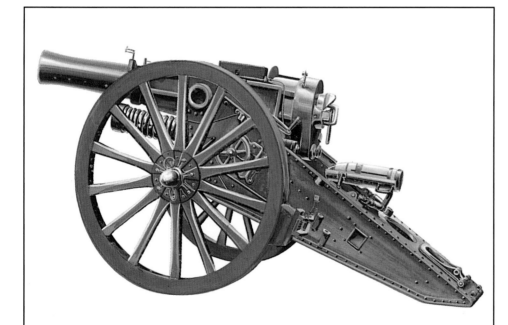

Breech-Loading 6in 30cwt Howitzer

Calibre: 152mm (6in)	**Elevation:** -10° to 35°
Weight: 3507kg (7733lb)	**Traverse:** nil
Length: 2.38m (94in)	**Muzzle velocity:** 237m/s (7777ft/s)
Barrel length: 14 calibres	**Country of origin:** Great Britain
Effective range: 4755m (5200yd)	

All these guns were kept busy during the war. Max E was the biggest of the lot, but they were all important. Shell weights varied among this class of guns from a lightweight 41.6kg (92.4lb) for the 150mm (5.91in) to the amazing 380mm (14.96in) Max E's 1008kg (2240lb). Virtually all were made by Krupp, with one exception, one version being built by the English firm of Elswick; this was really a gun captured and put to use against its former owners.

German Paris Gun
Late in World War I, German artillery astounded the French and everybody else on 23 March 1918 by firing into Paris with a cannon located almost 130km (80 miles) away, in the St Gobain Wood, not far from Laon. The trick was accomplished by a huge, nearly immobile gun of 220mm (8.6in) calibre and with a barrel 39.62m (130ft) long, based on a modified naval gun and designed by a team of Krupp engineers.

Each whole weapon weighed 144 tonnes (142 tons) and had some peculiarities. For one thing, both elevation and traverse were fixed. The barrel was mounted at an angle of 54 degrees and only fired at this elevation.

Traverse was only accomplished by moving the whole mount. The massive projectiles emerged from the muzzle at about 1524m/sec (5000ft/sec). The shell soared up 39km (24 miles), to the edge of space, on a journey that lasted two-and-a-half minutes.

Each round used so much propellant that the bore eroded at a very high rate, and each shell had to be slightly larger than the one fired before, the first being

■ABOVE: The *Canon de 194 Mle Saint Chamond sur Chenilles* looks like a self-propelled gun but is actually powered by another tracked vehicle. There were three variants.

210mm (8.27in) and the sixtieth 222mm (8.74in). After the sixtieth round, the barrel liner was replaced.

It was not an accurate weapon; the city of Paris is a large target, even from

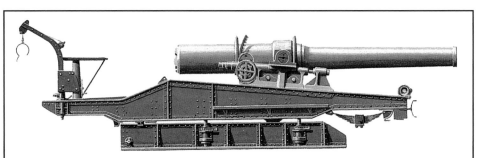

M1884 French 240mm

Calibre: 240mm (9.45in)
Weight: 31,000kg (61,000lb)
Length of complete gun: 6.7m (22ft)
Barrel length: 26 calibres
Effective range: 17,300m (18,920yd)

Elevation: 0° to 38°
Traverse: 10°
Muzzle velocity: 575m/s (1886ft/s)
Country of origin: France

130km (80 miles), and even so the *Pariskanone*, as the Germans called it, missed a few times. One round fired on Good Friday managed to hit the Church of St Gervais, full of worshippers at the time, and of course the Allied press suggested it was intentional.

Three of these cannons fired 351 rounds between March and August; however, aside from approximately 100 people killed or wounded, the whole effort was somewhat like using a million-dollar hammer to drive a two-penny nail. The original intention of the bombardment was never discovered, but it had little actual effect. Unless you were one of the 100 casualties, very little damage was done, as the shells were not very large or powerful, being only 120kg (264lb) each. The population of Paris, once they got over the novelty, went about their business without bothering about the occasional rounds from the gun.

The *Pariskanone* made the headlines and the history books, but was otherwise an expensive battlefield failure that accomplished nothing of military value. It acquired lasting fame, though, and several names: Long Max, Big Bertha (also the name of another German weapon), William's Gun (a reference to the Kaiser) and its official title, the Paris Gun. The tides of war ebbed away from Paris, and the Allied Forces, after much searching, finally located the gun – minus the barrel – as German forces withdrew from the area.

British Railway Guns

Britain began the war, as did the other powers, short of heavy artillery and with a good supply of surplus naval guns. Initially, a 230mm (9.05in) gun in a simple mount controlled recoil by the use of friction and an inclined plane. This basic approach was the Vavasseur mount, and it was used extensively during the war as an alternative to the more complex hydro-pneumatic or hydro-spring recoil systems.

These pioneering models were Mk 3 coastal defence guns, and they were placed on a 'well' railcar. A well car is designed to transport very heavy or tall objects by lowering the central portion of the car much closer to the tracks. These types of cars were, and still are, standard carriers for hauling massive objects by rail. The 230mm (9.05in) gun, with the 305mm (12in) calibre, was Britain's principal contribution to railroad artillery during World War I: not the biggest, nor

most unusual, but very good, useful and efficient weapons.

The first Marks in the 230mm (9.05in) calibre were essentially ranging shots. The Mk III mount added 360-degree engagement capability and a field-expedient modification that increased elevation to 35 degrees and permitted firing to 14,630m (16,000yd). This mount still used the simple Vavasseur recoil

device. A platform and crane at the breech end assisted with loading the 172kg (380lb) shells, and, with 30-degree elevation, the Mk X and Mk XIII gun versions could shoot at targets 20,665m (22,600yd) from the gun position.

A more ambitious gun was the immense 305mm (12in) Mk IX gun, firing an 386kg (850lb) shell to about 30km (19 miles). These big guns were equipped

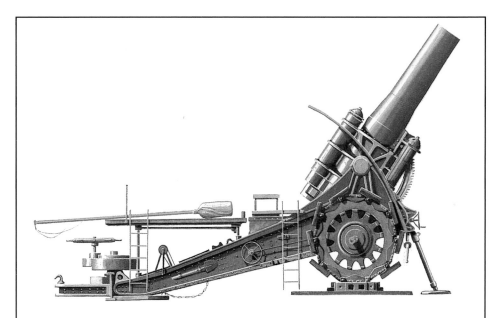

420mm Krupp 'Big Bertha'

Calibre: 420mm (16.53in)
Weight: 43285kg (85200lb)
Length: 5.88m (19ft)
Barrel length: 14 calibres
Effective range: 9375m (10,252yd)

Elevation: 40° to 75°
Traverse: 4°
Muzzle velocity: 425m/s (1394ft/s)
Country of origin: Germany

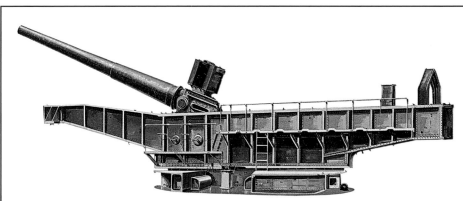

Schiffskanone L/35 'Max' Eisenbahn und Bettungs Gerust

Calibre: 380mm (14.96in)
Weight: 274,333kg (540,000lb)
Length: 31.61m (103ft 9in)
Barrel length: 35 calibres
Effective range: 47.5km (29.52 miles)

Elevation: -5° to 55° on pivot, -5° to 18.5° on wheels
Traverse: 4°
Muzzle velocity: 800m/s (2625ft/s)
Country of origin: Germany

with hydro-spring recoil systems and were ordered by the Royal Navy and presented to the Royal Artillery. They had been destined for HMS *Cornwallis*, but were declared surplus and sent to Vickers for conversion to railway gun use.

Vickers came up with a somewhat novel mount for the Mk I mount for these guns, a design with eight axles on one end and six on the other. On the ends of these axles are large-diameter wheels that appear to have been originally intended for use as driving wheels on locomotives. Vickers used them in the North American locomotive pattern, with the frame inside instead of out. Every other transport system used small-diameter wheels. The first two guns were

a success and inspired another pair, this time with a mount designed by Elswick Ordnance. All went promptly to France – and on to great glory.

Two 356mm (14in) guns originally ordered by Japan then turned up and were adapted to railway use. Double trucks supported the girder, with eight axles at the rear and seven at the front of the mount. Even in 1918, these mounts included petrol engines which served to power the gun's loading system, and, despite its size, the mount offered 2 degrees of traverse, both left and right.

French Railway Guns
As French military doctrine before the war emphasized speed and mobility, and

as the French presumed their M1897 was a war-winner, very little planning had been done for siege guns and extremely heavy artillery. The French had made some preparation, however, for using artillery on railcars. That programme expanded quickly in the summer of 1914, and, just like the Americans, Germans and British, the French started collecting every spare coastal defence and naval cannon that was not afloat and adapted it to railway operations.

Putting anything large on rails presents some interesting design problems for engineers. First, the railroad track gauge was standardized back in the mid-1850s at a very narrow width. The width varied somewhat at the time of

As usual, the French came up with new ways to do things. Although the French approaches were at times a bit unconventional, some of these designs were quite successful. The French, developed, as did all other nations subsequently, specialized rail cars which had been fitted with multiple axles to distribute the weight of the guns in transit to their firing site.

This was done first with multiple axles on a rigid car, then with a girder between two multiple axle trucks, a pattern also used by all other nations building such huge railway guns. Solving the great recoil problem in a short time was the major issue for armies of both sides, however, so the great French gun-maker, Schneider, came up with a simple, inexpensive and quite effective technique for dealing with the problem. Schneider's ingenious method basically reverted to the ancient technique of using friction to control recoil.

A firing position was designated and prepared by placing long steel beams parallel to the track, then pinning them firmly in place. The locomotive pulled the gun on its railcar over this prepared position, then large jacks were placed between the beams and fittings on the underside of the car. All the jacks were raised until the weight of the car was transferred from the wheels and tracks to the beams. The gun was aimed and fired, sliding backwards until friction brought it to rest only a metre or so behind its original position.

Now the jacks were cranked down, the wheels again supporting the gun and car, and it was carefully and slowly moved back to where it started, where the whole procedure was repeated. It was a slow process and required tremendous manpower, but had the virtue of putting very big guns in action without the development of complex hydro-pneumatic recuperators. It seems to have actually worked quite well on the very large guns of 275mm (10.83in) and above.

The *Canon de 320 Mle* 1870/93 *sur Affuit-truck Schneider* employed this simple friction recoil system. It used a gigantic war-surplus coast defence

World War I, but was normally not far from the current standard, 1435mm (4ft 8.5in). Clearances for bridges and tunnels, signal towers and everything else were standardized for those small, early locomotives. Anything that moved on the rails, including big guns, had to be designed to fit those standards. Recoil control was naturally a major issue when placing such large guns on comparatively small steel rails, especially when those rails are less than 1.5m (5ft) wide. This is a very narrow base for a big gun to fire from, and the rails themselves were far too weak to absorb the firing stresses or even the dead weight of any of the bigger guns in service on a conventional railcar.

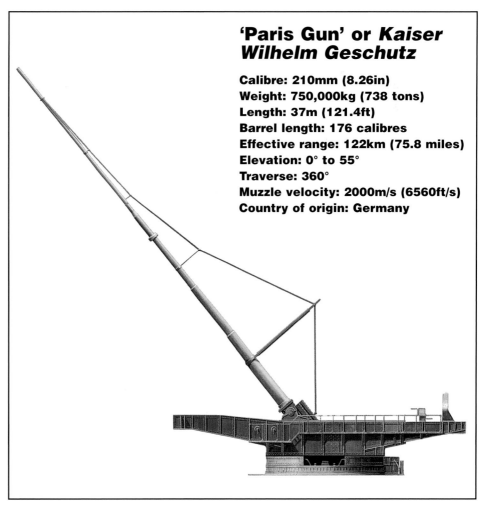

'Paris Gun' or *Kaiser Wilhelm Geschutz*

Calibre: 210mm (8.26in)
Weight: 750,000kg (738 tons)
Length: 37m (121.4ft)
Barrel length: 176 calibres
Effective range: 122km (75.8 miles)
Elevation: 0° to 55°
Traverse: 360°
Muzzle velocity: 2000m/s (6560ft/s)
Country of origin: Germany

cannon, a leftover from the previous war with Germany of 1870–71. This enormous old gun was installed on a girder between two five-axle trucks and connected to half a dozen supporting railcars with ammunition, a large detachment of men, spare parts and all the equipment needed to go to war. It fired a 338kg (854.5lb) shell out to 24,800m (27,120yd), several times, in fact, before it had to be jacked up again and rolled back up the track.

One example of another innovative railway gun is the *Canon de 240 Mle 1903 sur Affuit-truc St-Chamond et Schneider*. This 240mm (9.45in) gun employed the Canet rotary breechblock that was hemispherical in shape and turned along the long axis of the barrel, instead of at right angles to it.

The breech was semi-automatic, ejecting the spent case on run-out. The gun combined carriage-friction recoil control with the gun mount sliding backwards and up an inclined plane on the railcar itself. A hydraulic strut attached between the front of the gun mount and the railcar also helped manage recoil.

This gun, along with its more conventional cars, placed an excessive

load on the tracks when ready for action, so the barrel and carriage were carried separately. When ready for action, the gun had to be assembled with an accompanying crane, then moved into a prepared site. The car was positioned over a mound of earth placed on the tracks, then the railcar was lowered onto the mound until its weight was fully supported. The French M1903 240mm (9.45in) railway gun weighed about 48 tonnes (47 tons) when ready for action, elevated from 15 to 40 degrees and threw a 140kg (309lb) shell to a distance of 17,300m (18,920yd).

Another 240mm (9.45in) gun, the *Canon de 240 Mle 93/96 sur Affuit-truck St-Chamond*, recycled a simple coastal defence gun on a pedestal mount, attached to a girder all supported by 12 axles and 24 wheels. This gun could fire to any quadrant direct from the rails, but only after outriggers were mounted to the rear and brackets on the muzzle side to keep the whole gun on the tracks.

This French railway weapon weighed about a massive 140,000kg (138 tons) and could shoot a 162kg (357lb) high-explosive shell about 23,000m (25,159yd). As the gun could not traverse at all, the

■ABOVE: Most rail guns during World were naval rifles adapted to land use. The fixed, proportionately narrow width of the rails called for compromises. This is a British 406mm (16in) model.

only way to orient the tube was by positioning it along a curved portion of track and moving it forwards or back until it was properly orientated in azimuth for its target.

US Railway Guns
One of the oddities of US participation in World War I was that the first shot fired in ground combat by an American-designed gun, with an American crew, was actually from a US Navy crew firing a naval cannon many miles from shore. The American gun was an enormous 355mm (14in) weapon on an elegant railway carriage built by the Baldwin Locomotive Works.

The late entry of the United States into the war, after years of avoiding involvement, meant that the United States' major source of modern heavy artillery was either designed for use aboard ship or for use in fixed coastal defences. These cannons were all extremely large, with tremendous firepower and range, but very little thought had been given to employing them in any mobile ground role, at least until 1917. During that year, the pace of developments in US heavy artillery accelerated somewhat.

The navy and army both quickly developed plans for using 178mm (7in), 203mm (8in), 305mm (12in) and 356mm (14in) naval cannon in railroad mounts, the smaller calibres being first used for anti-submarine defences. The US Navy contracted with Baldwin Locomotive for 30 guns and supporting facilities.

Similar to German, British and French rail guns, each US system required a complete train with facilities for the large crew, ammunition cars, anti-aircraft car, a radio car, berthing and dining facilities, repair tools and parts, plus everything else required to support such a weapon in combat. Only five sets were completed in time to fight, arriving at the port of St-Nazarene in July 1918.

It is not often that a US admiral commands an artillery battery ashore, but this did take place in World War I. Under the command of Rear Admiral C.P. Plunkett, USN, these big railroad guns were assembled, test-fired and moved into position for their combat missions in early September 1918. The entire operation was owned and operated by the US Navy: the locomotives, the guns and the cars were all US Navy property, and everything, including the locomotives, was operated by sailors.

The massive German 'Paris Gun' had been firing into the city during this period, and a primary mission of the US 356mm (14in) guns was to silence this threat. By coincidence, the Paris Gun ceased fire about this time, and the US crew took credit for intimidating the Germans, implying that it was the threat of their counterbattery fire that silenced the gun.

Admiral Simms, one of the US Navy's senior officials in France, claimed, 'Expertly as this train had been camouflaged, the German airplanes must have detected its approach. As it neared the objective, the shells that had been falling on Paris ceased. Before the Americans could get to work, the Germans had removed their gun, leaving nothing but an emplacement as a target for our shells, though our men were therefore deprived of the privilege of destroying this famous long range rifle, it is apparent that our arrival saved Paris

12in Railway Howitzer Mk 5

Calibre: 305mm (12in)
Weight: 77,168kg (75.95 tons)
Length: 26.62m (87ft 4in)
Barrel length: 18.8 calibres
Effective range: 13,121m (14,350yd)

Elevation: 0° to 45°
Traverse: 240°
Muzzle velocity: 447m/s (1468ft/s)
Country of origin: Great Britain

Canon de 240mm Mle 93/96 sur Affuit-truck St Chamond

Calibre: 240mm (9.45in)
Weight: 140,000kg (137.75 tons)
Length: 19.5m (64ft)
Barrel length: 10.05m (33ft); 43.8 calibres
Effective range: 22,000m

(25,159yd)
Elevation: 15° to 35°
Traverse: 58°
Muzzle velocity: 840m/s (2755ft/s)
Country of origin: France

from further bombardment.' He forgot to mention that the German gun outranged the American by more than 80km (50 miles); the real threat was from aircraft.

But the American 356mm (14in) railway guns kept themselves and their huge crews busy for the next few months of the war, firing 782 635kg (1400lb) shells before the final ceasefire on 11 November 1918. One round fired at a railway junction at Laon landed in the middle of the switching yard, forming a huge crater, tossing one railcar up in the air and down on another and ripping up a large portion of the track.

The 356mm (14in) US Navy Railway Gun was produced in two mounts: Mk 1, the distinctive covered version; and Mk 2, with a more conventional uncovered mount. The original closely resembled a ship's gun turret that had been stretched severely over the entire weapon, but provided the crew with some protection. However, the layout of the gun and mount restricted elevation, unless a pit was dug and a special ground mount similar to that used with other World War I railway guns prepared, with the 356mm (14in) cannon placed upon it. It was a 36-hour job.

Another mount, the Mk 2, raised the gun enough so that it could fire at full elevation from the rails. The massive weight of the gun and mount were distributed on two huge trucks, each with 20 wheels on 10 axles. The Mk 2 employed a shell trolley to transport the 635kg (1400lb) shell to the breech.

The tube and breech alone were 50 calibres or 14.22m (560in) long and weighed almost 87.5 tonnes (86 tons). The whole system, in its Mk 1 mount, tipped the scales at 243 tonnes (239 tons). The gun itself could elevate to 43 degrees and traverse a total of 5 degrees; however, if firing from the rails, the Mk 1 was limited to 15 degrees and a maximum range of 21,031m (23,000yd).

COASTAL ARTILLERY 1914–45

Training and doctrine for artillery organizations of major nations from about 1850 to about 1940 strongly emphasized coastal defence using massive rifles, and this emphasis was reasonable at the time. In the days before instant communications by radio, an enemy could easily appear in strength off an essential seaport and take the place by storm long before friendly naval forces could be summoned for help.

In consequence, large naval rifles were emplaced at the entrances to important harbours. These big guns were extremely accurate, fired from fixed positions inside heavily fortified emplacements and used 'disappearing mounts' that exposed the cannon only very briefly. As they fired from a known elevation above the surface of the water, precise range-finding was another advantage. Simple triangulation told the gunners exactly how far away each target was, further enhancing the likelihood of a first-round hit.

While any adversary would be on a moving platform firing at a tiny target at a range that could only be approximated, the big coastal rifles had the advantage of a perfectly stable platform. It was, during World War I, a winning combination that inhibited naval attacks on coastal defences, and the lot of the coastal artilleryman was, with a very few exceptions, a safe and dull one.

Britain designed and deployed 19 models of coastal cannon between 1885

■RIGHT: The huge amount of propellant used to launch heavy projectiles to extreme distances invariably results in large muzzle-blasts. The flash would invite enemy counter-battery fire.

and 1942, most appearing around the turn of the century. These included small-calibre weapons such as the 3pdr Mk 1, a 47mm (1.85in) gun with a range of just 6850m (7491yd), designed for use against small, fast craft. At the other extreme was the 254mm (10in) Mk 3, accepted for service in 1888, which launched a 227kg (500lb) shell to a maximum distance of 10.5km (6.5 miles).

The United States, in particular, placed great emphasis on coastal artillery and produced dozens of guns specifically

for such use during the same period, ranging in size from 57mm (2.24in) to 406mm (15.98in), capable of engaging targets out to 22.4km (13.92 miles). These included direct-fire, high-velocity guns, as well as gigantic mortars such as the 305mm (12in) M1900, a weapon designed to drop a 485kg (1069lb) shell.

US 16in Coastal Gun M1919

A good example of the best of the coastal gun breed is the US M1919 406mm (16in) rifle, developed during and immediately

after World War I and standardized in 1928. Exquisitely engineered and manufactured, this was the design work of hundreds of men over three or four years. One of them at the time said, 'This unit has been designed to incorporate the lessons taught by the World War, and will out range any guns now mounted or contemplated for battleships.'

The gun used wire-reinforcement construction, and the tube and breech assembly were together more than 12m (40ft) long. This naval rifle employed a

■LEFT: An American version of the railway gun, this M1918 12in (305mm) gun was an adapted naval cannon. Its barrel's 72 grooves needed replacement after just 350 rounds.

round consumed 385.56kg (850lb) of propellant and produced chamber pressures exceeding 261,993 kPa (38,000lb psi).

Seven assemblies were needed for the mount: base ring, racer, side frames, cradle, the loading trolley and its associated components, the gears for elevating and traversing the mount, and the electrical motors and wiring to move the system around. Fabrication of guns of this size took at least three years of painstaking work, and the process required very large, very specialized machine tooling.

The base ring of this gun was a cast-iron assembly 9.75m (32ft) in diameter, built up of five sections and weighing 51 tonnes (50 tons). The top of this base ring was accurately machined to form the lower bearing race. This operation, which would have been simple with a smaller version, proved almost impossible. When the surface to be cut was over 30m (100ft) in circumference, the cutting tool became dull before the work could be completed. This delay was further complicated because the cutting tool could not be changed while the operation was actually in progress.

There were 42 rollers supporting the gun on the ring, while electric and hydraulic motors powered the traverse and elevating mechanism. This mechanism would quickly serve to point the gun between minus 7 degrees and 65 degrees, with an accuracy of 1 minute of

angle, and was able to move it up to 3.5 degrees per second.

The cradle weighed 51 tonnes (50 tons) all by itself, which is more than any complete modern self-propelled artillery system. Together with the barrel, this assembly weighed in at 249,475kg (550,000lb), about as much as three modern main-battle tanks.

But the trunnions were so artfully placed and balanced, with low-friction bearings, that a single man could quickly adjust elevation anywhere within the system's range by using a hand wheel. The system was so well thought-out that the gun was slightly muzzle-heavy when unloaded, but slightly breech-heavy when loaded. The weight difference made it easy to drop the muzzle for loading, then run it up into firing elevation once it was loaded. Guns such as the 406mm (16in) M1919 were initially emplaced in the open. They were widely dispersed, each with its own ammunition supply, and were able to function autonomously.

The United States installed such guns at dozens of places along each US coast, as well as in strategic locations such as Hawaii, the Philippines, Puerto Rico and the Panama Canal. The port of San Francisco had several such 406mm (15.9in) guns dug into the rocky hills on the north side of the Golden Gate, with smaller guns covering the southern approaches to the harbour.

During World War II, a programme was initiated to get them all in protective casemates and behind 102mm (4in) armoured shields that were 3.66m (12ft) wide. A large pit below ground level allowed the crew to serve and service the gun while remaining protected from enemy fire.

vertical breechblock of the Smith-Asbury type, which was operated by compressed air. With cradle, this part of the system reached a weight of approximately 203 tonnes (200 tons).

It was designed to fire an armour-piercing shell weighing 1061kg (2340lb), intended to defeat 356mm (14in) of armour plate. According to its press releases, it could do this at all ranges. That type of performance was actually unlikely at the outer end of its effective reach, almost 45,720m (50,000yd). Each

16in M1919 Coastal Gun

Calibre: 406mm (16in)
Weight: 491768kg (484 tons)
Length: 20.32m (66ft 8in)
Barrel length: 50 calibres
Effective range: 44.9km (27.9 miles)

Elevation: -7° to 65°
Traverse: 360°
Muzzle velocity: 822m/s (2700ft/s)
Country of origin: USA

CHAPTER FOUR
MASTER OF THE BATTLEFIELD 1936–1945

World War II saw the self-propelled gun come into its own. Usually based on an obsolescent tank chassis, these artillery pieces could launch a devastating barrage and then quickly move to avoid any enemy counter-battery fire.

World War I had begun with field artillery capable of maximum engagement ranges of 6km (3.75 miles). By the time it was over, some weapons were firing at targets 10km (6 miles) away. The war had started with a general expectation of rapid movement of forces and direct-fire engagements for supporting artillery. Instead, it was typified by static siege warfare and prolonged indirect fire coming from weapons hidden from their targets by terrain. Clearly, modern artillery changed dramatically in order to meet the new battlefield challenges.

GERMAN ARTILLERY

After World War I, Germany's huge arsenal of artillery systems was melted down and recycled, except for those systems that were kept hidden. The knowledge accumulated by gun designers and gunners was forgotten. The Treaty of Versailles limited the tiny German Army to guns with calibres smaller than 105mm (4.13in), and it allowed very few of those. Only 204 77mm (3.03in) field guns were authorized, and just 84 105mm leFH 16s, with no more than 800 rounds in storage for each.

German gun designers went off to work in Sweden and Switzerland after the war, with round-trip tickets to their homeland. They continued to develop weapon designs, and, after the rise of the

■ **LEFT: An American M7 Priest, a system cobbled together from a gun and vehicle chassis that happened to be available, but which worked well across North Africa and Europe.**

National Socialist Party, or Nazis, most returned to work for Krupp and Rheinmetall. After the Treaty of Versailles was renounced in the 1930s, production of artillery, along with all sorts of other materiel, went into high gear. The 105mm (4.13in) leFH 16 light field howitzer was a proven design, but only 33 were left of the 3000 produced. More than 450 new leFH 16s were built by 1934, and the total was up to nearly 1000 when the much-improved leFH 18 first appeared in 1937.

Directly after World War I, the US Army assembled a board of artillery officers to consider the lessons learnt from the experience in Europe and to recommend new designs and methods of artillery employment for the future. This was the famous Westervelt, or Caliber, Board of 1919, and the result was a list of suggested new designs, most of which were based on the French cannons and howitzers which had been in American use between 1917 and 1918.

These designs were developed during the 1920s, but were not produced. The plans were filed for lack of money to implement them. That changed in the late 1930s, with the rise of Hitler and the Nazi Party in Germany and with the concurrent rise of Mussolini in Italy. The plans were dusted off, in some cases adjusted, and put into production.

One of the most important modern modifications had nothing to do with firepower. It was a feature neglected by other armies: the replacement of wooden wheels with pneumatic tyres. The US Army realized, earlier than other armies, the role that high-speed mechanized ground combat forces would play in the future. The old guns simply could not be moved at the speeds which were required in order to accompany vehicles such as the then-new M3 Scout car, or M3 Half-Track, particularly when riding over broken ground.

During World War II, American gunners relied primarily on four guns: the 114mm (4.5in) M1, the 155mm (6.1in) M1 ('Long Tom'), the 203mm (8in) M1 and the M85 240mm (9.45in) gun. In addition, US 'redlegs' typically used five howitzers: the 75mm (2.96in) M1A1 Pack Howitzer, the 105mm (4.13in) M1A1, the 155mm (6.1in) M1, the 203mm (8in) M1 and the M1 240mm (9.45in).

Most of these systems revealed their French ancestry, albeit one generation removed. The most celebrated weapon at the outset of the war was the already obsolete but highly imitated French M1897 75mm (2.96in) cannon. By the end of World War II, the lower velocity howitzer had overtaken it in popularity as the field artillery weapon of choice.

The amounts of ammunition consumed by artillery units during World War II were huge. As one example, a US infantry division, the 104th 'Timberwolves', fought for about six months in Belgium, the Netherlands and Germany. During that period, they fired 101,221 60mm (2.36in) mortar rounds, 148,101 rounds for their 81mm (3.19in) mortars, 281,716 M2 105mm (4.13in) howitzer shells, and 51,470 rounds for their 155mm (6.1in) howitzers, and millions of rounds for their rifles and machine guns.

This division lost 1447 killed in action or died of wounds, and it inflicted an estimated 18,000 casualties on enemy personnel. When it was all added up, the old adage that it takes a man's weight in bullets to kill him was as true an observation in World War II as noted before and after that conflict.

FIELD ARTILLERY

Among the really stalwart cannon of World War II must surely rank the British 25pdr, developed in the mid–1930s

as a replacement for the then-standard 114mm (4.5in) Quick-firing gun and the 18pdr. It was one of those systems with many failings and handicaps and at least as many virtues that nonetheless somehow managed to get the job done.

More than 12,000 units were manufactured, and it was the basic artillery weapon for Commonwealth nations for three decades. The 25pdr first made an impression during the desert battles of World War II, where its massive anti-tank projectile demolished German and Italian tanks in wholesale lots. It was still giving good service 30 years later in 1971, when both India and Pakistan would use it against each other.

Three basic models of the gun were issued. The first – known originally as the Ordnance 88mm (3.45in), then as the

■ **BELOW: Canadian soldiers prepare to fire their 25pdr, one of the great guns of World War II, with a large, effective shell, a stable, pivoting carriage, and incremental propellant charges.**

1825pdr, then as the 25pdr Mark 1 – appeared in 1937 and used the carriage of the 18pdr as an interim economy measure. This carriage was not strong enough to handle firing forces from the extra increment added to the 'supercharge', and that limited the range of the Mark 1 to 11,704m (12,800yd), 549m (600yd) less than with the additional propellant.

Mark 2 versions finally got a stronger carriage and the extra range. The cartridge designers decided that the gun could handle even more propellant, so an additional powder charge was issued with the solid shot anti-tank projectiles. The 25pdrs have a bore 88mm (3.46in) in diameter, substantially bigger than the 75mm (2.95in) common at the time.

Combined with a separate-loading cartridge with three propellant charges and an alternate 'supercharge', the gun did not have the many choices or extensive firing tables of some other weapons. Many kinds of ammunition were available: all the normal types, plus a heavy solid shot anti-tank projectile, and a canister anti-personnel (AP) round.

The gun would elevate to 45 degrees and depress to minus 5, but it could only traverse 8 degrees unless it was on its 360-degree firing platform. Several self-propelled (SP) gun systems were developed around it, including the Bishop (on an old Valentine tank chassis) and the Canadian Sexton (on a Ram chassis). The Bishop modification did not allow elevation over 15 degrees, severely restricting the gun's range and usefulness, but the Sexton was a very successful gun and served long after World War II was over.

It was a heavy gun, though. At 1741kg (3838lb), it took a truck to move it around. The 25pdr used a limber to help distribute its weight and to provide a supply of ready ammunition. It could be ready to fire, however, 60 seconds after rolling to a stop, and just one of its crew could turn the gun on its rotary firing platform, a very convenient feature during defence against tanks in the desert or even the bocage.

5.5in Medium Howitzer

A stalwart British gun of the World War II years and after, the 5.5 was first issued to the Royal Artillery regiments in 1941 and served with distinction until the 1970s. Five and a half inches works out to 140mm, an odd calibre for a howitzer and unique in British service at the time.

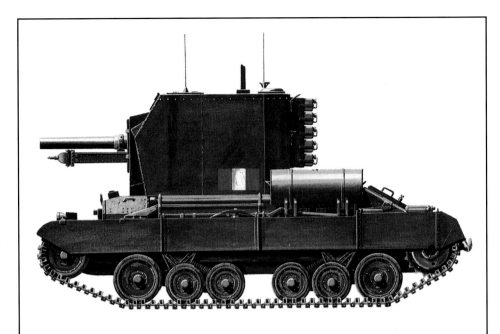

Bishop

Calibre: 87mm (3.45in)	Elevation: -5° to 20° (est)
Weight: 7879kg (17,333lb)	Traverse: 8°
Length: 5.64m (18ft 6in)	Muzzle velocity: 532m/s (1745f/s)
Barrel length: 2.4m (2.6yd)	Country of origin: Great Britain
Effective range: 5852m (6400yd)	

The 5.5in Howitzer was unusual in other ways, too. It used a tapered tube without muzzle brake and with the look of a small naval gun that had wandered far from its element. Its tall, spring-loaded, equilibrators alongside the breech were far taller and more distinctive than those on similar medium guns.

A 36.3kg (80lb) high-explosive shell was the normal projectile, with

Sexton

Calibre: 87mm (3.45in)	(13,400yd)
Weight: 25,300kg (55,660lb)	Elevation: -9° to 40°
Length: 6.12m (20ft 1in)	Traverse: 65°
Barrel length: 2.4m (2.6yd)	Muzzle velocity: 532m/s (1745f/s)
Effective range: 12,253m	Country of origin: Canada/GB

illumination and smoke separate loading rounds also available. Four charge increments could be used, and all of them launched the HE round out the front at 510m/s (1673ft/s) and to a maximum range of 16,400m (17,935yd). Elevation was up to 45 degrees and the gun would traverse 60 degrees total. Ten men filled the usual detachment, all of whom had to be retrained when the 155mm FH-70 replaced the 5.5in Howitzer in British service, using the standard NATO ammunition, beginning in 1970.

German 105mm leFH 18 and similar

Despite the Versailles Treaty, German artillery planners went to work on improved systems immediately after World War I, and a major project was the re-design of the standard field gun of that conflict, the leFH 16. Between 1914–18, Germany had fielded more than 11,000 guns of all types.

At the outset, these systems were, by and large, mostly high-velocity direct-fire guns, as well as just a few howitzers, at a ratio of five cannon to one indirect-fire howitzer. Four years later, the ratios were nearly equal; there were two howitzers for every three direct-fire cannon in the German Army, and, in addition, the value of indirect fire was well appreciated.

On 1 June 1927, the German Army Ordnance Office issued a request for an improved light field howitzer based on the proven 77mm (3.03in) leFH 16 that had served so well during the war. During the next three years, work on this project was slowly developed by Rheinmetall; in 1930, a new and improved field gun was demonstrated, called the leFH 18.

This system was based on a 105mm (4.13in) gun using a variable charge semi-fixed metallic cartridge. The tube was longer than the leFH 16 – at first 25 calibres, later 28 – and this improved muzzle velocity to 470m/s (1542ft/s) and range to over 10km (6 miles). It was a tremendous improvement, and one which was seen for the first time in a German field gun. Part of this improved performance was the decrease in projectile weight, 1kg (2.2lb) less than before. A large family of projectiles was developed for the gun: several shaped charge designs, smoke bombs, high-explosive charges, anti-tank charges as well as others.

The leFH 18 was loaded with features appreciated by artillerymen. It had a tremendous range of traverse – 28 degrees left and right – and the split trails and spades made the gun very stable while firing. Both of these features, added to good velocity and range, plus a wide choice of anti-tank projectiles, variable-charge propellants and good

sights, made the system a natural for both direct- and indirect-fire missions. It quickly became the standard light howitzer of the German Army and provided reliable service throughout the war. It was also popular after the war, with other armies.

This field-piece was a technically advanced design at the time, introducing features that would later become standard on other systems. It introduced a new sight that simplified and sped up engagements, an improved case-ejection mechanism, as well as other features, all of which combined to make the light howitzer heavier by a total of about 500kg (1111lb).

This penalty resulted in somewhat wider solid rubber tyres on the pressed-aluminum wheels, and made the leFH 18 too heavy for reliable transport by horsepower. Instead, it was typically pulled by a 5 tonne (5 ton) half-track at up to 40km/h (25mph), 10 times faster than artillery moved by horses. However, when fired with Charge Six for maximum range, especially at high elevation, the lightweight trails sometimes developed cracks that required depot repairs.

It was officially adopted in July 1936. More than 19,000 leFH 18s were manufactured during the war, mostly for use by the German Army, although some were sold to the Netherlands, Spain, Norway, Sweden, Slovakia, Hungary and Finland. Over the next 9 years, it would appear in 28 variants and serve reliably in every theatre and climate.

Some variants used muzzle-brakes, while others did not. Several lightweight models intended for transport behind horses were issued, while others had features customizing them for mechanized transport. The cannon was adapted for use on the *SturmGeschutz* III SP assault gun, on the Panzer IV tank, on the *Sturmhaubitzwagen* 638/14 SP howitzer and the *Wespe* (Wasp) SP gun.

German 75mm Recoilless Rifle

The first recoilless rifle appeared during World War I, a somewhat primitive American device called the Davis Gun, developed by USN Commander Cleland Davis. Inspired as a method to put a heavy gun on a light aircraft, this gun used two projectiles in a single tube open at both ends and with a powder charge in between. When fired, one went towards the target and the other, a mixture of lard and lead pellets weighing exactly the

Ordnance Breech-Loading 5.5in Gun Mk 2

Calibre: 140mm (5.5in)
Weight: 6190kg (12,120lb)
Length: 4.38m (14.3ft)
Barrel Length: 31 calibres
Effective range: 14,813m

(16,200yd)
Elevation: -5° to 45°
Traverse: 60°
Muzzle velocity: 510m/s (1673f/s)
Country of origin: Great Britain

■ABOVE: At full recoil, the German light field howitzer leFH 18, one of the most prolific guns of the war, fires its 105mm (4.13in) shell, while the crew try to keep the trail spades in position.

same as the working projectile, went out the rear as a counterbalance; the launch tube scarcely twitched.

The Davis Gun made little impact during World War I and was nearly forgotten afterwards, until resurrected by Germany's Rheinmetall in the 1930s. The company re-examined the basic principle of the weapon, and a whole new family of weapons was introduced. The Germans, however, omitted the lard and birdshot. Krupp and Rheinmetall both became involved in development of the

technology, and both came up with designs. Rheinmetall's design was selected for the first production weapon, designated *Leicht Geschutz* 1 at first, which was then later re-christened *Leicht Geschutz* 40, with reference to its year of introduction into service.

First of these was a lightweight 75mm (2.95in) gun for anti-armour use by the airborne troops, a weapon that could be delivered in five parachute-dropped bundles and assembled quickly. It was a very compact system, only 750mm

(29.5in) long, but a lot heavier than such rifles would become later, initially weighing 145kg (320lb). Maximum range was 6798m (7434yd) with special ammunition. An improved recoilless rifle followed in 1942, a 105mm (4.13in), designated the LG 42, which could fire to

■RIGHT: Germany pioneered the use of recoilless guns, like this 75mm (2.96in) Model 40. Light and effective, but producing noise, flash and dust, they were an adequate weapon.

8000m (8749yd) and offered variable-charge, separate-loading rounds.

Both these designs, and all such weapons since, trade the virtues of light weight and lack of recoil for a huge flash, incredible noise and a back-blast that is likely to be fatal to anybody within 50m (164ft) to the rear. Such weapons also require about three times the propellant needed to fire a similar projectile an equal distance from a conventional gun. The Germans were unable to drop a 105mm (4.13in) cannon with their airborne soldiers at the time, however, and neither could anybody else for some time to come. However, recoilless rifles, despite their problems, were to be important artillery weapons in the years following World War II.

German 50mm PaK 38

German commanders recognized fairly early in World War II – especially after the experience of the *Blitzkrieg* – how impotent towed anti-tank weapons had become. This was due to the thickening in the late 1930s of the armoured hide of vehicles. The 50mm (1.97in) PaK 38 was the result of the need for increased armour penetration.

Here was a serious artillery piece, firing what was then a hard, heavy, tungsten kinetic-energy projectile that could punch through up to 120mm (4.72in) of armour. Although a high-velocity gun, it was additionally issued a useful high-explosive round that could defeat 75mm (2.95in) of armour, as well as destroy thin-skinned enemy vehicles and similar targets within its 2500m (2735yd) range.

The first of these appeared in 1939 and were being produced by the thousands by 1941, about the time Hitler decreed that henceforth all tungsten would be reserved for use in machine tool production. That decree all but killed off the PaK 38 as a serious anti-tank weapon, but the gun and its high-explosive round continued the fight until the end of World War II.

German 75mm PaK 40

The PaK 40 was an evolutionary design and extension of the 50mm (1.97in) PaK 38. This 75mm (2,94in) high-velocity

cannon was quite effective against most Allied tanks, except, that is, against the T-34 fielded by the Russians. The gun first appeared in November 1941, and it went on to become the standard towed anti-tank gun to be used by the German Army until the end of the war.

It is a low, light, 1425kg (3142lb), very mobile gun, small enough to hide easily in almost any terrain. A double shield of spaced steel plates, raked back at a sharp angle, helps provide the crew with some protection against oncoming small-arms fire. As the PaK 40 was utterly unsuited to indirect fire, elevation was limited to 22 degrees and minus 5 degrees, but it would traverse 32 degrees left and right of centre.

Its standard round was an anti-tank projectile weighing 6.8kg (15lb), which left the muzzle at 792m/s (2598ft/s) and was able to defeat 116mm (4.57cm) of homogenous steel armour at 1000m (1094yd) if hitting it square on. Its maximum engagement range was about 1800m (1969yd); however, unless the gunners got a very lucky hit at that maximum range, they were more than likely to find themselves in a losing duel with an enemy tank.

Many kinds of anti-tank rounds were developed for the PaK 40, including several tungsten carbide kinetic-energy penetrators, shaped charges and conventional HEAT, as well as high-explosive rounds.

German '88'

Perhaps the most famous and feared gun system of World War II was the German high-velocity anti-aircraft gun known as the '88'. Properly designated the 8.8cm (3.46in) *Flugabwehrkanone* (Flak) 18, 36 and 37, this system evolved from a 1925 request for a high-velocity gun that could successfully engage aircraft at the extreme altitudes then being tested by bombers. The concept evolved during the 1920s, and Germans working in Sweden largely designed the gun. The prototype was built and tested in 1931, and series production began soon thereafter. By 1933, the Flak 18 was being issued to artillery units.

The 88, along with the entire German war machine, was tested from the beginning of 1936. During the Spanish Civil War, it performed quite well against ground and air targets. It did just as well in 1940 against French and British tanks during the *Blitzkrieg*, when German forces quickly overran most of Europe.

The 88 used an ingenious automatic breech system and a complex sighting system for aircraft, but conventional telescopic sights when engaging ground targets directly. Its velocity, range and large projectile all made it an excellent candidate for a dual-mission gun, so it was designed to depress to minus 3 degrees and elevate to 85. Anti-aircraft, anti-tank and combination projectiles were issued for the 88, including several novel incendiary, high-explosive, shrapnel, shaped charge and tungsten kinetic-energy versions.

Although the performance of the gun was good, it was not the best of its type. It had a muzzle velocity of 820m/s (2690ft/s), an effective ceiling range against aircraft of 8000m (26,248ft) and a maximum engagement range of 14,815m (16,202yd) for ground targets. The crew could fire up to 15 rounds per minute, partly due to an automatic fuse-setting device on the left-hand side of the breech.

Although it was a large and complex weapon, and it was too tall to be easily camouflaged, the 88 could go into action quickly. Normally fired from a secure ground mount with four outriggers, it could also shoot at ground targets from its wheels. Other weapons were technically superior, such as the US 90mm (3.54in) anti-aircraft system, but the Germans made 88s by the thousands and put them exactly where they could do the most damage.

While the US 90mm AA guns were restricted to guarding port facilities in North Africa, the Germans put the 88 out in the desert where it could engage both tanks and aircraft. It handled both missions quite well. More than 10,700 Flak 88s had been produced by the end of 1944, and they took a terrible toll on Allied ground- and air targets. The 88 continued to be used and produced after World War II, and Spain kept them in the inventory for years.

Japanese 70mm Howitzer M92
A very light, easily portable howitzer, the M92 was ideally suited for the jungle fighting conducted by Japanese soldiers during the war. Weighing less than 227kg

(500lb) and with a barrel that offered extreme elevation close to that of a mortar, it could fire 10 rounds per minute at targets up to about 10,000m (10,936yd). Although it only fired an 3.81kg (8.4lb) high-explosive round, it was better than nothing at all.

Japanese Type 35 75mm Gun
Japan already had plenty of combat experience before World War II began for Britain, the United States, France and the Soviet Union, but the Japanese had few modern or capable guns. The Type 35 could not be towed by truck, only horse or mule, but nonetheless, it was their most modern field gun available in 1945.

Weighing about 1000kg (2200lb) and with good elevation and traverse, it was a reasonable weapon for its time and place. The Type 35 could depress to minus 8

degrees and elevate to 43 degrees, with a 50-degree traverse. It fired a 5.90kg (13lb) high-explosive shell to a distance of 10,700m (11,700yd).

Soviet 76mm M1942 Field Gun
The battle of the calibres continued to escalate rapidly during World War II, with the Soviets upping the ante for light towed anti-tank guns to 76mm (3in) when they introduced this very useful combination gun. Characteristic of most such cannon of the period, it was a long-barrelled, high-velocity gun with a low profile that could be easily camouflaged from the enemy. It was light, with tubular split trails and small spade, but not much else. It could elevate to 37 degrees, however, 10 or 20 degrees more than typical anti-tank guns such as the PaK 38 or PaK 40. Its maximum range was 13,300m (14,545yd) with a 6.2kg (13.7lb) high-explosive shell.

Soviet 76mm SU-76 SP Gun
Soviet forces in 1941 battled the German invasion with towed artillery systems during the first months of the war, but had no self-propelled artillery to provide mobile fire support for armoured units. That began to change in late 1942 with a decision by the Defence Ministry to combine a good gun with a so-so hull and drive train, an improvisation that its

PaK 40

Calibre: 75mm (2.95in)
Weight: 1425kg (3141lb)
Length: 5.7m (6.23yd)
Barrel length: 3.7m (12.13ft)
Effective range: 2000m (2190yd)

Elevation: -5° to 22°
Traverse: 65°
Muzzle velocity: 990m/s (3248ft/s)
Country of origin: Germany

crews would soon give the nickname 'The Bitch'. Now, it wasn't really that bad. This vehicle was designated the SU-76, and in the Russian language 'SU' (for *Samokhodnaya Ustanovka*, or 'self-propelled mount') is pronounced in a way that sounds very similar to that derogatory term.

The first SU-76s certainly were mongrels, though. They used a modified T-70 light tank hull and drive train, with the two engines moved forward in the hull, and the hull itself stretched. These first versions used liquid-cooled engines, with the radiators installed on the track fenders or over the engines, while later versions would get air-cooled powerplants for simpler maintenance.

Their battlefield role initially was as tank-destroyers but that quickly evolved into any direct- or indirect-fire mission. Each was crewed by four men and armed with a 76.2mm ZiS-3 M1942 or –43 gun. These vehicles were assigned to self-propelled gun regiments within mechanized infantry and armour corps, each regiment of which included four or five batteries, and each battery had five SU-76 guns.

Simple yet Deadly
These were really simple vehicles, open at the top and, in the early versions, at the rear. The SU-76 needed a crew of four men to operate it. It could travel 320km (199 miles) on a tank of fuel, at a speed of up to 45km/h (28mph) on roads. Fuel tank capacity was only about 400 litres, with the two little 64kW (85hp) GAZ 6cyl engines working in tandem. Sixty rounds

for the main gun could be stowed in its racks, plus others lashed to any available deck space, where they were vulnerable to enemy fire. It had up to 35mm (1.37in) armour at the front and about 15mm (0.59) at the sides.

Despite its flaws, the SU-76 was one of the most important self-propelled guns in Soviet service during the war. Many thousands of these SU-76s were made and rushed into service: 12,600 were built in 1942 alone, and another 12,645 before the war was over. It may have been a mongrel, but it turned out to be a

■ ABOVE: American soldiers on Siapan fire a captured Japanese 70mm (2.75in) howitzer. Japanese artillery was not highly developed, but even such a small gun as this could be useful.

successful one, second only to the
legendary T-34 tank in production
numbers and a self-propelled gun system
that would live for over 40 years after the
end of the war.

US 105mm Howitzer M2

After World War I, the Westervelt, or
Caliber, Board report suggested that the
US Army needed a howitzer of
approximately 105mm (4.13in), with 65
degrees of elevation and a 15.88kg (35lb)
shell. This report proposed semi-fixed
ammunition and a maximum range of
10,973m (12,000yd). Such a weapon was
quickly developed, and by 1920 the
105mm (4.13in) M1 Howitzer was ready
for production. It was not built, however,
but instead was left on the shelf, along
with many other designs.

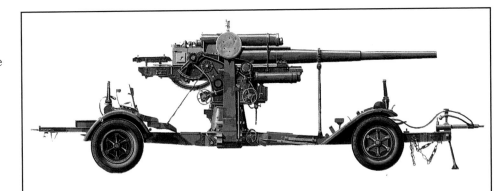

FlaK 18 '88'

Calibre: 88mm (3.46in)
Weight: 925,300kg (25 tons)
Length: 7.62m (8.33yd)
Barrel length: 4.93m (16.17ft)
Effective range: 14,815m

(16,200yds)
Elevation: -3° to 85°
Traverse: 360°
Muzzle velocity: 820m/s (2690ft/s)
Country of origin: Germany

Then, in 1936, the army decided it was
time to start getting serious about its
weapons and took another look. Instead
of issuing the weapon, a whole new
development programme was initiated,
and, in 1940, the design for the M2 was
accepted. This weapon became the
standard weapon for US Army infantry
divisions' artillery units, providing direct
supporting fires for the infantry.

The M2 consumed millions of M1 high-
explosive projectiles, each weighing
14.97kg (33lb) and typically initiated
with the M51 point detonating or M67
mechanical time fuses. The semi-fixed
ammunition offered seven charge zones;
with all the bags in the case, the M2
delivered its projectile on target out to
11,156m (12,200yd).

US 37mm M3A1

It may look a lot like a toy today, but
when the 37mm (1.46in) M3 anti-tank
gun first went to war in 1938, that small
projectile and cartridge were a serious
threat to most vehicles on the battlefield.
With few exceptions, such as Britain's
heavy Matilda tank, armoured vehicles
used steel plate that could be defeated by
the M3's armour-piercing round, good for
about 64mm (2.5in) if it hit squarely and
the target was less than 457m (500yd)
away from the gun.

The idea of this little 37mm (1.46in)
anti-tank gun was that it could be
extremely mobile and travel behind any
mechanized vehicle then in use,
particularly the jeep. Tyres and all, the
cannon and carriage did not weigh 454kg
(1000lb). Two men could easily move it
around. It had good traverse and velocity;

if the solid anti-tank shot had weighed
more than 907g (2lb), it would have been
more useful. A surprisingly wide variety
of ammunition was developed for the
37mm family of cannons. In addition to
the basic projectile, a small, high-
explosive round with only 45g (0.1lb) of
explosive and a very tiny canister round
that turned the M3 into an oversized but
not very effective shotgun were also used.

M3s were made at the Watervliet
Arsenal at the rate of 150 per month
until 1943, but the design was soon
overwhelmed by improved threat
systems. The 37mm (1.46in) gun proved
utterly inadequate for the kinds of
targets and the long ranges that anti-
tank gunners encountered in North
Africa and everywhere else.

The 57mm (2.24in) M1, a scaled-up
version of the M3, was soon introduced
and almost as soon was proven also to be
inadequate. Although this little cannon
served to train thousands of gunners
economically and effectively, it did not
kill many tanks. That work was soon
assigned to a much bigger, much better-
equipped cannon.

US 57mm Gun M1

Britain developed an excellent, almost
adequate anti-tank gun designated the
6pdr Mark 2. By 1942, the United States
quickly adapted the design for its own
army, designating it the 57mm (2.24in)
Gun M1. This version had a barrel
406mm (16in) longer than the British
gun, a feature that resulted in 30m/s
(100ft/s) better muzzle velocity, at 853m/s
(2800ft/s). This gun was useful and issued
in large numbers, but could not defeat

the very thick armour on the front glacis plates of the German Panther and Tiger heavy tanks that began appearing in the last year or so of World War II.

The 57mm (2.24in) gun and its carriage together weighed about 1270kg (2800lb) in firing order, and was still compact enough for a small detachment to move quickly during engagements. Its primary projectile was the M86 HEAT round, which was capable of defeating

about 76mm (3in) of armour at 305m (1000yd). As its rounds were fixed, it was possible to maintain a high rate of fire: up to 15 rounds a minute. A solid shot, the M70 projectile, was also available for this weapon.

As appropriate for an artillery piece intended to engage moving targets, the 57mm M1 had extremely good traverse at 45 degrees left and right. It elevated to only 15 degrees, however, and could be

depressed to minus 5 degrees. Maximum range was more than 9144m (10,000yd), but at half that range it was only effective against personnel carriers, lightly armoured vehicles and similar targets. With such a small high-explosive shell, the 57mm (2.24in) was quite limited in the kinds of targets it could engage, so it was soon phased and replaced by the 76.2mm (3in) M5 anti-tank gun.

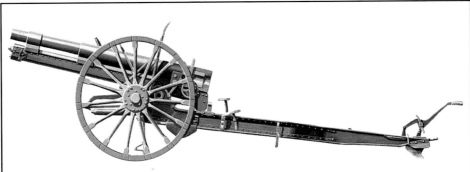

Type 35/75 Gun

Calibre: 75mm (2.95in)
Weight: 1007kg (2220lb)
Length: 4.8m (5.25yd)
Barrel length: 2.35m (91.37in)
Effective range: 10,700m
(11,700yd)

Elevation: -8° to 43°
Traverse: 50°
Muzzle velocity: 520m/s (1700ft/s)
Country of origin: Japan

■ABOVE: An American gun crew manoeuvre their M2A1 105mm (4.13in) howitzer into a new position during the battle for Okinawa. The role of artillery had become more important than ever.

US 3-inch M5 gun

Every time the United States fielded a new anti-tank gun, the new model was about twice the size of the previous one. The M5 76.2mm (3in) gun evolved from a 1940 requirement, one that combined the tube of an anti-aircraft gun, re-chambered for a hybrid cartridge using the propellant capacity of a 105mm (4.13in) howitzer round, with a 76mm (3in) projectile. The 'wildcat' cartridge fired a 7kg (15.4lb) projectile out of the muzzle at almost 800m/s (2600ft/s) and to a maximum range of 14,630m (16,000yd). It could pierce 100mm (3.94in) of armour at 1000m (1094yd).

■ABOVE: US Army soldiers inspect a captured howitzer far from its Russian home. The M1942 76.2mm (3in) gun had been captured originally by the Germans and adapted to their own use.

As often happens when cartridge cases from one design are married to a projectile from another and then fired in the barrel of a third, there were problems. The M5 did not see much

M3 37mm Anti-Tank Gun

Calibre: 37mm (1.49in)
Weight: 414kg (912lb)
Length: 4.25m (4.65yd) (est)
Barrel length: 2.1m (82.5in)
Effective range: 457m (500yd)

Elevation: -10° to 15°
Traverse: 60°
Muzzle velocity: 884m/s (2900ft/s)
Country of origin: USA

action until after the Normandy invasion in June 1944. As it was the only towed American anti-tank gun with any authority over German main battle tanks, the 57mm (2.24in) M1 being utterly inadequate, the M5 began to see serious action. The same cannon and cartridge were used in the M10 Tank Destroyer, with fair success, but the 90mm (3.54in) gun superseded both.

US 75mm M1A1 Pack Howitzer

An odd little weapon, one that was an unlikely success, was the US 75mm (2.96in) Pack Howitzer M1 and its several variants. With its small shell, limited range and low velocity, it was outperformed by nearly everything on the battlefield. Its essential blessing, however, was that the Pack 75 could go places no other similar artillery could. In this role, it was an important asset.

The key to its success was a modular design that allowed it to be quickly assembled or disassembled, as well as its extremely light weight for a gun of that calibre. Broken down into six major assemblies, the Pack 75 could be delivered by parachute, transported by mule or even carried by soldiers or hired porters. It was intended for use in difficult terrain where other artillery could not go, and places such as Italy and Burma became its playground.

ROCKET SYSTEMS

Another famous and deadly artillery system of the World War II period, the *Nebelwerfer* rocket launcher also had its origins in the early 1930s. The Treaty of Versailles prohibited heavy tube artillery, but did not proscribe light launchers with

big rockets. It was a fairly simple, light, economical system for use in area, rather than aimed, fire, and it featured six launcher tubes supported by a carriage also used by the German 37mm (1.45in) anti-tank gun.

Each rocket weighed about 32kg (70lb) and at maximum elevation would reach about 7000m (7655yd). These rockets were spin stabilized by rails inside each tube, spinning the rocket somewhat like rifling as it fired. All six rockets could be ripple-fired electrically in about 10 seconds; when they began to impact the target area, the effect was devastating. They were first used in combat on 22

■**BELOW: An anxious moment in Germany, 1945. This American gun crew are ready for action with their M1 57mm (2.2in) anti-tank gun, with a round fired every 4 or 5 seconds.**

June 1941, during the opening assault on Russia, Operation Barbarossa. Four regiments of artillery participated in this surprise attack.

Germany fielded seven types of rocket artillery, from 150mm (5.91in) *Nebelwerfer* 41 up to 300mm (11.81in) *Raketenwerfer* 56 variants, some towed and others mounted on vehicles as self-propelled systems. The actual design of the rocket motor was somewhat unusual, as it was in the forward section of the projectile, while the warhead was actually a 'war-tail' at the rear. Propellant gasses were exhausted through vents around the midsection of the rocket, a feature that enhanced both accuracy and effectiveness on impact.

Among the many types that were developed by Germany was the 150mm (5.91in) *Panzerwerfer* 42 *Auf Sf* (SdKfz 4/1), built by Opel. This was an armoured personnel carrier with a fully armoured cab, on which was mounted a 10-barrel *Panzerwerfer* 42 launcher. This launcher could elevate to 80 degrees and had a 270-degree traverse towards the front. Opel also provided some vehicles with 24 launch tubes for the 80mm (3.15in) *R-Vielfachwerfer* used by the *Waffen-SS*.

Soviet Rocket Launcher M13

The Soviets answered German rocket artillery with rockets of their own. About two weeks after the first *Nebelwerfers* were fired, Soviet rockets were fired from simple, truck-mounted rails, first appearing on 7 July 1941, near the town of Orsha. This was designated the M-13 system, the development of which began about the same time as the German rocket programme in the early 1930s.

Using a ZIL-151 6x6 truck as a foundation, the M-13 was actually used with many different kinds of vehicles: obsolete tanks, farm tractors and Studebaker trucks, shipped to the Soviet Union from the United States by the thousands. Eight rails, each supporting two rockets, top and bottom, were attached to a simple rack that could be raised and lowered by a hand crank. The rails could be loaded with M8 82mm (3.23in) rockets or M13UK 132mm (5.2in) rockets. The 132mm rockets could hit area targets at about 8500m (9300yd).

Although not intended as a precision weapon, vibration from firing rocked the vehicle so much that stabilizing platforms were added to the rear. This worked well enough, and the rockets were effective, so many hundreds were produced for the Red Army. Rockets up to 310mm (12.2in) were fired from them and similar, simple launch assemblies.

The awesome firepower of this simple system made it one of the legendary artillery weapons of World War II, and it earned immortal fame as the *Katyusha*. The odd, eerie sound of this early multiple-launch rocket system (MLRS) earned it another nickname: 'Stalin's Organ'. It was a sufficiently sound design that 132mm (5.2in) rockets are still being produced and fired from simple rail launchers, with their distinctive noise.

US 4.5in Rocket M8

Rocket artillery use among US forces during World War II was less extensive than in Germany or the Soviet Union, but a 114mm (4.49in) rocket was designed and produced for use on ground attack aircraft such as the P-47 Thunderbolt. Designated M8, it was a powerful rocket with a range of 4200m (4593yd) and a reasonably potent 1.95kg (4.3lb) high-explosive warhead.

ABOVE: Somewhere in the Pacific, 29 December 1943. American gunners have dug their 75mm (2.95in) howitzer into an emplacement to fire support for their infantry against the Japanese.

The M8 rocket looked something like a fire extinguisher and was just about the same size; in fact, that is just what was used for the prototype. There were similar models intended for different applications, for use from launchers on aircraft, from assault ships and boats, and from ground vehicles.

An M12 variant was used with a simple ground mount, while the M16 version was designed for the 60-tube 'Hornet's Nest' launcher. Individual rockets could be used with simple, one-tube launchers or even with field-expedient launchers which were hastily concocted from scrap wood or metal, and communications wire.

Unlike the German version, the M8 placed the rocket motor at the rear, with the warhead up front. It was fin-stabilized by spring-loaded vanes that popped out after launch. The motor used smokeless powder and a central venturi in a conventional, simple layout. These rockets reached speeds of up to about 965km/h (600mph); a 'Super 4.5 Incher' that attained about 1500km/h (900mph) and flew about 3.25km (2 miles) was tested but not used during the war.

The M8s were, like the Russian versions, fired from all sorts of launchers. A 60-tube model, designated the T-34, bolted to the turret of the M4 Sherman tank. A link to the gun tube allowed the gunner to elevate the launcher. Like the Russian version, the T-34 acquired a musical nickname: the 'Calliope'. Few were issued because of the system's poor accuracy. Additionally, in this configuration, there was no practical re-load procedure.

The US Army also employed larger rockets, such as the 183mm (7.2in) demolition munition fired from a 20-tube launcher called the 'Whiz Bang', a potent weapon for use against enemy fortifications such as bunkers. These munitions were fired from the Mk 20 and Mk 21 'Mousetrap' launcher.

MORTAR SYSTEMS
Mortars became very important weapons systems for small units during World War II. They provided organic, indirect-fire support that was immediately on call.

ABOVE: Each Nebelwerfer 41 launcher was light, highly mobile, and inexpensive to produce, but also inaccurate, greedy for propellant and with a very showy firing signature.

They were essential to the battalion, company or platoon commander who could not wait to see if supporting fires from other units was available.

Developed in France by Edgar Brandt, the mortar is a very simple system and represents the last vestige of the muzzle-loading smoothbore. The barrel of most

infantry models will, as long as the calibres are the same, fire the ammunition of any other mortar. Projectiles, called 'bombs' by some operators, use a common propellant component that is nearly identical to a common 12-gauge shotgun shell. This is fitted to the base of the projectile and is typically surrounded by stabilizing fins. Small holes vent the propellant gases and send the round downrange. The basic propellant charge is quite small, although additional powder increments in the form of small bags or capsules have been used at various times to customize the ballistics of mortars, just as with higher-velocity guns and howitzers.

French Mortier Brandt de 81mm
Sir Wilfred Scott-Stokes invented the mortar in 1915, a lightweight, highly portable indirect-fire weapon, but it was Edgar Brandt of France who refined the idea and fine-tuned the design. The French 81 model, designed between World War I and World War II, has set the pattern for such weapons ever since. The most modern issued today are different only in the smallest details, and Brandt's original version could fire today's ammunition without modification.

This design used Stoke's concept of a smoothbore tube, base-plate, bi-pod and shotgun cartridge propellant, but perfected it. Brandt used a barrel 1.27m (50in) long, a ball-and-socket mount and a sturdy bi-pod with geared elevation and traverse controls. He combined this

M13 Rocket and Launcher
Calibre: 132mm (5.2in)
Weight of rocket: 42.5kg (93.7lb)
Rocket length: 1.42m (53.9in)
Effective range: 8500m (9300yd)
Elevation: 10° to 30° (est)

Traverse: none
Maximum velocity: 355m/s (1165ft/s)
Country of origin: USSR

elegant weapon with a round weighing 3.25kg (7.16lb) and containing enough propellant to travel 2850m (3115yd). The weapon was designed to be 'drop' fired, inserted in the muzzle and allowed to slide down onto the fixed firing pin, which then struck the primer and sent the bomb on its way.

Many nations produced copies, either under licence from Brandt or by simply counterfeiting. The United States, Italy and the Soviet Union all used the design before, during and after World War II, and still use it today.

In its original 81mm (3.18in) configuration, the Brandt M27/31 weighed about 59kg (132lb) and could be easily broken down into three basic loads for transport. Today's US M1 mortar is still 81mm, weighs about 59kg (132lb) and fires ammunition of about the same weight to about the same range. At least some things on the battlefield have not changed much in all that time.

German 50mm GrW 36

Germany's basic light infantry mortar during World War II was the 50mm (1.97in) *Granatwerfer* 36, built by Rheinmetall from 1936 to 1943. It was a light little thing, only 14kg (30lb), but more complex than a short-range weapon ought to be. Its maximum range was 520m (569yd) with its only projectile, a high-explosive type containing 120g (4.25oz) of bursting charge, could be either drop- or trigger-fired.

Other contemporary mortars were just about as effective without any sights at all, as the GrW 36 included a complex sighting system that was so inaccurate that any mortar team using this weapon was lucky to get within 35m (38yd) of the aiming point. Even so, nearly 26,000 of them were manufactured, and more than 22 million rounds of ammunition were provided to feed them.

Despite the large numbers produced, German soldiers seem to have been disappointed with the design. They used captured Soviet 50mm (1.97in) mortars whenever they were available because they not only weighed far less at just 11.8kg (26lb), but also had far better range, out to 800m (875yd).

80mm GrW 34 *Granatwerfer*

A better 'morser', as the Germans called them, was the 80mm (3.15in) GrW 34, a 1932 Rheinmetall design that entered service in 1935. This was the basic organic heavy mortar for the infantry

battalion, firing a high-explosive 3.4kg (7.5lb) projectile 2400m (2625yd). About 4600 of these had been issued by the beginning of World War II and were followed with nearly 72,000 more before the end of the conflict. The entire system, including the bipod, the base-plate and the tube, weighed in total about 56kg (125lb), so it took a whole squad to crew this weapon when it was operational in the field.

A lighter version with a shorter barrel, the GrW 42, was developed for the airborne forces. This weapon weighed just 26kg (58lb). It was sometimes called the *Stummelwerfer*, or 'Stump Projector', because of its stubby little tube. The penalty for the short tube was short range – 1200m (1312yd) – and only about 1600 were made. German forces also employed a few Austrian 80mm (3.15in) mortars based on the French Brandt design, the GrW 33 (o), a 62kg (137lb) system with a 3.5kg (7.7lb) round and 1900m (2078yd) range.

US 60mm Mortar M2

US infantry units during World War II relied on a slightly modified 60mm (2.36in) mortar, the M2. This weapon was a near copy of the French Brandt design and manufactured in the United States under licence. Of very simple and conventional design, the M2 had three major component groups: the barrel, base-plate and bi-pod.

■ABOVE: Rocket launchers became popular on the battlefield. American soldiers had a version of their own; this example being loaded with 23.6kg (52lb) rockets.

Together these components weighed 19kg (42lb), so the load was spread normally among three men. One carried the 5.4kg (12lb) barrel, another got the 5.9kg (13lb) base-plate and a third man packed the 7.3kg (16lb) bi-pod, all in addition to their personal weapons and equipment, plus at least a few rounds of mortar ammunition.

The M2 was the smallest mortar routinely issued to US soldiers. It could engage targets from 91m (100yd) to just under 1829m (2000yd) and fired both high-explosive and illuminating rounds. Normal sustained fire was up to 18 rounds per minute, up to 35 per minute for short periods.

There were times when nobody bothered to check their watches and simply dropped those little rounds down the tubes as fast as they could prep the fuses. One such occasion was during the 8 March 1943 fight for Hill 700 on Bougainville in the South Pacific jungles. Soldiers from 2nd Battalion, 145th Infantry, fought off waves of suicidal Japanese in the dark and pouring rain. When the Japanese soldiers began to infiltrate the position, Staff Sergeant Otis Hawkins called in 60mm (2.36in)

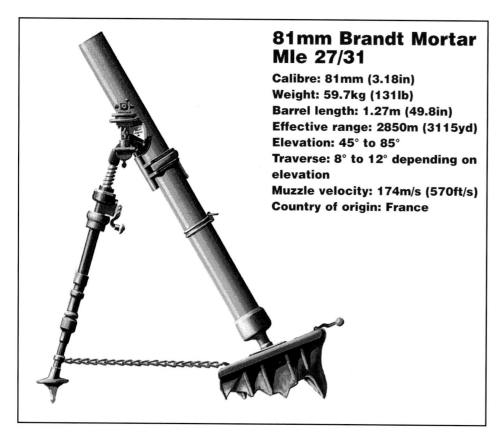

81mm Brandt Mortar Mle 27/31

Calibre: 81mm (3.18in)
Weight: 59.7kg (131lb)
Barrel length: 1.27m (49.8in)
Effective range: 2850m (3115yd)
Elevation: 45° to 85°
Traverse: 8° to 12° depending on elevation
Muzzle velocity: 174m/s (570ft/s)
Country of origin: France

SGrW 34 81mm Mortar

Calibre: 81mm (3.18in)
Weight: 56kg (125lb)
Barrel length: 1.143m (45in)
Effective range: 2400m (2625yd)
Elevation: 40° to 90°
Traverse: 9° to 15° depending on elevation
Muzzle velocity: 175m/s (574ft/s)
Country of origin: Germany

illumination rounds, then high-explosive – and lots of it. The battalion's organic mortars, and those of supporting field artillery battalions, pounded the enemy assault with hundreds of 60mm (2.36in) and 81mm (3.18in) rounds, while keeping the Japanese visible to the infantry rifles and machine guns.

US 81mm Mortar M1
While the small, light 60mm (2.36in) mortar went along on just about every US infantry operation at company level and above, it was still a slightly awkward weapon. The system's components were not all that heavy by themselves; however, when added to the rest of the

kit that was carried by the soldiers, it was a load. The real challenge was carrying enough rounds of ammunition to keep it fed, and that was a chore the entire platoon or company shared. The 60mm was a great weapon in battle, but limited in its performance. Backing it up in the US Army – and in most others, too – was something bigger, the 81mm (3.18in) M1 mortar.

This system evolved from the British 76.2mm (3in) Mk 1 Stokes 'trench mortar' which was issued to US units during World War I, and, like just about every other US artillery system, it went through a development process before being placed on the back burner during the 1920s and 1930s. During this time, however, the French firm owned by Edgar Brandt worked towards perfecting the Stokes and managed to convince the American War Department that this design was appropriate for the US Army's use. It was manufactured under licence in huge numbers and served around the world during and after the war.

Typical of the breed, the US 81mm (3.18in) was too heavy for travelling very far without a mule or vehicle. Ready to fire, the tube, base-plate and bi-pod weighed 61.7kg (136lb), each component accounting for a weight of about 20.4kg (45lb). But it all paid off in firepower – the high-explosive round weighed about 3kg (7lb), more than double that of the 60mm (2.36in) equivalent. Any target from 274m (300yd) to more than 2286m (2500yd) was fair game for the M1's gunners, who were quite capable of putting 18 rounds downrange every minute, as long as their ammunition could hold out.

Soviet World War II Mortars
In the Soviet scheme of infantry support weapons, 50mm (1.57in), 80mm (3.15in) and 120mm (4.72in) mortars fit in in just about the same way they did with other nations: at company, battalion and regiment levels, respectively.

However, the Soviets quickly realized that the 50mm (1.57in) mortar was not worth the effort and so it was replaced by the 82mm (3.22in). So effective was it that production of the larger 82mm mortar went from 16,000 in 1941 to more

■ RIGHT: German soldiers ready to fire their 50mm (1.9in) LeGrW 36, a weapon with all the attendant problems of a mortar of its calibre: a small warhead, short range and limited effectiveness.

than 100,000 in 1942. Conversely 50mm (1.9in) mortar production slowed drastically in 1942, and would stop altogether a year later.

The Soviet quest for greater weight of metal on target progressed to larger and still larger mortars. A 107mm (4.21in) design for mountain troops was issued, but 120mm (4.72in) and then 160mm (6.29in) mortars were also developed and successfully employed. The largest of these, the 160mm (6.2in), was the only all-new artillery system produced by the Soviets in World War II, and it appeared in 1944. This weapon weighed one-third as much as a 152mm (6in) howitzer, while delivering more explosive and steel on the target, although to a much shorter range. Independent mortar brigades used it extensively during the final two years of the war.

The 120mm (4.72in) M1938, however, was one of the real success stories for the Soviets during the war, and, whenever the Germans managed to capture one, it was quickly put into service. The Germans went so far as to copy it, too, using it instead of their own 150mm

(5.91in) sIG 33 gun. It was light for a 120mm mortar, at 280kg (617lb), and fired a 16kg (35lb) bomb 6000m (6562yd) with reasonable accuracy. The 120mm mortar could be either drop- or trigger-fired, and it came with a special trailer that could pick the entire thing up from its firing position and have it rolling on the road long before its last rounds were impacting their target. Ian Hogg has called this 'undoubtedly one of the great designs of World War II'.

COMBINATION ARTILLERY

There are not too many weapons that can elevate so much that they can effectively shoot at themselves, but anti-aircraft guns are an exception, and one of the dominant designs during World War II was the Swedish 40mm Bofors. Aircraft had become a serious threat to armies during World War I, and systems were improvised to engage these targets. By the end of the war, bombers were operating at altitudes well out of the range of small arms. The French 75mm (2.95in) Quick-firing gun and British QF 76.2mm (3in) were propped up on

improvised mounts in an effort to deal with these targets (and sometimes they actually scored), but an effective anti-aircraft system was not developed until after World War I.

Civil and military aviation developments in the 1920s demonstrated that the threat from these bombers would be becoming more dangerous to ground forces in future conflicts. The British Army therefore requested an anti-aircraft gun in 94mm (3.7in) calibre for the new, high-altitude threat. Rather than re-invent the wheel, they looked to a foreign manufacturer for the solution to their problem, and ordered 100 40mm (1.57in) mobile quick-firing guns from the Bofors company in Sweden.

This basic design turned out to be tremendously successful, and variants are still in production. The design as used during World War II had a vertical

BELOW: Two US Marines prepare to fire the M2 60mm (2.3in) from a mortar pit. Mortars are the premier close-in indirect fire weapon, particularly when organic to the company or battalion.

breechblock operated by recoil. Four rounds were fed into the gun at a time, attached by clips, and the gunner fired the gun by depressing a foot pedal. Empty cases were ejected to the front, out of the way of the gunners and ammunition bearers. The 40mm (1.57in) round fired a high-velocity 907g (2lb) projectile 2560m (2800yd) vertically, sufficient to engage enemy close-air support aircraft effectively, but not enough for high-altitude bombers.

Most of the ammunition issued by the crews was a high-explosive tracer with an impact fuse, intended to detonate on contact with the target. The tracer element was thoughtfully designed to self-destruct the shell at 'burn-out' if it did not strike a target; this feature prevented the rounds causing casualties and damage among friendly forces. An anti-personnel round was provided in addition to this.

The Bofors could be aimed at targets from minus 5 to 90 degrees from the horizontal and rapid all-round traverse. When firing at ground targets, the range of the gun was 5299m (5795yd). As the primary mission of the Bofors was to engage aircraft, the aiming system was designed for fast-moving aerial targets. Initially, that was a fairly simple ring sight used by the gunner to guess at aim-off angles, a very complicated business.

This complicated ring sight system was augmented in 1944 by adding a third gun-layer using an additional sight system called a 'stiffkey stick'. One layer centred the target in his sight, setting elevation only, while another centred his sight to give horizontal data; the third stiffkey stick gunner's sight computed approach angle. The combined result was more accurate engagements.

Engaging aircraft was, and continues to be, a tremendously difficult mission, and computers were introduced quite early on in the development of artillery in order to help compute solutions for these targets. The 40mm (1.57in) Bofors used one of these during World War II, a device called a 'predictor'. It was a large, heavy, electrically powered device that was ill suited to mobile combat operations, but worked well in static defensive positions.

At this time, many nations manufactured the Bofors 40mm under licence: Britain, the United States, Canada and Austria, as well as France and Poland, among others. Bofors still manufactures and sells a similar weapon to this day.

PM-37 82mm Mortar

Calibre: 82mm (3.22in)
Weight: 56.25kg (125lb)
Barrel length: 1.22m (48.23in)
Effective range: 3040m (3325yd)
Elevation: 45° or 75°
Traverse: 6° to 15° depending on elevation
Muzzle velocity: 211m/s (692ft/s)
Country of origin: USSR

M1943 160mm Mortar

Calibre: 160mm (6.29in)
Weight: 1170kg (2580lb)
Barrel length: 3.03m (9ft 11in)
Effective range: 5150m (5630yd)
Elevation: 45° to 80°
Traverse: 25°
Muzzle velocity: 245m/s (804ft/s)
Country of origin: USSR

US Mobile Anti-Aircraft/-Tank Gun
Until July of 1941, US mobile anti-aircraft systems were essentially single-purpose weapons. The existing M1A1 mount could be used for direct-fire missions against ground targets, but only after a long and complicated emplacement. A requirement was published for a triple-purpose weapon,

one that could engage aircraft at typical bombing altitudes, tanks and armoured vehicles on the ground, and fast torpedo boats offshore.

This latter specification included the ability to depress the tube below the horizon, something the existing M1A1 mount could not accomplish. The design process began in September 1942, and, in

May 1943, the M2 90mm (3.54in) was standardized and put into production. The result looked quite a bit like a close relative of the German 88, and it was.

A bore diameter of 90mm (3.54in) allows use of a heavy, effective shell, and the M71 high-explosive round went downrange weighing more than 10.43kg (23lb). A long tube, 50 calibres in length, helped that projectile attain a high velocity of 823m/s (2700ft/s). The result was excellent range both vertically at 12,043m (13,170yd) and horizontally at 17,830m (19,500yd).

The M2 used an automatic breech that helped achieve an excellent rate of fire, one round every two-and-a-half seconds being an average firing cycle. Once the first round had been loaded manually, the breech would cycle mechanically

thereafter, opening and ejecting the cartridge case after each round and closing as each new cartridge was rammed fully into the chamber.

One feature of the M2 was a fuse-setting and power ramming system controlled by electrical cables from the battery director during anti-aircraft missions. This feature was automatically disabled when any ammunition used exclusively for ground targets was fired: anti-personnel, base-fused or point-detonating projectiles.

Power loading was an essential feature for all modern heavy anti-aircraft guns during World War II, the only way large, heavy, time-fused rounds could be delivered at high rates of fire. The rammer was used during both air- and ground engagements. In the event of a

power failure, loading and fuse setting could be done manually, but at a great penalty for the system's rate of fire.

The crew, unlike those serving the German 88, had a platform surrounding the breech on which to work, and most of the crew did not have to trip over the outriggers during firing. A large shield offered some protection to the gun crew from small-arms fire and artillery shell splinters, as long as they came from in front of the gun. Those outriggers folded upwards for travel, as did the platform, but the M2 was still a bulky package.

The 90mm (3.54in) M2 gun was certainly better than the Flak 88, but it was, in many respects, too late for the party. Had it been available in North Africa, and used in the ground role, it might have been the most famous gun of on the K18 100mm (3.94in) gun. The entire 18 family was a joint project of Krupp and Rheinmetall, and the line would become the foundation for German medium field artillery units during World War II. Each heavy artillery battalion from each German infantry division was normally supplied with 12 of these large guns, in 3 batteries of 4 FH-18s. These guns were light enough to be moved by teams of horses, standard motive power for many units, although some groups had the services of tractors or other motorized transport.

A 43.5kg (96lb) high-explosive round was the most common projectile, although a concrete-piercing and shaped-charge anti-armour round were also provided, along with a pioneering sabot round with discarding sabot. Eight charge increments were available, although only the seventh and eighth were dangerous enough that special authorization was required to fire them. At Charge Six, the sFH-18 could reach almost 10,000m (10,936yd) and, with the other two increments, all the way to a distance of no less than 13,200m (14,436yd).

US 155mm Gun M1A1
One of many ancient designs from World War I warmed over during the 1920s and 1930s, the 155mm (6.10in) Gun M1A1 (and later the M2), was distinctive for its exceptionally long barrel of 45 calibres, something that earned it an enduring nickname, the 'Long Tom'. The expression is an old American one and has been applied to long-barrelled cannon for many years, including one during the Civil War, but it is now understood to describe this stalwart cannon.

As with so many other US designs, this one is of French heritage, descended from the 155mm (6.1in) gun M1917 GPF, which had been issued to the American Expeditionary Forces in 1917 and 1918. Although many weapons fired 155mm (6.1in) projectiles during World War II, the Long Tom was able, thanks to its immense tube, to deliver rounds much farther downrange, more than 22,860m (25,000yd), or more than 14 miles.

Such extreme range was especially valuable during counterbattery duels, a common but critical fire mission during World War II and, later, Korea. But the Long Tom was more than just a common howitzer. This weapon could also conduct direct-fire missions against enemy vehicles and positions, usually with devastating effect.

The original M1917 was a good weapon to begin with, firing a 43kg (95lb) shell out to 16,093m (17,600yd). That was improved during World War I in the M1918, which was modified yet again with a longer barrel, larger powder capacity chamber, an improved breech mechanism and a better obturator.

During World War I, the massive weight of the weapon made it very difficult to move around the battlefield. In World War II, this was still a big challenge, but a new hinged split trail and 10 pneumatic tyres made movement a lot more practical.

As fielded during World War II, the entire gun and carriage weighed about 15,241kg (15 tons), most of which was the carriage, not the cannon and recoil system, which only accounted for a third of that figure. Everything about the system was big: the high-explosive shell weighed about 43kg (95lb) and the anti-personnel version was 45kg (100lb), both with around 6.8kg (15lb) of explosive as a bursting charge.

Approximately 13.6kg (30lb) of propellant sent the projectile downrange at 853m/s (2800ft/s), and that was good enough to slice through 76mm (3in) of armour at 5486m (6000yd). The cannon was 7m (23ft) long, and, with the trunnions placed very far back on the tube, massive equilibrators were required to permit mechanical aiming controls. The Long Tom could traverse 30 degrees left and right, and elevate to 65 degrees and depress to 0 degrees. Normally, a crew could get one into action in about 20 minutes and get off one round about every 60 seconds, although up to 4 per minute could be fired in an emergency.

A crew of 14 men was required for the weapon, and it was used well in Europe, the Pacific and, later, Korea. Long Toms moved with Patton's Third Army towards Germany and helped beat back the Nazi counterattack at the Bulge with a 'time-on-target serenade' on 23 December 1944.

US 155mm Howitzer M1
A much more compact and mobile weapon firing the same projectiles as the Long Tom was the very common 155mm (6.1in) Howitzer M1 (or M114). Yet another adaptation of a World War I French design from the Schneider company, it had been brought up to World War II American standards. First issued to artillery units in 1942, its actual heritage went back to the M1917 155mm Howitzer, but it was modified with a

■**ABOVE: US Marines man their 40mm (1.57in) Bofors anti-aircraft gun on an important airstrip, Bougainville, New Guinea, during the campaign to recover the Western Pacific from the Japanese.**

World War II. Even so, it served effectively around the globe: a example being the time when a provisional battalion from the 251st Anti-Aircraft Artillery equipped with M2s poured their 90mm fire directly into Japanese positions during the fight for Hill 700 on Bougainville in 1944.

HEAVY ARTILLERY
A new family of gun designs emerged as a result of the lessons learnt by German gunners in World War I, one of which was the 150mm (5.91in) field howitzer based

carriage designed to be pulled by mechanized equipment, instead of the horses which had first been used with the M1917 and M1918.

More than 6000 of these large-calibre howitzers were built, and in one version or another, they served through the Korean War and the war in Vietnam before being retired in the 1970s. Eleven men operated this cannon. With seven propellant charges available, they could fire a wide variety of projectiles to a maximum range of 14,552m (15,914yd). That shorter range was a direct result of the 20-calibre barrel length, less than half of the Long Tom. The ammunition is NATO standard and available in the normal types and, with the maximum Charge 7, a muzzle velocity of 564m/s (1850ft/s) was produced. Four rounds per minute can be fired briefly, then two per minute for sustained missions.

The 155mm (6.10in) Howitzer M1 elevated to 65 degrees up and minus 2 degrees down, and it could traverse 3 degrees left and right. Although a telescopic sight M25 was issued with the gun, most engagements were indirect fire with the M12 panoramic sight. Other equipment issued with the gun included a gunner's quadrant, aiming circle, bore sight, rangefinder M7, two hand fuse-setting tools, telescope M65 and two sets of firing tables.

The 155mm (6.10in) Howitzer M1 got a complete makeover and a new name after World War II. Rechristened the M114, the weapon became a standard in field artillery divisions of the US Army and Marine Corps, and in modified form with Israel, the Netherlands, Brazil and many other nations.

German 210mm K12 Railway Gun
An outgrowth of the World War I Paris Gun, the K12E (E for *Eisenbahn* or railway) was another somewhat experimental long-range cannon without a clear mission. The project began in the mid–1930s, about the same time as the K5E and other programmes, with a 105mm (4.13in) test barrel. One of the major problems with the earlier gun was rapid bore erosion, something the K12E's designers tried to avoid by cutting grooves into the driving band that

■RIGHT: The American 90mm (3.54in) was good at engaging threats both in the air and on the ground, although the gun was rarely used by the US in the anti-tank role.

precisely matched the rifling in the bore, rather than forcing the band into the rifling, as with conventional systems. This was somewhat successful, but required specialized production. An operational 210mm (8.26in) prototype was produced in 1937, tested in 1938 and sent to the field in 1939. Even though it was able to throw a shell 115km (70 miles), there was not much control over where the shell would ultimately come down to land.

The barrel was so long, at 33m (109ft), that it had to be braced to prevent excessive warping. On its railcar, it weighed 302,000kg (297 tons), and the whole vehicle was more than 42m (140ft) long. The tube could fire from 25 to 55 degrees, but not before either a large pit had been dug to make room for the breech as it recoiled, or otherwise the whole girder supporting the mount was elevated by jacks.

As with the first Paris Gun, once it was ready to fire, there was not an obvious military target suitable for its capabilities. So, somewhat like its parent, it was used as a technology demonstrator, a terror weapon and for domestic propaganda. A very few rounds were fired across the English Channel in late 1940, landing around the town of Rainham in Kent, England, about 100km (62 miles) from the gun line. Some landed in the countryside, entirely unnoticed by anyone, a feat that is very difficult to accomplish with noisy artillery during a war, but perhaps not such a bad thing after all for the English.

German 280mm K5(E) Railway Gun
The clear winner in the long-distance shooting match was clearly the German *Kanone* 5 *Eisenbahn* (K5(E)) 280mm (11.02in). Developed during the mid-1930s and test-fired in 1936, this weapon system was one of the very few railway guns that saw much use in World War II.

It was a success from the beginning; despite all the problems of constructing and fielding such an immense cannon, five were already in service at the beginning of the war, with many others on order. It would be produced at the rate of two or three a year until 1945 and conducted fire missions that were

M2 155mm 'Long Tom'
Calibre: 155mm (6.1in)
Weight: 13,880kg (30,536lb)
Length: n/a
Barrel length: 6.97m (22.86ft)
Effective range: 23,220m (25,395yd)
Elevation: -1°40' to 63°20'
Traverse: 60°
Muzzle velocity: 853m/s (2800ft/s)
Country of origin: USA

memorable for people on both ends of the trajectory. A total of 22 were delivered of the 36 which had been ordered.

Despite its official designation, the bore of the gun was actually 283mm (11in), and its barrel was 21.54m (70.08ft) long. Ready for action, the K5(E) weighed in at about 218,000kg (215 tons), including its mount. The tube elevated to 50 degrees and traversed only 2 degrees, but it could fire a standard 256kg (563lb) high-explosive shell to a distance of about 62km (39 miles).

That high-explosive shell was the *Granate* 35, filled with about 31kg (68lb) of explosive and with pre-rifled driving bands. The bands were difficult to manufacture and were one of the problems that kept the gun from being used even more than it was. Only about 255 projectiles were made every year.

Also manufactured were special 'sighting shot' rounds that produced a large, highly visible cloud of smoke to help determine just where the round struck, a serious difficulty when shooting at targets at such distances, even with the help of forward observers up in aircraft or hunched down in foxholes.

Also issued was the RGr 4331 rocket-assisted projectile. This extended the reach of the 280mm (11.02in) K5(E) to 85.3km (53 miles), but accuracy and effectiveness were both minimal with this

shell. Even greater range was achieved with the K5(E) and a smoothbore barrel combined with an 'arrow' projectile that had a maximum range of 101km (63 miles), but only one was built before the war ended. Four powder charge bags and a metallic case to seal the breech propelled all these projectiles.

Each K5(E) needed two trains to provide support for its operations, pulled with diesel-electric locomotives. One train pulled the cannon, a magazine car, kitchen car, three sleeping cars for the gun crew, two cars carrying 113 projectiles each, another two for propellant bagged charges and a flatcar mounting an anti-aircraft gun. The other train included more ammunition, the battery's wheeled vehicles, another anti-aircraft gun and more carriages for the detachment. It also included the specialized track and turntable used by the K5(E). Normal K5(E) batteries included 2 guns, each with 5 officers and NCOs, plus 37 soldiers.

Many of these guns were sent from France to support the invasion of Russia, Operation Barbarossa, in 1941, but a few stayed behind. Two K5(E)s from Battery 712 made a name for themselves at the Anzio beachhead during May 1944, when they shelled Allied forces, who nicknamed the guns 'Anzio Annie'. Several guns stayed in the Calais area, watching over

the English Channel until they were withdrawn or captured during 1944. By late 1944, nearly all the 22 had been captured, except for 2 that participated in the futile Ardennes offensive. Three have apparently survived and are still here today: one in Russia, one at Cap Griz Nez in France, and one at the US Army's Aberdeen Proving Ground in Maryland.

German 800mm KE Railway Gun

These two 800mm (31.4in) guns, 'Dora' and 'Gustav', brought an entirely new definition to the concept of 'heavy' artillery. Both were built by Krupp, and each was named for a member of that fabled clan. Weighing 1,350,000kg (1329 tons), these were the largest guns in history, past, present or, very likely to be in the future.

Each gun required a detachment of more than 1400 men, and the gun captain was a colonel. It fired a projectile about 3m (9ft) long and weighing 4800kg (4.73 tons) to a distance of 38km (23.61 miles). Instead of a normal bore brush on a pole, the tube was scrubbed out by one of the detachment who crawled up inside, a very dirty job, as that tube was more than 32m (106ft) long.

Originally ordered by Hitler and intended to help fire the opening shots of World War II against the Maginot Line fortifications, these two guns were unfinished in September 1939. Not until two years later did a potential target materialize, the fortress of Gibraltar, but Spain refused to allow the Germans within range. Another opportunity developed in 1942 during Operation Barbarossa, the invasion of Russia, and this time one of the guns was prepared for a fire mission.

Far too large to move on conventional railway track, the 800mm (31.4in) K(E) was transported by five complete trains of five cars each, which were assembled on specially laid track near a village called Bakhchisaray, just outside Sevastopol. The gun team alone involved about 500 men, plus a large support organization and two anti-aircraft battalions. All this manpower reached the approximate strength of a brigade. Six weeks were required in order just to prepare the gun to fire. The first round

■LEFT: July 1944 – the Allies grind away at the Germans, securing the Normandy beachhead. This crew digs in its heavy 155mm (6.1in) M1 Howitzer, with scant protection.

went downrange on 5 June 1942 and the port fell about a month – and 500,000 artillery shells of all calibres – later.

Gustav's targets were well within its maximum range, about 25km (15.5 miles) from Bakhchisaray, and included Russian coastal defence artillery batteries. Forward observers in the little Fi-156 *Storch* (or 'Stork') aircraft provided corrections, and eight rounds from the gun destroyed the target. Four more rounds were fired at another fortification, destroying it as well.

Two kinds of projectiles were available for this weapon: a concrete-piercing, base-fused version, and a somewhat more conventional high-explosive type. After the success of the first day's shooting, the gun team opened fire on a magazine that had been excavated under water. Nine rounds were fired at this magazine, fused to detonate after penetrating about 30m (100ft) of water, mud and concrete. At the ninth round, the magazine was flooded. Gustav fired on several other targets before Sevastopol fell on 1 July. It had been in action for 13 days and fired about 300 rounds, before being disassembled and loaded back onto its 25 railcars. All those cars and all those components were dispersed across Germany and never assembled again.

Soviet 100mm SU-100 SP

A beefy alternative to the heavy German Panthers and Tigers, the Soviet SU-100 first appeared in 1944, when the SU-85 proved to be under-gunned for the job. The 100mm (3.94in) D-10S cannon with its long, 56-calibre barrel, was based on a long-range, high-velocity naval gun. With HEAT ammunition, it could punch through 380mm (14.96in) of armour at 1000m (1100yd) range, or 180mm (7in) with dual-purpose high-explosive rounds at the same distance.

SU-100s could fire up to eight rounds per minute, if they had to and were not knocked out first. They were very heavily armoured, though, with a huge cast steel mantlet and up to 45mm (1.8in) of armour plate steeply angled at the front and sides. Inside the fighting compartment were bins for 52 rounds of HVAP, HEAT, APHE and standard high-explosive rounds. As with other tank-

■LEFT: After huge expense and effort, Germany managed to develop the 210mm (8.26in) K12 (E), a gun that fired across the English Channel, but failed to hit anything of value.

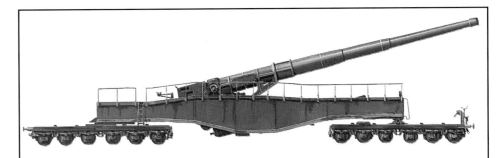

280mm Railway Gun K5(E)

Calibre: 280mm (11.02in)
Weight: 21,8000kg (214.59 tons)
Length: 41.23m (135.28ft)
Barrel length: 21.54m (70.08ft)
Effective range: 62.18m (38.64 miles)
Elevation: 0° to 50°
Traverse: 2°
Muzzle velocity: 1128m/s (3700ft/s)
Country of origin: Germany

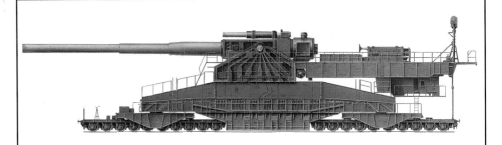

800mm Railway Gun 'Gustav'

Calibre: 800mm (31.4in)
Weight: 1,350,000kg (1328.9 tons)
Length: 42.976m (141ft)
Barrel length: 32.5m (106.6ft)
Effective range: 47m (29.2 miles)
Elevation: 10° to 65°
Traverse: none
Muzzle velocity: 820m/s (2690ft/s)
Country of origin: Germany

killers of the era, the SU-100 driver had to be alert and quick; traverse on the gun was very limited, only 4 degrees, so he had to have the vehicle pointing directly at the target before the gunner could engage the target.

The commander had the advantage of an armoured cupola on the right of the SU-100, providing all-around visibility, a feature inherited from the T-34 tank. The gunner sat behind the driver on the left of the gun, and the loader served the piece from the right rear of the fighting compartment. A 12-cylinder 395kW (530hp) engine provided a road speed of 53km/h (33mph) and road range up to 320km (200 miles), good performance for a vehicle that weighed a total of about 32,000kg (70,400lb).

Many nations begged or borrowed SU-100s after World War II – Algeria, Cuba, Mongolia, Korea, Syria and a dozen more

countries – some of which may still be fielding it today. Egypt and Syria used it against Israel, and Yemen still seems to have 70 SU-100s in its inventory for self-propelled artillery.

Soviet 122mm Howitzer M-30

The Soviet standard howitzer that the Soviet Union provided for its divisions during World War II was the M-30 122mm (4.80in) towed howitzer, churned out of state factories by the tens of thousands during the war. A product of the prolific Petrov Design Bureau, this stalwart design was fielded in six-gun batteries, three batteries to a battalion and three battalions per tank division, which made 54 M-30s in total.

It was a simple howitzer without a muzzle brake and sharing the same carriage with a larger howitzer, the D-1 152mm (6.0in). A small shield protected the crew of eight men. They currently use a MTLB personnel carrier or truck to move it into firing positions, but during the war it was commonly found behind ZIL and imported Studebaker trucks.

The M-30 would elevate from minus 3 to 63.5 degrees and traverse 24.5 degrees left and right. In service in many nations today, a normal unit of fire for this howitzer is 80 rounds of high-explosive or HEAT ammunition. The OF-462 high-explosive round weighs about 22kg (48lb), while the anti-tank projectile is 15kg (33lb). Maximum range for the M-30 is 11.8km (7.3 miles), but the rated effective range against armour with the BP-436 HEAT projectile is only 630m (688yd).

Soviet 152mm ISU-152

Developed in just a month, after the capture of the first German PzKpfw VI Tiger in January 1943, the ISU-152, also

called the Ioseph Stalin, combined an extremely powerful howitzer with the hull and drive train of the KV-2 tank. Normally, such hybrids trade one feature for another, and in this case the Russians got a vehicle that was able to destroy anything on the battlefield, including the dreaded Tiger, but the ammunition ran out after only 20 rounds. However, it ate up Panthers, Tigers and even lumbering Elephants that were once immune to almost anything else, so its Russian crews called it *Zvierboy*, which translates as 'Animal Killer'.

Several howitzers would be used with the basic design, and it would stay in production until 1945. The 152mm (6in) ML-20S was common; it could elevate from minus 3 to 20 degrees, traverse 10 degrees left or right, and was protected by a large cast steel mantlet. The chassis had up to 90mm (3.54in) of armour on

both front and sides, one of the reasons for the vehicle's approximately 45,500kg (100,100lb) weight. A V-12 diesel provided the power for the ISU-152, generating 803kW (600hp) and a maximum road speed of 37km/h (23mph).

Along with stowage for the 20 main gun rounds, the ISU-152 carried 1000 rounds for the heavy 12.5mm (0.49in) DShK machine gun. More rounds for both were often lashed to the engine cooling grills on the rear deck, along with additional drums of fuel. With full tanks, this heavy vehicle could only travel 145km (90 miles) by road before filling up again. ISU-152s fought well against the

■BELOW: Soviet vehicles were brutally simple and reliable, with powerful guns, and could be mass produced in huge numbers. Anti-tank guns like this SU-100 slaughtered German tanks.

Germans, and they were part of the Soviet vanguard entering Berlin.

US 240mm Howitzer M1918M1A1

American gunners did not have any of their own heavy guns during World War I, but 330 French 240mm (9.45in) howitzers were manufactured in the United States for their use. During World War II, a similar weapon, the 240mm Howitzer M1918M1A1, was designed and standardized for US Army heavy artillery units. This howitzer fired a 156kg (345lb) shell to a maximum range of 14,996m (16,400yd), but not very often. The sustained rate of fire was just one round every five minutes, or one every two minutes for short periods.

This was an extremely heavy system in every way, especially for one used in mobile warfare. Ready to fire, the 240mm (9.45in) howitzer weighed more than 18,590kg (41,000lb). This system, and others like it, was most suitable for coastal defences and similar tactical situations. They could be moved, but only on specialized transporters and divided in two loads.

Even so, they were used across Europe. The 29th Infantry Division's 269th Field Artillery Battalion put them to work and moved them on fat balloon tyres through the dust and mud of France and then on to Belgium and Germany during the winter of 1944–45. The 269th went ashore at Normandy in July 1944 and christened its big guns with names such as 'L'il Abner', after a hulking, muscular Sunday comic character of the time.

US 8in Gun M1

World War I experience suggested that US artillery units would need very long-range cannon if they wanted to successfully defend high-priority fixed targets and conduct extremely deep fire missions. A family of very large guns was accordingly developed to meet such a standard, and one of these was the 203mm (8in) Gun M1. The United States produced many weapons designated M1, including several with 203mm (8in) bores, but this particular version was easily recognized by its extremely long barrel and heavy mount.

■ABOVE: Russian gunners have been sending 122mm (4.8in) projectiles out of their cannons for many generations, and here is a battery of some World War II examples, the M1931/27.

Developed on the basis of the Westervelt, or Caliber, Board report issued in May of 1919, this cannon was intended to provide heavy reserve combat power at the corps level. Some work on the gun was begun, but later suspended in the mid-1920s, and the design hibernated until events during 1939 awakened the US Army. The result finally appeared in 1941, and it was almost too large for field use.

The breech and barrel assembly was 50 calibres or 1.04m (409.5in) long and, without the recoil mechanism, weighed 15,241kg (15 tons). The entire package tipped the scale at more than 31,298kg (30 tons). It was so large and heavy that the cannon assembly had to be transported separately from the carriage and the system reassembled with the aid of its own dedicated 6 x 6 truck, the Cannon Transport Wagon M1.

SU-152 Self-Propelled Assault Gun

Calibre: 152mm (6in)
Weight: 45,500kg (100,100lb)
Length: 9.8m (10.7yd)
Barrel length: 4.42m (4.83yd)
Effective range: 17,265m

(18,880yd)
Elevation: -5° to 18°
Traverse: 24°
Muzzle velocity: 655m/s (2150f/s)
Country of origin: USSR

Each high-explosive shell weighed more than 108kg (240lb) and was backed by almost 48.5kg (107lb) of propellant. Inside that shell was 9.5kg (20.9lb) of TNT. Even the primer was huge, a 4.54kg (10lb) naval type operated by electrical impulse or percussion. The consequence of all this was a projectile that left the muzzle at 899m/s (2950ft/s) and that with 50-degree elevation, travelled 32,000m (35,000yd). This cannon was so powerful its minimum range of 20,117m (22,000yd) was more than the maximum of almost any other artillery weapon on the field.

US 8in Howitzer M1

The Westervelt, or Caliber, Board suggested that the US Army needed a 203mm (8in) weapon with not only the power and range to destroy deep targets, but also the agility to shift position with some ease on what was likely to be a more mobile battlefield than that of World War I. American artillerymen at the time used British Mark V, Mark VII and Mark VIII howitzers, of both British and US manufacture.

These systems became the foundation for the new specification. Part of the specification proposed that the carriage for this weapon should be shared with another of similar weight, the 155mm (6.1in) gun, and that is exactly what was developed in the immediate post-war years. The common carriage for both, after some teething problems, was finally standardized as the T2E1, the cannon and its associated components were designated the T3, and the entire package became the 203mm (8in) Howitzer M1 in 1940.

The barrel for the cannon was initially intended to be cast using the centrifugal technique developed during the American Civil War, but was instead cold-forged. A breech ring was shrunk on the tube, using the same technique developed by Armstrong nearly 100 years before. During World War II, an American gunner on this piece might have a further sense of déjà vu, as the 203mm (8in) M1 had the option of being fired with the same type of friction primer and lanyard used with the Napoleons and Parrott cannon of 1863.

In its World War II format, the 203mm (8in) used about 5kg (11lb) of propellant to send a 90kg (200lb) shell out the muzzle at just under 610m/s (2000ft/s), to a maximum range of 16,926m (18,510yd). That shell, the M106 high-explosive version, included 13.6kg (30lb) of bursting charge, which made it just the thing for destroying bridges, observation points, troop concentrations, massed vehicles and especially bunkers and fortified positions. It was also useful for engaging enemy artillery batteries, most of which it could easily outrange. A near miss from one of these massive projectiles could flip the largest German tank over on its back, and sometimes did.

SP ARTILLERY AND ASSAULT GUNS

In February 1945, the US Army accepted two very similar self-propelled gun systems into service, just in time for the end of World War II. These were the M-40 (155mm/6.10in Gun M1A1 or M2) and the M43 (203mm/8in Howitzer M1 or M2 on Mount M17), systems that were badly needed to provide long-range, high-power

mobile artillery support. Of the two, the M40 would become highly successful and go on to be produced in large numbers, 418 units being made by the Pressed Steel Car Company.

The M40 was needed to replace the GMC M12 with its worn-out and obsolete M12 chassis and World War I vintage M1918 155mm (6.10in) gun. This new design used the automotive foundation from the Sherman tank and its 298kW (400hp) nine-cylinder Continental R975 radial engine, excellent suspension and, for a self-propelled gun, good armour protection, with up to about 113mm (4.5in) on the front glacis plate. However, there were some changes required to the vehicle design for its intended use, and so the engine was moved forwards from the rear of the vehicle, and the hull lengthened and widened.

The cannon was the same as used in the M1 towed gun, with the same performance; it was installed on the M13 mount, attached to the rear of the hull in an open-top compartment with light armour panels at the front and side. Stowage for 20 of the big rounds in their fibre containers was provided around the perimeter of the fighting compartment, along with racks for the crew's weapons, small-arms ammunition, bins for sights, binoculars and all the trivial but essential kit issued with such a vehicle.

Eight men formed the normal M40 detachment, a large number for a self-propelled gun, but a number required because of the difficulty of preparing such large rounds of ammunition.

M7 105mm SPH Priest

US armour and artillery units found themselves under the same pressures applied to German and English gunners, and came up with similar solutions. One of these answers was presented in April 1942: a self-propelled howitzer designed to keep up with the leading edge of rapid mobile operations, christened the 105mm (4.13in) Howitzer Motor Carriage M7 by the US Army and soon nicknamed the 'Priest' by its users.

The nickname Priest came from British gunners, accustomed as they were to christening their self-propelled artillery with the titles of churchmen. In the case of the M7, they were further inspired by the pulpit-like compartment at the extreme right front of the vehicle, from which vantage point one of the crew would sermonize with an M2 .50 calibre machine gun.

Imitating the Germans, who were then developing their *Wespe*, or Wasp, SP gun, the Americans also took a well-tested, plentiful, slightly obsolete tank chassis and bolted a 105mm (4.13in) howitzer to it, added a simple gun shield and started issuing them to the troops. The US version used the chassis of the M3 medium tank, the first of its breed, which by 1942 was badly outclassed by the competition. The M3s had seen combat, though, in North Africa, and their hull and drive train had shown themselves to be reasonably reliable.

M7s used this foundation as a mount for the M2A1 howitzer in a M4 mount at the right front of the hull. The vehicles were manufactured by two companies, the American Locomotive Company (ALCO) and the Federal Machine and Welder Company. They were produced in large numbers, with 3490 being delivered in all variants, and they went on to serve the US Army after the end of the war, until as late as 1953.

American armoured vehicles during World War II used petrol-fuelled engines, often of the air-cooled aircraft type, including the M7, the engine of which was a nine-cylinder Continental radial producing up to 298kW (400hp). Maximum speed reached by the M7 was 40km/h (25mph), and maximum range with full 788 litre (175 gallon) tanks was 136– 200km (85–125 miles).

Seven men crewed the M7: a section commander, a driver, a gunner and four cannoneers. Protecting them was a simple shield of 12.7mm (0.5in) steel plates around the sides, with no overhead cover. They served the M2A1 howitzer, an excellent weapon with good range, 45-degree elevation (minus 5 to 40 degrees) and traverse (30 degrees to the right of centreline, 15 degrees to the left).

Sixty-nine main gun rounds could be stored in racks along the sides of the compartment, with most of the semi-fixed rounds stored in their cardboard shipping tubes, but six rounds partially prepared

■ **ABOVE: Italy, April 1945, and the skies are clear. A crew of the 12/54 Super Heavy Regiment, Royal Artillery, re-assemble their American 240mm M1 Howitzer in a new firing position.**

and stowed in a ready ammunition rack near the breech if the possibility of combat threatened.

Sexton Mk 2 SPH

British experience in North Africa proved the importance of powerful, long-range mobile artillery. The towed 25pdr (87.6mm/3.45in) was an excellent weapon and was rather hurriedly adapted to employment on a self-propelled chassis. The basic vehicle was a modified Canadian Ram tank hull and drive train, to which the gun was attached. Armour up to 32mm (1.26in) provided some protection for the gunners from small-arms fire, but, like others of this type and time, the Sexton provided no overhead cover at all.

8in M1 Howitzer

Calibre: 203mm (8in)
Weight: 14,380kg (14.5 tons)
Length: n/a
Barrel length: 5.08m (16.66ft)
Effective range: 16,925m
(18,510yd)

Elevation: 2° to 65°
Traverse: 60°
Muzzle velocity: 595m/s (1952ft/s)
Country of origin: USA

M40 155mm Self-Propelled Gun

Calibre: 155mm (6.1in)
Weight: 36,400kg (80,080lb)
Length of vehicle: 9.4m (29ft 8in)
Barrel length: 6.97m (22.86ft)
Effective range: 23,220m
(25,395yd)

Elevation: -5° to 45°
Traverse: 36°
Muzzle velocity: 853m/s (2800ft/s)
Country of origin: USA

Like the US Sherman tanks which formed its ancestor, the Sexton was powered by a large air-cooled radial engine originally intended for aircraft. This engine used petrol and, like the Shermans, 'brewed up' and burned easily. When all the propellant and high explosive in the ammunition burned along with the petrol, the Sexton made an impressive sight.

Despite the improvised nature of its creation, the Sexton was an important and successful self-propelled gun system. Well over 2000 were made and the very last finally wore out, in the service of small nations in the more obscure corners of the globe, in the 1980s.

StuG III

Beginning as early as 1935, German commanders foresaw the utility of armoured self-propelled artillery, and thousands of very superior weapons systems of this type were manufactured throughout the war.

Perhaps the very best was the G-model StuG III, or more correctly, *Sturmgeschütz* III *Ausfuhrung* G, a very heavily armoured assault gun that could go toe-to-toe with any Allied tank while also delivering useful fire against conventional artillery targets. The series began in 1936 with a request for a support vehicle which was armed with a 75mm (2.95in) gun, resulting in a self-

propelled gun based on the PzKW III Ausf F tank hull and drive train, fitted with a Krupp *Sturmkanone* 40 for the main armament. More than 9000 of all variants were made between 1940 and the end of the war, but the G model was easily the most common, with 7893 produced or converted from earlier self-propelled gun types.

Four men crewed the StuG III: commander, driver, gunner and loader. Aboard, they carried 54 rounds of 75mm (2.95in) main gun ammunition and 600 rounds of 7.92mm (0.31in) for the MG 34 or MG 42 machine gun. They were protected by up to 80mm (3.15in) of armour. A 12-cylinder 223kW (300hp) petrol Maybach engine provided power through a five-speed transmission and could achieve a maximum of 39km/h (24mph) on good roads and a maximum range of 150km (93miles).

With the introduction of the G in 1942, and its longer cannon, the Germans were somewhat better able to deal with the brilliant Soviet tanks such as the T-34 that were threatening to dominate the battlefield. The StuG III was much cheaper to manufacture than contemporary tanks, as it did without a turret, forsaking all-around engagements for a very limited traverse.

The result was that the StuG could, and sometimes did, destroy amazing numbers of enemy vehicles – when in a protected position. One F model destroyed 9 Russian tanks in 20 minutes at Stalingrad in 1942, and the crew of another accounted for 43 T-34s and T-36s in 1943. The low profile, heavy frontal armour and excellent training helped attain these scores, but these results were possible only when terrain or other vehicles protected the StuG's rear.

Without the ability to traverse the gun, the crew had to be especially vigilant about threats from all quarters at the same time as they were engaging targets to the front. British, Soviet and US tankers learned they could defeat German vehicles by swarming them, hitting them with many rounds that might not penetrate the armour, but that would destroy the vehicle's tracks or sighting systems, or pierce through the thinner engine grill doors at the rear.

■**RIGHT: The M7 Priest 105mm (4.13in) Self-Propelled Howitzer adapted a standard M2A1 howitzer to a M3 light tank, replacing the armour with 12mm (.5in) plate to protect the crew.**

SP 105mm Howitzer *Wespe*

Battlefield experience during the later days of World War II indicated to German forces that more mobile artillery was essential, but industrial capacity and raw materials did not exist to manufacture new designs. The result was a series of improvisations, one of which was called the *Wespe*, or 'Wasp'.

Based on the then entirely obsolete Panzer II (the *Panzerkampfwagen* II, SdKfz 121) chassis and leFH 18 howitzer, this self-propelled cannon turned out to be remarkably successful. Originally intended as a stop-gap design until something better could be produced, no less than 682 'Wasps' stung Allied forces from 1942 until the end of the war in March 1945.

The development process was extremely brief and prompted by an order by Hitler on 4 April 1942 that existing weapons and vehicles be adapted as mobile artillery systems, rather than have new 'weapons carriers' developed. The Panzer II had just been pulled from front-line service and was available in huge numbers. That small, light, obsolete Panzer II chassis was still a good design. Although armour protection was slight by 1942, it was sufficient to protect from most small-arms fire and some artillery shell splinters. The 10mm (0.39in) thick gun shield, like that on most mobile howitzers, did not provide overhead protection – or protection from rain, wind or snow – but it was better than nothing.

The hull and drive train were well tested by 1942. With the transmission and track driving sprockets at the front and the engine amidships, the fighting compartment was located towards the back of the vehicle. The engine was moved forwards a bit, the suspension reinforced to take recoil forces and, later, the hull was stretched 220mm (8.7in). Power was supplied by a six-cylinder, 140HP Maybach engine and manual transmission with six forward- and one reverse gears.

Rheinmetall-Borsig designed the gun system, a variant of the standard cannon of the whole German Army, the lIH-81 105mm (4.13in) howitzer. As initially configured, the gun could only traverse 20 degrees and elevate 42 degrees. If a

■**RIGHT: The StuG III was a vehicle that specialized in line-of-sight, direct fire engagements with tanks, fortifications, or any target that could be effectively serviced with a high-velocity round.**

the cannon, behind which all four of the gun crew worked. The ready racks normally contained high-explosive, HEAT and anti-personnel rounds. As with the standard leFH 18, ammunition was of the semi-fixed type, and charges could be 'cut' for high or low velocity, as required.

Radio gear was also installed in the fighting compartment, along with personal weapons (MP38 or MP40 machine pistols), plus a MG 34 7.62mm (0.3in) machine gun for defence against aircraft and enemy infantry. Five men crewed the *Wespe*: a commander, three gunners and a driver, all of whom were 'cross-trained' in the duties of each of the others. The driver's position was at the left front of the hull, isolated from the other four in the fighting compartment.

Self-propelled artillery systems were given informal nicknames, and *Wespe* or Wasp was used when the system was first christened in 1942. Hitler, however, prohibited the use of that name in January 1944, and it was known thereafter by its formal name, Special Vehicle 124. Originally, 1000 were ordered, including the ammo carriers, but that was reduced to 835 in late 1943. Of the 682 that were actually completed, about half (370) survived the war intact. The Wasp, supplied to nine light armour divisions in France before the Normandy invasion and many more afterwards, was both highly successful and durable. Ten thousand rounds could be fired before the barrel needed replacement.

German 150mm SP Howitzer

Complementing the little Wasp, German artillery regiments had another SP gun with a bigger stinger, the *Hummel*, or in English, the 'Bumblebee'.

Officially the 15cm (5.9in) *Schwere Panzerhaubitze auf Geschutzwagen* III/IV (Sf), this fine self-propelled gun was the result of bitter lessons which had been learnt in Russia in 1941, when the need for a howitzer of large calibre and with enough speed to keep up with the tanks became painfully apparent.

Originally, a 105mm (5.9in) light Field Howitzer 17 was mounted on the hull of a converted Panzer III medium tank, but the combination wasn't quite up to standard. The automotive components proved to be inadequate, so the hull and drive train from the Panzer IV were tried in their place. This seemed to provide the vehicle with an acceptable level of agility, but the 105mm (5.9in) gun was not approved. It was replaced in July 1942

target developed anywhere but to the front, the driver had to quickly start and move the vehicle before the gunners could engage. *Wespes* could fly along at 40km/h (25mph) on decent roads and 24km/h (15mph) on open ground, and had sufficient trench-crossing and climbing ability to stay near the leading assault elements. With full tanks (170 litres/299 gallons), the *Wespe* could road march a total distance of 212km (132 miles).

Placing a heavy howitzer on top of any vehicle, even a medium tank, raises its centre of gravity, and that was a problem for the *Wespe*. Drivers had to be good at their job and chose their routes carefully or else they risked rolling the vehicle over

■**ABOVE: Three big *Wespe* (Wasp) guns protrude from their nests deep inside Russia. The gun was known as Special Vehicle 124 after Hitler prohibited the use of the original name.**

onto its side, with dire consequences for anyone in the gun compartment.

The cannon was the same basic 105mm (4.13in) weapon designed in World War I, with 32 ready rounds in racks on the vehicle and another supply aboard a dedicated ammunition supply vehicle. This ammunition vehicle looked almost exactly like the *Wespe* itself, but without the gun. Aboard this vehicle were 90 additional rounds. A shield protected with the heavy FH 18, which had a 30 calibre barrel but was manufactured without a muzzle brake.

Adapting a tank hull and drive train for service as a self-propelled gun is seldom as simple as bolting the carriage to the top deck and driving away to glory, and such was the case with the Bumblebee. The engine was moved forward and the whole hull lengthened in order to fit a proper fighting compartment and mount for the big howitzer. Flat armour plates provided some protection for the crew against small-arms fire, but nothing except a canvas cover to keep out rain, snow, and enemy artillery airbursts.

The first examples of the *Hummel* flew out of their nest towards the end of 1942, and they stayed in production for about two years, during which time a total of 724 self-propelled guns and ammunition carriers (using identical hull and drive train and armour, but lacking the gun) were manufactured.

These ammunition vehicles were nearly identical to the armed version and could be quickly converted if necessary. Their services were made essential because the *Hummel* had room for only 18 rounds for its stinger. *Hummels* saw their first serious action during the summer of 1943, during Operation Citadel, as part of *Wehrmacht* and SS divisional artillery batteries.

As efficient and successful as this armour-plated creature was, Hitler decided early in 1944 that he didn't think naming weapons of war after relatively harmless little insects quite created the right impression, and henceforth the vehicles were invariably described by their official designation and never again called 'Bumblebees' – not in Hitler's presence, at least.

US M101 or M2A1 105mm Howitzer

Of the many lessons of World War I studied by the US Army, the need for a good, mobile, long-range howitzer delivering a heavy shell was one of the most important. The Westervelt, or Caliber, Board report of 1919 called for a 105mm (4.13in) gun with 65 degrees of elevation, firing a 15.88kg (35lb) shell to a distance of up to 10,970m (12,000yd). Development of such a gun began in 1920, and the basic design was tested and finally approved eight years later – after several changes of name – and was given the moniker the Howitzer M1 and Carriage M1.

Budgets during the ensuing Depression years prevented production, and so the blueprints stayed in the files, awaiting their time. That came in 1933, when the US Army decided that it probably would not be using horses to pull cannon on the battlefield for much longer. This factor as well as the alarming rise of militant German and Italian nationalism, meant that it was time to get serious about artillery.

The cannon was modified to take a specialized shrapnel round in 1934, and the modified gun became the M2. The old M1 design received a makeover and an entirely new carriage, and it was accepted by the Army for production in 1940 and christened the 105mm (4.13in) Howitzer M2 on Carriage M2. The result was a weapon that quickly became the standard artillery piece for the entire US Army, and which was produced in huge numbers and employed by dozens of other armies around the globe for many years afterwards. In fact, it is still in service with many nations worldwide right up until today.

The gun and carriage together weigh 2030kg (4475lb) in firing order (M2A2), light enough to be pulled by many light vehicles. It is a simple, mostly 'soldier-proof' system with sliding wedge breechblock, percussion ignition and, with its World War II ammunition, a maximum range of 11,156m (12,200yd). The high-explosive projectile weighs 15kg (33lb), and the whole round weighs a total 19kg (42lb). As originally suggested

in 1919, it elevates to 65 degrees and depresses to minus 4 degrees, with a useful traverse of 22.5 degrees, left and right of centreline. The weapon got another name after the war – M101A1 – but only after a staggering 8536 M2s and its variant 105mm (4.13in) towed howitzers had been produced. Rock Island Arsenal produced nearly 2000 more until 1953, when manufacture of the system was completed.

About 50 armies around the world have employed the weapon since its conception, and a great many still do. It saw very extensive use during the Vietnam War, where US helicopters delivered it to tiny clearings on ridge tops and right into the middle of the jungle in order to establish American firebases in what would have been otherwise impossible locations.

Virtually all kinds of projectiles have been made for this weapon and its NATO-standard cartridge design. These include four different kinds of high-explosive, plus HESH, HEAT, smoke, illumination, chemical, leaflet, 'beehive', tear-gas, rocket-assisted, as well as others. Seven propellant charges allow M2 gun batteries considerable flexibility in the delivery of their fire.

If it had a longer barrel (and it is rather short at 22.5 calibres), the weapon's range would not be quite so modest. All weapons are compromises, however, and the ones accepted for this howitzer made it a tremendously successful package.

Hummel (Bumblebee)

Calibre: 150mm (5.9in)
Weight: 23,927kg (52,640lb)
Length: 7.17m (7.84yd)
Barrel length: 4.13m (4.51yd)
Effective range: 13,250m

(14,490yd)
Elevation: -3° to 42°
Traverse: 30°
Muzzle velocity: 495m/s (1624f/s)
Country of origin: Germany

XXVI
ЛЕНИНСКИМ КУРСОМ –
К ПОБЕДЕ КОММУНИЗМА!
ПЛАНЫ ПАРТИИ –
ПЛАНЫ НАРОДА!
ЕШЕНИЯ XXVI СЪЕЗДА КПСС - ВЫПОЛНИМ !

CHAPTER FIVE
COLD WAR KILLERS

Artillery had played a key role in the defeat of Nazi Germany, but in the Cold War it seemed, initially at least, likely to be eclipsed by nuclear weapons. However conflicts like Korea and Vietnam proved artillery still had a role.

The story of the M109 Self-propelled 155mm (6.1in) Howitzer is a long and successful one, extending back over half a century, and it may keep going for another 50 years. The M109 was conceived in 1952 as a system to replace the M44 SP 155mm (6.1in) howitzer that had served so well in World War II and Korea. After a gestation period of 10 years, the first production vehicle was delivered. Many thousands followed it, and the basic design is still in service and in production with many nations from around the world.

All of the many variants of the M109 are large vehicles shooting a large projectile. Even so, they are still transportable by cargo aircraft and can almost keep up with the Abrams tanks and Bradley APCs during offensive combat operations. M109s can get up to 56km/h (35mph) and have a range of 354km (220 miles). Combat loaded, the M109 is a hefty 24,948kg (55,000lb). It is about 3m (10ft) high, 3.1m (10ft 4in) wide and 9.1m (29ft 8.4in) long.

The M109 has been through quite an evolution. The first version used a very short barrel with a quite short maximum range: only 14,600m (15,966yd). The first modification, the A1, extended the tube and the range out to 18,100m (19,794yd). A2 and A3 models improved performance a bit, but the A4 finally gave the crew some NBC (nuclear/biological/chemical) protection, although through use of MOPP suits and masks instead of a fully pressurized hull and turret. Unlike some

■**LEFT: The 2S3, with 152mm (6in) gun, has a top speed of 55km/h (34mph)! Here brand new, carefully painted and polished Soviet 2S3 SP guns parade through Red Square in 1981.**

other self-propelled systems, standard M109s do not have overpressure NBC protection; the crew has to suit up in MOPP4 gear when threatened by nuclear, biological or chemical agents. This requires the crew to don masks attached to ducts supplying clean, cool air.

The heart of the M109 in its most common A2/A3/A4 versions is its M185 cannon. This weapon will fire a very wide variety of ammunition, all with projectiles weighing about 45kg (100lb), out to 23,637m (25,850yd). The A5 uses the M248 gun with a maximum range of 22,128m (24,200yd). The most recent member of this large tribe is the A6 Paladin version, a model which uses the M284 cannon, elevates to 75 degrees and depresses to minus 3 degrees, with a 360-degree traverse and the ability to reach out to 30,175m (33,000yd). It can even fire the W48 nuclear projectile.

In combat, the crew may fire one round per minute for as much as an hour, but then only one round every three minutes for a sustained bombardment. In an emergency and with a cold tube, however, 1 round every 15 seconds can be sent downrange for 3 minutes before the breech gets too hot. Two precision Copperhead projectiles and 37 conventional rounds are normally stowed on the vehicle ready for use, plus an additional supply in a separate, dedicated ammunition vehicle always parked nearby. M109s generally are equipped with a M2 .50 calibre heavy machine gun for self-defence against personnel, aircraft and thin-skinned vehicles.

This self-propelled howitzer is comparatively simple, sturdy and reliable, and uses traditional gunnery systems and procedures. Loading and re-supply are entirely manual, each 44.45kg

(98lb) projectile being carried by hand from the re-supply vehicle, inserted in the breech, then followed by the propellant bags. Its simplicity and economy of operation have made it a standard with dozens of nations, and, although it is being superseded by more complex and costly systems in some armies, the M109 will be around for many more years, perhaps long enough to celebrate 100 years of service.

D-30 HOWITZER

A seasoned veteran of Soviet, and now Russian, artillery batteries is the D-30 towed 122mm (4.80in) howitzer, now a very versatile and capable example of post–World War II design. The D-30 uses three, instead of two, trails, all of which fold neatly for towing. In action, the three trails, along with a firing pedestal, form a platform that permits the gun to be rapidly traversed through a full circle while giving excellent stability.

This design first was issued to Soviet forces during the 1960s and is still very common in armies around the world. Dozens of nations currently use it, and the cannon has been copied and installed in a Chinese self-propelled system. It was a product of the Petrov Design Bureau and has been upgraded several times

since its introduction, with changes in the wheels and suspension, muzzle brake, cradle and recoil components.

Besides the three trails, the D-30 has another novel feature. Both components of its recoil system are installed on top of the tube instead of the usual over-and-under arrangement, and both are covered with a distinctive metal shield. The wheels elevate much higher than on most other systems using a firing pedestal, a necessary feature for them to clear the trails as the gun is swung around to engage moving targets. Instead of typical spades, the D-30 uses spikes to secure the ends of the trails.

The gun will elevate to 70 degrees and depress to minus 7. Maximum range is 15,490m (16,940yd) with standard projectiles and 22,028m (24,090yd) with the rocket-assisted type. A long barrel helps the gun's performance. D-30s fire most of the available 122mm (4.8in) projectiles issued by the Russian artillery supply system, plus a fin-stabilized HEAT round, the BK-6M, which can defeat 480mm (18.9in) of conventional armour. Ammunition is of the variable-charge, semi-fixed type. Up to 8 rounds per minute may be fired during sustained missions. Each D-30 is authorized 80 rounds as its basic unit-of-fire.

■ABOVE: Hiding in its fresh hole in the sand, a M109 during Operation Desert Storm. The advance went forward too quickly, but the SP guns still made a telling contribution to the attack.

During February of 1986, a platoon of D-30s executed an artillery ambush against Mujahedeen insurgents in Afghanistan. The platoon, commanded by Lieutenant V. Kozhbergenov, first emplaced sensors along a known infiltration route. These Realii-U sensors could, when operated by skilled operators, identify the passage of troops, vehicles and pack animals. Kozhbergenov's unit designated three target areas along the route, and pre-planned fires for all three. These targets were spaced 100m (328ft) apart along a road between high hills and designated 110, 111 and 112.

One night soon after the sensors were installed, the operator reported passage of 2 vehicles, 15 personnel and several animals, all in a group. As the infiltrators entered the middle target area, 111, the battery fired a single-round volley. One of the D-30s then shifted fire to the left target, 110, while the other shifted to the right, 112, to catch any escaping Mujahedeen. At first light, two destroyed

M109A3G

Calibre: 155mm (6.1in)
Weight: 24,948kg (55,000lb)
Length: 9.2m (30ft)
Barrel length: 33 calibres

Effective range: 18,105m (19,800yd)
Elevation: -3° to 75°
Traverse: 360°

Muzzle velocity: 585m/s (1919ft/s)
Country of origin: USA/Germany

Toyota trucks, four dead pack animals and six rebel soldiers were found along the road, with weapons and ammunition scattered nearby. The battery had achieved this count by firing just 12 rounds of ammunition.

According to Janes' Information Services, Russian motorized rifle regiments are authorized a battalion of 18 D-30s, tank divisions get 36 and MR divisions 72. D-30s and their clones are still in production in four other nations,

and the Chinese version is an almost perfect copy, except for the white sidewall tyres. This same cannon system, with some modifications, is the heart of the 2S1 self-propelled howitzer described in a later section.

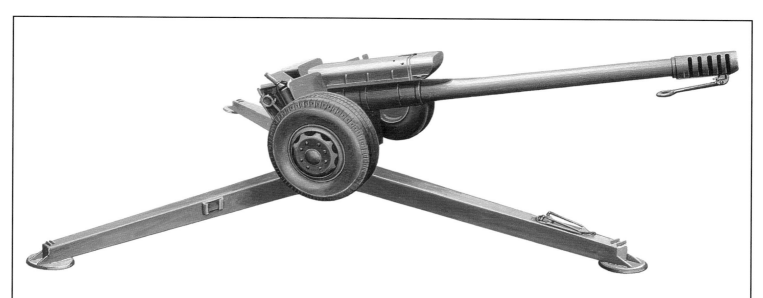

D30 122mm Gun

Calibre: 122mm (4.8in)
Weight: 3150kg (6945lb)
Length of gun: 5m (16.4ft)
Barrel length: 4.875m (16ft)

Effective range: 15,400m (16,840yd)
Elevation: -7° to 70°
Traverse: 360°

Muzzle velocity: 690m/s (2264f/s)
Country of origin: USSR

■LEFT: A battery of Soviet 122mm (4.8in) D30s, complete with smoke pots. This is a rugged workhorse gun, and the pivoting mount gives it a real advantage on the battlefield.

for the 122mm (4.8in) M30. It uses several high-explosive projectiles of about 40kg (88lb) and can fire to about 12.4km (7.75 miles). Elevation limits were minus 3 to 63.5 degrees, with the traverse 35 degrees in total. D1s are still commonly found in the artillery parks of nations such as Afghanistan, Iraq, Iran and Mongolia, among many others.

RUSSIAN 152MM GUN-HOWITZER

Petrov designed the M1955 D20 combination gun, with a longer barrel and much improved range – but also with a substantial weight penalty. It weighs

SOVIET 130MM M46

Although quite elderly today, this long-barrelled cannon is another Soviet success story with a diverse combat history. Its origins go back to the late 1940s and a period when Russian planners were anticipating war with NATO nations. Artillery commanders wanted something with more punch and reach than the 122mm (4.8in) systems, especially for counterbattery fire missions, and they wanted something quickly. The result was a 130mm (5.12in) naval cannon adapted to service ashore, with a tremendously long tube 55 calibres, or 7m (23ft), long. It is so long that the gun has to be dismounted and moved to the rear of the trails before being towed, a characteristic of many long-barrelled systems that cannot safely be moved in firing order.

Other than the tube length, the M46 is of conventional layout. Its elevation is from minus 2.5 to 45 degrees, and it will traverse 45 degrees left and right from the centreline. Nine men form a standard gun crew, and they can put six or seven rounds downrange in 60 seconds. It has a distinctive 'pepper pot' muzzle brake and unusually high box trail legs. Also, the spades fold and are stowed on top of the trails when the gun is moved. These three features help make the M46 easy to identify in the field. Ammunition is semi-fixed type and is available in a wide range of projectiles made in Russia, China, Israel and France. The standard anti-tank round will defeat 240mm (9.45in) of homogenous armour plate at 1000m (1094yd).

The M1946 is still in service half a century after being introduced. That longevity is probably based on the gun's tremendous range – 27km (16.8 miles) – and excellent overall performance. It can outrange most other guns and is especially valuable in counterbattery duels, a capability that got an extensive and successful trial during the Arab–Israeli wars.

It has been produced under licence by the Chinese and sold by them to India, Pakistan and other nations. India uses the cannon on tank chassis as a home-grown self-propelled gun, the 'Catapult'. The M46 has been employed by Israel, North Korea, Syria, Cuba, Poland, Nigeria and even Mongolia, as well as Russia, and is likely to be in service for many years to come.

RUSSIAN 152MM HOWITZER

Another battlefield classic from the F.F. Petrov Design Bureau, the M1943 D1 is a simple gun which has been sold around the world, been copied by several nations and fought in wars large and small for six decades. It was designed during World War II to be a lighter and more powerful version of the M1938 M10 152mm (6in) howitzer. It weighs about 900kg (1984lb) less than the earlier version and was a mainstay of Soviet artillery units throughout the Cold War years.

Petrov installed a large two-baffle muzzle brake on the tube, permitting this fairly compact gun to fire high-power variable-charge separate-loading ammunition without excessive recoil forces on the carriage, originally designed

about 2000kg (4400lb) more than the D1, being 5650kg (12,456lb) instead of the 3600kg (7937lb) for the smaller gun. That paid off in an extra 5000m (5470yd) in range, with a maximum engagement distance of 17.2km (10.7 miles). The carriage is small, with split trail, platform and caster wheels to help swing the gun quickly towards its target. It limits elevation to 45 degrees, one legacy of its 122mm (4.8in) origins. Eight men are normally assigned to this gun.

The D20 pioneered the sliding wedge vertical breechblock, and with it, the gun can fire a very respectable six rounds per minute. D20s are still in service with infantry divisions' and fronts' artillery regiments and brigades; in the 2S3 self-propelled version, it is found in the artillery units of motorized rifle and tank divisions. It is fielded by more than 13 nations and copied by at least one, China, and a longer barrelled version was produced by Yugoslavia, where it is designated as the M84.

RUSSIAN 180MM GUN S23
Based on a naval cannon and developed during the 1950s, the S23 is the largest of the Soviet Cold War towed artillery. It is a very hefty gun weighing 21,450kg (21.1 tons) ready to fire, about four times that of many other heavy artillery pieces, but delivering an 84kg (185lb) projectile to ranges that were, at the time it was introduced, quite extreme.

Unlike most Russian artillery, the S23 fires bagged charges instead of cased propellant, and it fires them to very long range: 44km (27 miles) for the RAP type and about 30km (18.6 miles) for standard projectiles. Included in its arsenal are massive high-explosive and concrete-piercing types, as well as a .2 kiloton nuclear device. Twelve are the normal complement of an artillery division's heavy artillery brigade. They are transported by an AT-T heavy tracked artillery tractor and require a detachment of 16 men. This crew can fire up to two rounds per minute in emergencies, one per minute for sustained missions.

Although no longer manufactured in Russia, the S23 is still in service with some former Soviet client nations, including Syria, Iraq and Egypt.

■BELOW: A pair of Soviet 130mm (5.1in) M-46 Field Guns. Developed in the 1950s by the Soviet Union, these weapons have seen action with Egypt, Iran, Iraq, and 24 other nations.

■LEFT: Three 130mm (5.1in) M-46 Field Guns in travelling order and on parade in the Middle East. Too long in its firing position for towing, the gun it slides to the rear before it is moved.

(6in) calibre, its ammunition is not interchangeable with other designs of the same bore measurement. Besides the normal high-explosive and anti-tank projectiles, a 60-round unit-of-fire for the 2A36 can include base-bleed, chemical, nuclear, concrete-piercing and Krasnopol laser-guided types of ammunition.

It has good elevation and traverse, from minus 2.5 degrees to 57 degrees vertically and 25 degrees left and right. This makes it a compelling device for sniping at tanks and similar moving targets. A trained crew can have it ready to fire in 5 minutes and be on the road, after firing, in 10.

RUSSIAN 152MM FIELD GUN

The Russians like guns, the bigger the better, and the 2A36 M1976 is a very hefty 152mm (6in) example. It uses a long tube on a long carriage, and the whole gun weighs 9870kg (21,760lb) ready to fire. But it can deliver fire to 27km (16.8 miles) with normal ammunition and 40km (24.9 miles) with

RAPs. It is so large that four wheels are needed to support it, and the 13m (43ft) length makes it awkward to fit into dark alleys. It has a multi-baffle muzzle brake.

The 2A36 can fire quickly for such a hefty piece, with an emergency rate of six rounds per minute and sustained rate of one per minute. And, although it uses the standard and traditional Russian 152mm

RUSSIAN 152MM SP GUN

Despite the Russians' fondness for towed artillery systems, they have fielded and exported some sturdy, stalwart self-propelled designs. One of the most popular has been the 2S3, known to NATO as the M1973. This design actually entered service in 1971. Based on the

standard 152mm (6in) calibre, this system was intended to provide supporting fires at division level for motorized rifle and tank divisions. Eighteen systems are authorized per motorized or tank division.

The hull and drive train are adapted from a design used to transport the SA4 anti-aircraft missile system and the GMZ mine-laying vehicle, but with modifications to suit this somewhat demanding role. It is powered by a 520HP V-12 diesel engine that will move the vehicle at speeds of up to 55km/h (34mph) and distances of up to 300km (186 miles) on a tank of fuel.

The hull has NBC protection for the crew of six, but is not capable of the kinds of river-crossings that have been a tactical feature of Russian/Soviet operations, and this gun can only ford streams to a depth of 1.5m (5ft). The detachment is protected against small arms and artillery threats by steel armour up to 20mm (0.79in) thick.

The layout and external appearance of the 2S3 is quite similar to the M109, and the two would be easily misidentified on the battlefield. Both use a turret with sloping sides and a fairly short barrel, and have road wheels of similar size and

placement. The M109, however, is a bit higher and uses a fume extractor with a noticeably different shape.

The driver sits at the left front with the engine to his right and an emergency escape panel under his seat. The commander's station is at the left rear of the turret, where he has the only roof hatch and a set of vision blocks installed in a rotating cupola for an all-round view. He also has control of the 7.62mm (0.36in) PKT machine gun for defence against air- and infantry threats. This weapon can be operated conventionally or can be remotely controlled from inside the turret.

The gunner sits in front and below the commander. He has sights for direct- and indirect-fire missions, an OP5-38 5.5-power telescope for firing at visible threats and a PG-4 panoramic sight with 3.7-power magnification. To the gunner's right is the 152mm (6in) 2A33 gun, a variant on the D-20 towed cannon, but with a fume extractor fitted behind the large, two-baffle muzzle brake. The gun will depress to minus 4 degrees and elevate to 60, and it has all-round electrically powered traverse, with manual backup. Because of the relatively short barrel, the maximum range for the

2S3 with unassisted high-explosive projectile is only 18,500m (20,232yd).

The loader works on the right side of the turret. Behind him, at the rear of the compartment, are racks for 33 projectiles at the top of the turret and racks for the propellant cases below. During sustained operations, the loader will typically get his rounds from handlers outside the vehicle, who will pass prepared projectiles and propellant through hatches at the rear of the turret.

Soviet artillery 'front' divisions massed the M1973 in batteries of 6 or 8, up to 24 systems per regiment, 72 per brigade. Janes estimates that more than 10,000 2S3 systems have been manufactured, but no production data are available. Many of these have been supplied to Iraq and other traditional Soviet client states.

RUSSIAN 2S5 SP
The Soviets placed special emphasis on self-propelled guns, capable of extreme range, during the Cold War. Part of that

■BELOW: The large Soviet 180mm (7in) S23. It has been in service since the 1950s; with rocket-assisted projectiles, the gun could reach a target more than 43km (26.7 miles) away.

emphasis was based on their planned use of artillery-delivered, small nuclear weapons. Although not the biggest of these guns, the 2S5 was included as one of the systems capable of delivery of such projectiles, along with standard high-explosive rounds, out to 28,500m (31,168yd). Introduced in 1981, the 2S5 replaced M46 towed howitzers, in artillery brigades and regiments in both front and army formations.

The system uses a long, 52 calibre 152mm (6in) cannon mounted on a proven chassis used on other Russian self-propelled systems. This weapon is exposed and has very limited traverse, like the larger and similar S203, but it nonetheless has room aboard for the crew of five, while 15mm (0.59in) of armour provides them with substantial ballistic and NBC protection.

A mechanical and semi-automatic ammunition handling system allows the crew to fire up to six of the massive rounds per minute. Automatic loading has been an important feature of Russian armour and artillery systems for many years, and they are generally reliable and efficient designs.

On the 2S5, the loader selects and sets the fuse on the gunner's command, then places the projectile in a loading tray set at an angle below and behind the breech. He then selects and 'cuts' the propellant charge and places the case in the lower part of the loading tray. When ordered to load, he actuates the chain-drive loader, which then feeds the projectile into the throat of the chamber, followed by the propellant case and its integral primer. The breech then slams shut, ready to fire.

Each 2S5 goes into action with 60 rounds of ammunition, 30 on the vehicle and another 30 on a supporting vehicle. A carousel at the left rear of the turret is used for on-board stowage of the projectiles, and the propellant cases are carried in a dispenser that is mounted below the turret basket, an arrangement very common on many kinds of Russian combat vehicles. A rocket-assisted high-explosive projectile with a maximum range of 40km (25 miles) is one option, along with the usual broad spectrum of 152mm (6in) projectiles available to Russian artillery commanders.

The gun has good range of elevation, from minus 2 to 57 degrees, and it can

ABOVE: A carefully painted and polished Soviet 2A36 152mm (6in) Field Gun and its detachment taking part in a military parade somewhere in the former Soviet Union.

traverse 15 degrees left and right; however, it is an indirect-fire system only. It lacks the gun display unit and fire-control computer systems found on all modern guns, making it somewhat primitive by current standards.

A 2S5 can be ready to fire within three minutes of arrival, once the barrel is released from its travel lock, and it takes about a minute to get ready to leave. Finland and several other nations have acquired the 2S5, but the hazards and limitations of such an exposed cannon, and the basic fire controls, have restricted their popularity during the past several decades.

RUSSIAN 122MM 2S1 SP

Warsaw Pact forces began fielding a new self-propelled howitzer in 1972, a 122mm (4.8in) gun system installed on the very successful MT-LB hull and drive train, officially designated SO-122. When NATO

2S3 SP 152mm Gun

Calibre: 152mm (6in)
Weight: 24,945kg (54,880lb)
Length: 8.4m (27ft 6in)
Barrel length: 34 calibres

Effective range: 18,500m
(20,230yds)
Elevation: -3° to 65°
Traverse: 360°

Muzzle velocity: n/a
Country of origin: USSR

2S1 (NATO M1974) SP 122mm Gun

Calibre: 122mm (4.8in)
Weight: 15,700kg (34,540lb)
Length: 7.3m (23ft 11in)
Barrel length: 5m (16.4ft)

Effective range: 15,300m
(16,730yds)
Elevation: -3° to 70°
Traverse: 360°

Muzzle velocity: 690m/s (2264f/s)
(est)
Country of origin: USSR

■LEFT: A chore for the junior men on the crew of any self-propelled gun is setting up the camouflage netting. The vehicle is a 2S1, its 122mm (4.8in) gun properly stowed in its travel lock.

observers first noticed it two years later, they decided to identify it as the M1974 and also as the 2S1, the latter designation being used by the Kharkov Tractor Works where the system was developed. Over the years, the 2S1 became a standard fixture in motorized rifle, artillery and armour divisions of the Warsaw Pact and its allies and customers. More than 10,000 have been made and fielded, some of which have actually gone to war. Vast numbers of Iraqi 2S1s were either destroyed or captured during the 1991 Gulf War.

The foundation for the 2S1 is the welded steel MT-LB personnel carrier. It is very low, with a superb suspension and drive train, good speed and excellent reliability. The hull has three major sections: one for the driver on the left front, the engine and transmission in the middle of the vehicle, and the turret system and ammunition storage bins at the rear. The MT-LB is amphibious with minimal preparation, will zoom across the battlefield at 60kHz, and its seven road wheels and torsion-bar suspension provide its crew of four a smooth ride. A 300HP V-8 diesel and a transmission with five forward and one reverse gears supply the power. The hull uses 15mm (0.59in) steel, suitable protection against

most light weapons and shell fragments; the turret is a bit tougher, having 20mm (0.79in) of armour. The 2S1's optimum load of 550 litres (121 gallons) of fuel are carried in cells installed just forward of the turret, enough for a best-case road range of 500km (310 miles).

Onto this hull is attached a very compact turret and its gun system. Ready rounds are stowed in racks all around the turret interior, with additional rounds in bins at the very rear of the vehicle. It is a fairly tight fit, but the gun uses an automatic loader, which helps somewhat. Three men fight from the turret: the commander, gunner and loader. Two others from the 2S1's dedicated ammunition supply vehicle provide rounds for conventional-fire missions, so the actual crew is six, consisting of four inside and two outside.

The heart of the 2S1 is the 2A31 122mm (4.8in) howitzer. This cannon's range of motion is from minus 3 degrees to 70 degrees elevation, and it has 360-degree traverse with electrical primary controls and manual alternates. The cannon is a modified version of the Russian's very common D-30 towed howitzer, and it fires the same ammunition: high-explosive, HEAT-FS, illuminating and smoke. All of these projectiles weigh about 22kg (48.5lb) each and leave the gun at about 690m/s (2264ft/s), with the exception of the HEAT-FS round. This fires at 740m/s (2428ft/s) and can engage targets out to almost 22,000m (24,059yd). Other

specialized projectiles are available, too, including a precision-guided laser-homing Kitolov 2M, fleshette anti-personnel, incendiary and chemical. Sustained fire rate is one or two per minute, but a rate of five rounds per minute is possible for short emergencies.

While most of the fire missions for a 2S1 will be indirect, using a PG-2 sight with 10.5-degree field of view, direct engagements are possible with the OP5-37 sight mounted just to the left of the gun. It does not have either a dozer blade for entrenching or a spade. The 2S1 does, however, have an overpressure NBC system and is well sealed for operations in dusty environments. The 2S1 is much more compact and more agile than the M109, with an exceptionally low silhouette, but it also fires a smaller projectile. According to Janes' Information Services, motorized rifle divisions are authorized 36 2S1s, the same for artillery divisions and 72 for a tank division.

RUSSIAN 152MM SP HOWITZER
The 2S19 is Russia's newest and most advanced self-propelled artillery system, similar to equivalent modern systems fielded by other nations, but with some distinctive Russian characteristics. The hull and drive train are based on the well-tested T-72 and T-80 tank designs, and the cannon uses the same 152mm (6in) round that is standard for Russian forces. That engine is a big 626kW (840hp) V-12 diesel that burns almost as

SCUD A/B
Diameter: 880mm (34.6in)
Weight (missile): 4400kg (97,000lb)
Length (missile): 10.7m (35ft 2in)

Effective range: 280km (173 miles)
Elevation: 90°
Traverse: none

Muzzle velocity: n/a
Country of origin: USSR

much oil as fuel, but that starts every time, even in the dead of winter, thanks to several ingenious innovations, one of which is a backup starting system using compressed air that actually works.

Development of the 2S19 evolved during the late 1970s and early 1980s, with the first systems delivered in 1984. The vehicle looks a bit like the French GCT, a vast, spacious turret positioned amidships, with a very long gun of 48 calibres. It is equipped with the same kinds of bells and whistles installed on US and British systems of modern design: automatic fire suppression, automatic loading systems, power feeding for ammunition from outside the vehicle, improved sights and fire-control data processing. Its shock absorbers can be locked up before firing, giving the gun a rigid, stable platform and improving the weapon's accuracy, without the use of either spades or stabilizers.

As with other modern systems, much of the ammunition handling during firing operations is automated; the gunner selects, fuses, loads and fires each round through a control panel, instead of the manual methods required with previous systems. The cannon itself is not

materially different from its predecessors, but everything behind the breech is new. Among these features is a chute at the rear of the turret that permits the ammunition handlers to supply the 2S19 with projectiles and propellant from an external supply, saving the onboard ammunition for emergencies. Unlike previous auto-loaders, the one on this cannon works at all elevations and does not need to have the gun lowered each time it is reloaded. There are 50 rounds aboard; any of the many types of 152mm (6in) ammunition can be fired, including the Krasnopol laser-guided projectile.

Seven men form the detachment for each 2S19: five on the vehicle and two ammunition handlers on the support truck. Each of the four men in the turret has his own roof-mounted hatch. This crew can, with the help of the ammo handlers, put up to eight rounds downrange in one minute. Unlike other self-propelled guns, the spent cases are ejected to the front of the turret, rather than to the rear or sides. A battery of eight 2S19s can fire a TOT mission that will deliver 3048kg (3 tons) of high explosive on a target in 60 seconds and retreat before the enemy can reply.

■ ABOVE: Russian soldiers erect an R-17 SCUD B missile. The SCUD A was accurate to within 3km (1.86 miles) at 180km (11.8 miles); the B is rated to 450m (492yd) at 300km (186 miles).

One feature common to Russian self-propelled systems that is not common elsewhere is a dozer blade attached to the front of the hull. With it, the 2S19 crew can dig its own protected emplacement in about an hour and a half, or prepare its field of fire by uprooting trees that would otherwise require the services of an engineer detachment.

A new variant of the 2S19 is currently being offered for export sales and issued to selected artillery units, the 2S19-M. This system uses computerized fire-control components that automate the process of mission execution even further and in ways similar to those used by NATO and other nations. In a bid for even more export sales, the Russians are even offering a variant with a 155mm (6.1in) cannon that will fire NATO-standard ammunition, but do not expect the United States or Britain to order many as replacements for the Paladin or AS90 systems.

RUSSIAN VASILYEK 82MM MORTAR

Leave it to the Russians to come up with an imaginative way to design an automatic weapon! This model was first produced in 1971 and used in Afghanistan. It is still issued to light infantry units, including airborne divisions, but the larger 120mm (4.72in) mortar has since replaced it with heavier organizations. It looks a lot like a small howitzer and can function like one, too. The 2B9 in its towed version has a split trail wheeled carriage quite like that on howitzers; during firing, it rests on these trails, and a firing platform is lowered from beneath the tube.

It can be either breech- or muzzle-loaded, and used with semi-fixed rounds for high-angle indirect fire or for high-velocity direct-fire engagements. When breech-loaded, its ammunition can be fed to the mortar from the right side in four-round clips, each of which can be fired in one-and-a-half seconds. Its practical rate of fire is 40–60 rounds per minute in bursts. This system does not have a great range; it can engage enemy targets directly out to just 1000m (1094yd) and from 800–5000m (875–5468yd) in indirect-fire missions.

Some 2B9s have been mounted on MT-LB personnel carriers, but the mortar is normally carried on a GAZ-66 truck equipped with a crane to facilitate unloading. This truck carries a ready supply of ammunition that includes 96 rounds in clips and fused, ready to fire, plus another 130 unprepared rounds. Hungary licensed production of the 2B9, and China's NORINCO operation recently announced production of a near duplicate of the 2B9 and offered it for export sale as the W99.

SOVIET SCUD

During the final weeks of World War II in Europe, the United States and Britain were in a race with the Soviets to capture German rocket experts and their technologies. Both sides succeeded; long-range rocket and missile systems soon became a feature of the arsenals on both sides of the Iron Curtain.

An early product of this programme on the Soviet side was the SS-1, or SCUD, missile, essentially a new and improved

■RIGHT: SCUD B missiles can carry nuclear, chemical, biological or conventional warheads, and have been supplied to a number of former Soviet allies, including Iraq.

German V-2 rocket on a mobile launcher. Like its parent, the SCUD had limited range and accuracy, but could deliver a nuclear warhead 180km (112 miles) downrange, and nuclear weapons do not require precision accuracy.

The early SCUD A entered Soviet service during the 1950s. Transported on an erector mounted on a modified JS-3 assault gun chassis, each rocket had to be set up before being fuelled and launched, a process that took 30–90 minutes. Part of this setup time involved filling the rocket's tanks with a two-part propellant,

a very hazardous job, as the crewmen had to work on a very small ladder while pumping aboard large quantities of nitric acid and kerosene.

This first version has been replaced by a long sequence of improved SCUDs with longer range, larger payload and better accuracy. The first versions were rated to hit within 4000m (4374yd) at 130km (81 miles); the latest improve that to within 50m (55yd) at 700km (435 miles). All variants are about the same size – between 10.25m (33ft 7.5in) and 11.25m (36ft 10.9in) in length and 88mm (3.5in)

artillerymen on both sides of the Iron Curtain. It was the first serious attempt in modern times to field a heavy artillery system on a wheeled, rather than tracked, chassis. A wheeled system is much cheaper to build and operate, and is faster on the road, but cannot follow tracked vehicles across some kinds of battlefield obstacles and some kinds of broken ground. Most tracked vehicles, for example, can cross a trench of one-and-a-half to two metres (five to six-and-a-half feet). Many wheeled vehicles, by contrast, are blocked by such ditches. But where a good road network exists, or where engineer support is likely to be available,

in diameter – and weigh about 6300kg (13,890lb) at launch. An inertial navigation system provides guidance only during the powered phase of flight for the earlier versions, until the motor cuts off about 80 seconds after firing. Thrust is generated when the two components of the fuel are mixed in a chamber, and the resulting propellant gases exhaust through a ring of nozzles at the base of the rocket. Four motor-driven vanes are mounted in this exhaust path and control the flight of the rocket by redirecting the gases coming from the exhaust.

Iraq used modified SCUDs during its wars with Iraq and with the coalition forces during the 1991 Gulf War. Eight of these rockets were fired at Israel on 18 January, the effect of which was much more political than tactical. SCUDs can carry chemical and biological warheads, as well as nuclear and conventional high-explosive, and there was serious concern that they would be used to deliver such unconventional munitions. After these launches, SCUD hunting became a priority for coalition air forces and special operations forces on the ground.

CZECH DANA 152MM SP GUN

When the DANA self-propelled howitzer first appeared in 1980, it must have seemed preposterous to most

a modern gun can still reach any target that might need to be engaged, and Czechoslovakia has a very good road network for it to run on.

Skoda, the old and very inventive Czech gun-maker, adapted a long-tube 152mm (6in) gun to an excellent and already standard military vehicle, the Tatra 815 truck. This was a very large vehicle, with a chassis 10.5m (34.4ft) long and 2.8m (9.2ft) wide, eight driven wheels and a 242kW (325hp) engine. Capable of 80km/h (50mph) on the road and able to cross ditches 1.4m (4.6ft) wide, this was one self-propelled system that could keep up with the tanks, on or off the road. Five men crew the DANA: commander, driver, gunner, loader and ammunition handler. Loading is fully automatic and at all angles of elevation, but each round must be prepped manually and the fuse set by hand before being fed to the power loader.

The howitzer system was nothing special when it was introduced, but the chassis received a lot of attention. Like many other Warsaw Pact wheeled vehicles such as the BRDM, the DANA was well thought out. Air pressure in the tyres could be raised or lowered from the cab: higher for better fuel economy on the highway, lower for better traction off road. These tyres had 'run-flat' inserts that prevented the vehicle from being immobilized by potential road hazards, such as small-arms bullets and sharp artillery fragments.

One problem with the DANA – and indeed all wheeled vehicles (or any self-propelled system with a high centre of gravity) – is that recoil forces can roll the vehicle when the gun is fired to the side. Another is that the suspension does not offer the stability during firing offered by tracked vehicles. Skoda dealt with these issues by requiring that the gun be fired in a limited frontal arc and by installing stabilizing struts and pads that are deployed before firing.

Although the DANA's gun system is essentially the same as installed on the 2S3 self-propelled gun, Skoda's installation is slightly different than on the tracked vehicle. Traverse is restricted to 225 degrees, and, although the turret appears to be one fighting compartment like most other self-propelled guns, it is actually two smaller cabins arranged like those on the Swedish *Bandkanon*.

On the right side of the gun is the ammunition handler's station; he prepares the projectiles by manually setting the fuses. Both of these cabins are

sealed off from the gun, preventing inhalation of the propellant fumes. This arrangement, however, requires a rubber glove to be installed on the panel on the left side of the gun permitting the breech to be opened manually for the first round. One of the virtues of such a large chassis is plenty of storage space; the DANA carries 60 rounds, twice the normal combat load carried by most self-propelled systems.

Other than the South African G-6, there have been very few imitators of the DANA, although it has been a very popular design and more than 750 have been built for domestic and export clients. Several variants have been developed, including one with a longer barrel and another with twin 30mm (1.18in) anti-aircraft cannon in a modified turret.

BRITISH ABBOT
British weapons designers have a reputation for doing things just a bit differently, often in ways that are superior to the competing systems of both friend and foe. The Abbot is one such example. This self-propelled system, the first complete British version that was

ABOVE: A cutaway drawing of the Abbot, showing the amphibious screen and a view inside the turret. It could reach 48km/h (30mph) on roads for 390km (240 miles) with one tank full.

not cobbled together from other components, was designed in the 1950s. Prototypes were presented in 1961, and it entered service in 1965. The Abbot displaced the towed 25pdr for most missions and became the stalwart standard close-support weapon for British Royal Artillery regiments.

Abbot married a chassis derived from the FV430 armoured personnel carrier with the L13A1, a superb gun and cartridge that easily outranged the NATO 105mm (4.13in) round. Good to 17,000m (18,591yd) – a distance far beyond the NATO version – it had an auto-loading system that pumped 12 rounds downrange per minute and accuracy twice that of the previous 105mm British gun. This weapon used eight charge zones; that made for large firing tables, but great flexibility. Additionally, the gun would fire the NATO round, even if only to 15,000m

(16,404yd). The tube elevated to 70 degrees and depressed to minus 5 degrees, and the traverse was 360 degrees.

The Abbot and the L118 Light Gun both used the same powerful ammunition of the separate loading type, and 40 ready rounds were secured in racks in the turret, with a mix of projectiles stowed near the breech.

Crews fought from air-conditioned comfort; the fighting compartment was protected against nuclear, biological and chemical weapons and dust by an overpressure system. The vehicle was reasonably fast, rated at just under 50kHz in top gear, thanks to a Rolls Royce 197kW (240hp) six-cylinder multi-fuel powerplant. Road range was 390km (242 miles) on 386 litres (85 gallons).

The Abbott was, undoubtedly, the best 105mm (4.13in) self-propelled howitzer around, in any army. It would still be around, too, if it were a 155mm (6.1in) system like other contemporary self-propelled howitzers such as the M198; its range and payload were determined to be about 50mm (1.97in) too small. Abbots, along with other 105mm self-propelled systems used by most other nations, were withdrawn from British service beginning in 1990, to be replaced by the AS90 155mm (6.1in) Self-propelled Howitzer.

US 8IN M55 HOWITZER

Among the most beloved weapons of US Army and Marine Corps 'redlegs' is the now-retired 203mm (8in) Howitzer in its many evolutions. Renowned for its extreme accuracy, monster 90kg (200lb) projectile and devastating effectiveness, it was a fixture in the US arsenal for several decades.

Its final gestation in US service was the M2A1 cannon installed on the same big M1 carriage used by the 155mm (6.1in) Long Tom. The barrel was relatively short – 25 calibres, or 5.1m (16.8ft) long – without a muzzle brake and conventional hydro-pneumatic recoil system. Ammunition choices for the 8in Howitzer were somewhat limited, but impressive: a high-explosive round and several anti-personnel rounds using submunition 'grenades'. Charge Seven will propel these to 16,800m (18,373yd).

A crew of 14 was needed to keep the weapon in action, and it took all of them to attain its 'burst' rate of fire of one round per minute or a sustained rate of one round every two minutes. The tube elevated from minus 2 to 65 degrees, and it traversed 30 degrees left and right.

Some 203mm (8in) Howitzers are still in service around the world with smaller nations, as towed weapons and as the

M110 203mm (8in) Self-propelled Howitzer. The 8in Howitzer served with distinction during Operation Desert Storm, but has now been superseded by MLRS and the M198.

US 280MM M65 GUN

While many artillery systems have been rated as being capable of firing nuclear projectiles, the only American one to do so was this cannon, the M65 'Atomic Annie'. The gun and carriage (excluding transporter) of this 280mm (11.02in) gun weighed more than 84,332kg (83 tons). It was capable of launching an approximately 225kg (500lb) shell as far as 29km (18 miles).

The shot happened on 25 May 1953 at the Nevada Test Site, the one and only time such a round has been fired. Code-named 'Grable', the result was a 15 kiloton explosion. This shot was fired by 1st Gun Section, Battery A, 867th Field Artillery Battalion, based at the US Army's Artillery School at Fort Sill, Oklahoma. The 1/A/867FA trained for this momentous test by driving their big gun out to the range at Frenchman Flats, where they fired conventional but nonetheless very large high-explosive rounds for several weeks.

On 25 May, they all climbed into trenches around the gun and somebody 'pulled the tail' of the piece. After the T-124 shell and the Mk 9 warhead detonated 160m (524ft) above the desert, the gunners were allowed to take a look at a towering dust cloud boiling up into the sky. It must have seemed like a good idea at the time, as the gun and its huge transporter were paraded through the streets of Washington DC for the inauguration of President Dwight Eisenhower. Atomic Annie is on display to this day at Fort Sill.

US M198 TOWED 155MM

American artillery gunners have been sending 155mm (6.1in) projectiles

■**BELOW: The 280mm (8.1in) M65 Atomic Annie certainly wins the prize for steel on target. In 1953 this gun fired the first nuclear artillery projectile during a test in the Nevada desert.**

downrange for more than 80 years, first with guns designed by the French, then with domestic designs in the 1930s. The current version, in its towed variant, is the M198 Towed Howitzer. This is really a combination gun-howitzer, and a very successful one. Both the US Marine Corps and US Army field them in large numbers. The M198 is light, can fire a very wide range of projectiles, is extremely accurate and has proven to give quite an effective performance in varying combat situations.

Development began on the M198 during the height of the war in Vietnam, during 1968, with different government arsenals designing the weapon's major components. The gun tube and breech were designed at Watervliet Arsenal, ammunition came from Picantinny and the Harry Diamond Laboratory, the fire-control system from Frankford and the recoil system and carriage from the Rock Island Arsenal. The first designs were completed in 1969, and first test shots were made the following year. Ten prototypes, designated XM198, were built and tested. A refined design went into full production in 1978.

Air mobility was then a fundamental feature of US Army doctrine, and the new weapon needed to be light enough for the CH-47 Chinook medium-lift helicopter to carry. The final design was much bigger and a bit heavier than the existing M114 howitzer, but still light enough to be carried as an external load by the Chinook and other larger helicopters. Barrel length was one of the noticeable features of the M198 – about 6m (20ft) long compared to 3.8m (12.5m) on the M114. The barrel uses a two-baffle muzzle brake.

This cannon is of standard layout and features, with split trail and wheels that can be raised to permit the gun to be operated from a stable firing platform. It will elevate to 72 degrees and depress to minus 5 degrees, while the gun's traverse is 22.5 degrees to the left and right of the centreline.

The M198 is a separate-loading weapon with eight charge zones and many projectiles. The standard high-explosive round is the M107, a projectile that weighs 42.91kg (94.6lb) and has a maximum range of 18,100m (19,794yd), about 10 miles. In addition, the 155mm

M20 75mm Recoilless Rifle

Calibre: 75mm (2.95in)
Weight: 52kg (114.5lb)
Length: 2.08m (6ft 10in)
Effective range: 6400m (7000yd)

Elevation: -2° to 50° (est)
Traverse: 360°
Muzzle velocity: 328m/s (1000ft/s)
Country of origin: USA

(6.1in) projectile is big enough for submunitions, and many varieties are available: the M449 with 60 anti-personnel grenades, the M718 carrying nine anti-tank mines, the M864 with DPICM munitions, plus illuminating, smoke and nuclear versions. There is also a rocket-assisted projectile that can range out to 30km (18.6 miles).

Many nations have purchased the M198, but most have been issued to US forces: the Army took 745 and the US Marine Corps took 566.

US RECOILLESS 75MM M20

During World War II, the recoilless 'Davis gun' principle was revived in several nations. It offered the opportunity to provide fairly heavy firepower in a fairly light package. The United States fielded 57mm (2.24in) and 75mm (2.95in) designs, followed by a 105mm (4.13in) version, the M40, during the 1950s. Britain tested a 94mm (3.7in) model and then issued 120mm (4.72in) recoilless weapons at the time of the Korean War.

Of all of these, the 75mm (2.95in) M20 has probably seen the most action. US special forces weapons sergeants still learn to use and maintain this weapon, as it can be found in the arsenals of small nations around the world. It evolved from the need for an effective infantry anti-armour weapon that could reliably kill the big German tanks that were resisting the early bazookas and 57mm (2.24in) anti-tank guns. The first 75mm version was tested in 1944, and full-scale production started in March 1945.

Two M20s were used by Task Force Smith's heroic and near suicidal rearguard action on 5 July 1950, the very beginning of US involvement in the Korean War. Both M20s engaged North Korean T-34s at short range, but the HEAT rounds failed to penetrate the enemy tanks.

The M20 can deliver about the same terminal effect on a target as the legendary German 88mm (3.46in) from World War II, but from a package that is only about 2.1m (7ft) long and that weighs just 52kg (115lb). It can engage targets to about 6400m (7000yd) with an approximately 10kg (22lb) projectile. Its anti-armour HEAT round was effective against tanks of the previous generation, particularly those encountered in Korea fighting for the Communist forces.

Finally, the infantry had a portable support weapon of its own, something that could be carried by a squad up a mountain and used to take out bunkers, fortified positions and especially tanks, without begging for help from some artillery battery which was perhaps miles and miles away. One thing these infantrymen learnt instantly, however, was to cover their ears and to stay off to the side when it was time to cut loose: the bangs from these recoilless rifles are extremely loud.

■**RIGHT: The new breed of lightweight towed guns developed during the Cold War: the M198 can be lifted by helicopter, has extreme range and fires various projectiles with accuracy.**

US SP 106MM RECOILLESS RIFLE

There are very few tube artillery systems with as much bang for the money as this one, officially named Ontos M50 Multiple Self-propelled Rifle, that joined the US Army in 1955. This small tracked vehicle carried just three crewmen, but was capable of mounting six 105mm (4.13in) recoilless rifles, any one of which would have been enough for most combat vehicles of the time.

This was an unusual gun system in several ways. For one, it had a 105mm (4.13in) bore, but it was intentionally identified as a 106mm (4.17in) system; this decision was taken to try to avoid the possibility that ammunition for an earlier, incompatible gun of the same calibre might be fired. Another unusual feature was that it had almost no protection for the crew, very much unlike its contemporaries.

Two variants were used, the M50 and M50A1. Both very similar, having a combat weight of 8641kg (19,050lb), a small hull manufactured from welded 12.9mm (0.5in) steel, and being fitted with a small, six-cylinder, 92.4kW (124hp) petrol engine. this powerplant could move the little M50 Ontos along at a good top speed of 48km/h (30mph).

On top of the hull was a small turret, inside of which was the station for the gunner/commander. Mounted on this turret were six powerful M40A1C recoilless rifles, three to a side. Four of these rifles included .50 calibre spotting rifles, M8C, which were electrically fired and which were each loaded with 20 tracer rounds. When fired, the spotting rounds clearly showed the point of impact for the 105mm (4.13in) recoilless rifles. The turret used manual drive for both elevation and traverse, from minus 10

degrees to 20 degrees vertically and 40 degrees to the left or right.

In addition to the main armament and spotting rifles, the M50 mounted a M1919A4 .30 calibre machine gun for close-in defence. Eighteen rounds for the recoilless rifles could be carried: 6 of these would be in the weapons, and another 12 rounds would be carried in bins inside the hull. Reloading required the loader to dismount, which could certainly be a hazardous activity for those engaged in close combat.

Originally intended as a cheap – but somewhat suicidal – anti-armour gun platform that would help repulse the Soviet 'Red Horde' as their T-55s poured westwards into Germany at the beginning of World War III, the Ontos, teamed up with M48 tanks, made a major contribution to the US war effort in Vietnam during January 1968.

CHAPTER SIX
SEARCH AND DESTROY

Modern artillery systems are state-of-the-art killing machines, designed to 'shoot-and-scoot': in other words, to deliver a lethal volley of fire and move quickly before the enemy can react with any counterbattery fire.

Artillery systems and their tactics of employment on the battlefield have been through a radical series of changes during the past few years, and especially since the demise of the former Warsaw Pact and the Cold War. Nations all over the globe have been re-evaluating the threats that face them and the proper way to counter those threats. Artillery remains an important tool for all military forces, but the kinds of guns, the projectiles they shoot, the way they move on the battlefield and the way in which they execute their missions are all new and different.

Generally, the armed forces of most nations have shrunk to a shadow of their former selves. This is particularly true of the United States, British and Russian armies, all of which have had their budgets and formations severely pruned. At the same time, these forces retain their global missions and are expected to accomplish them without excuses. These nations, and others, have responded by applying information and manufacturing technologies developed during the 1980s and 1990s – computers, digital data transmission, composite materials and laser technologies – to permit fewer people and fewer guns to accomplish the same mission assigned in the past.

The result has been smaller units of almost all kinds, manned by professional specialists and equipped with much more sophisticated weapons and support systems. Within US Army forces, for example, the trend has been to lighter,

■**LEFT: A Multiple Launch Rocket System sends its round downrange. The MLRS is a free-flight rocket, but offers rapid-response and accurate area fires of 45km (28 miles) ranges.**

more mobile and rapidly deployable brigades and divisions, armed with air-mobile guns and supporting vehicles. Members of these units are linked to each other and to their chain of command with entirely new communications systems that are revolutionizing the way artillery and other ground combat units fight.

Guns today have to be light enough to be carried as external loads by helicopters; anything heavier will be left behind. This process began in the 1960s with the US Army's interest in air mobility and the development of the M198, but the process has continued with even lighter weapons, such as the United Kingdom's 155mm (6.1in) Ultralight-weight Field Howitzer and L118 Light Gun, in service with the US Army.

The really revolutionary things happening in artillery today, however, involve the application of space-age technologies in communications between units and even between gunner and projectiles. Combat units can be smaller and lighter than they were before simply because they are, as units and as weapon systems, much more lethal and much faster to react than before.

The US Army is currently connecting its units to each other with secure digital communications systems that let every unit, right down to the infantry squad and individual gun detachment, know exactly where they are on the ground, exactly where friendly and hostile units are and exactly what they are supposed to accomplish, in real time, all the time. Using global positioning system (GPS) transceivers, tiny but rugged computers and secure digital radios, individual gun teams can operate out of sight of other members of their battery and still fire coordinated missions ordered by the FDC.

Additionally, when modern artillery systems fire, each round is much more likely than in the past to be effective. In the past, destruction of, say, an enemy tank by indirect, observed fire could take hundreds of rounds. Bunker complexes, convoys, troops in the open, artillery batteries – all took many rounds and a lot of time to destroy.

Today, an artillery battery commander has at his disposal 'smart' munitions that have an extremely high probability of kill on the first shot when fired at point targets, laser-guided projectiles, and they can easily destroy the heaviest main battle tank. This commander, too, has other projectiles that are capable of scattering small submunitions across a wide area, and either suppressing or destroying area targets.

Modern guns used by most developed nations use GPS and computers to identify exactly where each gun is, and then use that data with specialized ballistic computers to design a fire mission. This speeds up the process of engagement tremendously, as the gun crew does not need to do a survey as previously. With towed systems, the gun rolls up into position, the gun data is transmitted to a terminal at the gun and the crew elevates and traverses as required, loads and fires on command, with good expectation of a first-round hit.

With modern self-propelled guns, the process is automated even further. Once the vehicle stops and the data are entered, the weapon is aimed and loaded automatically and in the most developed weapons systems, can even be fired by remote command as well.

MODERN MORTARS

Smoothbore muzzle-loading artillery is still around 100 years after most armies replaced it with breech-loaders. Mortars are light, effective, close-in, organic firepower for light infantry companies that are under the command of the company commander and that deliver indirect fires to places other weapons simply cannot reach.

Mortars, too, can light up the night with illumination rounds, provide smoke for screening and white phosphorus incendiary rounds that will literally burn an enemy unit out of its holes. They come in many sizes, but just one basic shape – a short tube with a base-plate on one end and, with the man-portable sizes, a bi-pod attached to the other. When organic to manoeuvre units, mortars provide

■ LEFT: The US M224 60mm (2.36in) Mortar has all the virtues of a light mortar: light weight, organic to the infantry company, plus the ability to trigger-fire its rounds at low trajectory.

■ BELOW: 81mm (3.1in) and 82mm (3.2in) mortars have given trusty indirect fire support for more than 50 years. This 81mm M-29A1 is owned by the US Army's 6th Infantry Division.

Brandt 120mm Mortar

Calibre: 120mm (4.72in)
Weight: 682kg (1530lb)
Barrel length: 2.06m (6ft 9in)
Effective range: 8135m (8900yd)
Elevation: 30° to 85°
Traverse: 14°
Muzzle velocity: n/a
Country of origin: France

weapons. Mortar fire, when part of an assault plan, will keep an enemy's head down while the rifle and machine-gun fire teams manoeuvre their way towards their objective.

US M224 60mm Light Mortar

This is certainly the smallest crew-served artillery in the US inventory, but the M224 has been a popular one. It is light, at 21kg (46.5lb) with base-plate and sight, and goes with most infantry units on operations. It will reach out to 3400m (3718yd) and will also drop rounds on enemies just outside the perimeter, only 70m (77yd) away. Like other man-pack mortars, the M224 is normally drop-fired, but it may also be hand-held and trigger-fired at targets which are at distances of up to 1300m (1422yd).

When necessary, and the ammunition supply permits, this little weapon can put out an amazing number of rounds: 30 per minute for the first four minutes, then 20 per minute for as long as there are rounds and targets left. The small size,

immediate and flexible indirect fires that destroy or disrupt enemy forces. Even the smallest of these will easily be able to outrange the direct-fire weapons of an infantry company.

Today, the smallest mortars will cause an enemy armoured unit to button up, and a direct hit on the vulnerable top armour of even main battle tanks can be defeated by these light, close-support

■**BELOW: The new breed of expensive precision munitions: this US Copperhead projectile fired from a 155mm (6.1in) M198 homes in on the laser reflected off the target's turret.**

high rate of fire and light weight make up for a small warhead. The 60mm (2.36in) mortar section can move with the rifle platoons and is able to provide supporting fires for its infantry faster than any other source.

The basic component is the M225 cannon, a 1m (40in) smoothbore tube with a finned cap at the base and a combination carrying handle-trigger assembly. The fins help cool the weapon during rapid fire. Inside the base is a firing pin and trigger system that allows the gunner to either drop-fire or trigger-fire the rounds. In common with all other infantry mortars, the M224 has an adjustable bi-pod that permits elevation and traverse of the tube and an optical sight, M24, that mounts to a dovetail bracket on the weapon.

Airborne, ranger, light infantry and mountain divisions are issued the M224 – which has now replaced the older 81mm (3.19in) and 60mm (2.36in) mortars for these units – at the rate of two mortar systems per company. Five soldiers comprise the normal 60mm mortar team: a gunner and his assistant, plus three ammunition bearers.

US M29A1/M252 Medium Mortars

Organic medium-range indirect fires for infantry battalions are delivered by the mortar platoons of the headquarters or weapons company, typically by the M29 or M252 Medium Extended Range Mortar. This weapon is a variant on a 1970s-era British design and breaks into the standard subassemblies: tube, base-plate and tripod.

This weapon is man-portable, but just barely; the tube weighs 15.8kg (35lb), the base-plate 11.5kg (25.4lb) and the bipod 12kg (26.5lb): about 40kg (88lb) total. When added to all the other gear a combat infantry soldier has to carry, these weights mean that the 81mm (3.18in) mortar will be usually getting a ride in some sort of vehicle – helicopter, HMWWV, truck or APC – rather than on a soldier's back, to somewhere which is close to its firing position.

The fireball from the rounds used with this weapon – particularly with all the propellant increments – can be substantial, so the M258 uses a flash

■**RIGHT: A SADARM (Seek And Destroy Armour), which senses an armoured vehicle's signature, flies to a position overhead, and then fires a slug of metal at extreme velocity through its roof.**

surpressor to reduce the weapon's firing signature. It will elevate from 45 to 85 degrees and will put rounds 5700m (6234yd) downrange with full charge. The mortar team can put out 33 rounds per minute for short-duration emergencies and 16 rounds per minute for sustained fire. Like the 60mm (2.36in) mortar, the M258 uses the basic M64 sight.

US M120 120mm Heavy Mortar

For serious infantry organic indirect artillery, motorized infantry units are authorized the M120 120mm (4.72in) Heavy Mortar, a weapon that is heavy in every way. The whole package weighs 144kg (317lb), and it is normally operated from a specialized vehicle, which is frequently either a M113 adapted for this mission or from the ground after transport in a specialized trailer towed by a HMWWV. The tube alone weighs an enormous 49.5kg (109lb), the ground-mount bi-pod another 70kg (154lb), and the base-plate 61kg (134lb).

A five-man squad crews the weapon: a squad leader, two gunners and two ammunition bearers. The gunners are stationed beside the cannon, one aiming the weapon and the other loading rounds. Just behind the base-plate and on the left, the mortar squad leader supervises the team, and the two ammunition bearers are positioned at the right rear of the base-plate.

The 120mm (4.72in) projectiles are quite powerful as well as lethal, with the anti-personnel versions reaching out to 7200m (7874yd) and having an effective bursting radius of 75m (82yd). The weapon can fire bursts of 16 rounds in 1 minute and, during sustained fire, fire bursts of 4 rounds per 1 minute.

ARTILLERY PROJECTILES

Although the basic cannon used in modern self-propelled cannons is not much different than that of many years ago, the kinds of projectiles these guns fire have evolved tremendously.

■LEFT: The M39 Army Tactical Missile System (ATACMS), a complex, costly weapon used for high-threat, high-payoff targets up to 300km (186 miles) from the launcher.

■RIGHT: A technician with a Brilliant Anti-Armour Submunition (BAT) prototype. Without laser designators or forward observers, BATs seek out, attack and destroy armour targets.

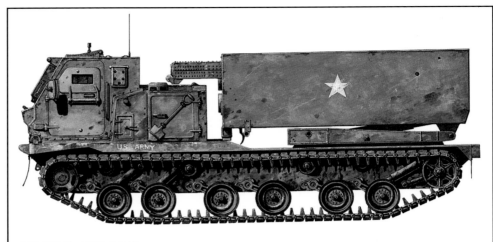

M270 MLRS

Calibre: 227mm (8.94in)
Weight: 25,191kg (55,420lb)
Rocket length: 3.94m (12.93ft)
Rocket weight: 308kg (679lb)
Effective range: 32.5km (21.1 miles) (M26 warhead)

Elevation: n/a
Traverse: n/a
Country of origin: USA

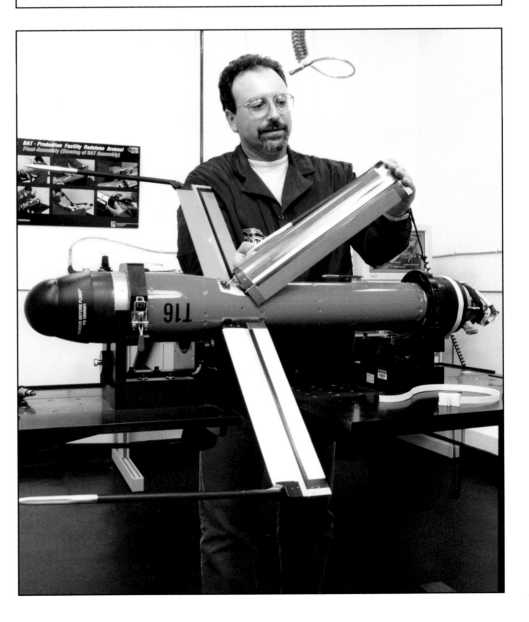

During World War II, the introduction of proximity fuses that detonated a shell at a predetermined distance from an object was considered a revolutionary accomplishment. Today, individual projectiles can seek out and home in on a target, adjusting their trajectory to intercept a moving tank, for example, with or without human interaction during the terminal phase of the projectile's flight.

Projectiles such as the US Copperhead and Russian *Krasnopol* and *Smel'chak* are laser-homing munitions. A forward observer (FO) using a laser designator 'paints' a target with a spot of invisible light that emits a specific coded frequency. An artillery crew fires sets the code into the projectile and fires it to the

■ABOVE: The ATACMS missile, an example of the new digital battlefield's capability to engage area and point targets at ranges considered impossible not long ago.

approximate location of the target. During the final phase of flight, the seeker in the projectile scans for reflected energy with the programmed code, and, using short wings or vanes that pop out after firing, adjusts its trajectory to strike directly on the laser spot.

These projectiles are extremely expensive and complicated, costing somewhere in the range of US$500,000 each for a Copperhead, and yet they are considered to be a very good investment for many situations on the modern

battlefield. As they have a very good probability of success – about 90 per cent – one round can achieve target destruction instead of hundreds, and the fire mission is completed quickly instead of over hours or even days.

Not all such munitions even need a laser designator. SADARM (sense and destroy armour) submunition projectiles are being developed that can be fired over an armoured formation and are dispensed several hundred metres in the air. As they fall, each submunition is stabilized and orientated towards the ground, then seeks the signature of the target vehicles. At a pre-programmed height, the device fires a metallic slug down on the thin top armour, penetrating it and destroying the vehicle.

Current SADARM warheads for 155mm (6.1in) cannon have been tested successfully, but are extremely expensive and not capable of defeating tanks. They are, however, effective against self-propelled howitzers as well as against similar vehicles.

Another set of wonder weapons is called DPICM, which stands for dual-purpose improved conventional munitions. These are also submunitions that scatter over a target area, but without guidance systems. There are many types available, some with anti-armour mines, others with top-attack shaped charges. They are called 'dual-purpose' because they are both anti-armour and anti-personnel devices. If one lands on top of a vehicle, it will blast a hole in its thin overhead armour; if it lands on the ground near exposed personnel, the steel shell of the device will produce casualties within a range of about 15m (49ft).

Then there is a large selection of FASCAM (family of scatterable mines) 155mm (6.1in) projectiles. Use of FASCAM projectiles allows a commander to slow or channel an enemy armour force by delivering large numbers of these potent explosive devices across a wide area. FASCAM submunitions create a small projectile of molten metal and blast it into the underside of any vehicle that triggers it, punching a hole in the armour and almost certainly causing the vehicle's complete destruction.

This 'bottom up' attack is particularly effective against combat vehicles that store their ammunition low in the hull, such as the Russian tanks and self-propelled guns; they are especially vulnerable to such weapons. The submunitions are easy to see in daylight and can be carefully cleared by combat engineers, but the process is slow and destroys an attacker's tempo of operations. Most submuntions automatically self-destruct after a fairly short period, from a few hours to as much as two weeks.

US M270 AVMRL MLRS

Back in 1976, Redstone Arsenal's Missile Command group began a development process that would result in one of the most successful modern weapons, the multiple-launch rocket system (MLRS). Fourteen nations field the MLRS at the time of writing, including Germany, Israel, Italy, Greece, Norway and Turkey, as well as Korea.

This success is based on several subsystems that were developed independently and then combined to make this excellent weapon. Lockheed Martin manufactures a version in the United States, while in Europe a consortium of companies work together to supply various NATO and other allied countries, including the United Kingdom, Germany, Italy and France.

MLRS delivers indirect fire with unguided rockets out to long range, operated by a crew of only three men: a driver, gunner and commander. The foundation for the MLRS is a hull and drive train from a Bradley Armoured Fighting Vehicle, an excellent and well-proven chassis that provides a speed, agility and dependability which is able to keep up with the main battle tanks and all their escorting armour during a modern land battle.

On the hull is mounted the launcher assembly that orients the rockets towards their targets, the associated electronics and a crane for loading and unloading. The basic MLRS weapon is a 227mm (8.94in) free flight, unguided rocket designated M26. This large rocket is packed in a container of six, fully sealed, with a shelf life of 10 years without maintenance. When launched, it will fly out to 45km (28 miles).

Twelve rockets are mounted on the launcher assembly M270 of each MLRS and are pre-programmed by the crew before launch. Within the warhead of each M26 warhead are 644 small submunitions, each given the designation

M77 Dual-Purpose Improved Conventional Munition (DPICM).

Using GPS and data from the battery fire direction centre, the crew programme the missile for launch and delivery. In fact, all the firing data can be pre-programmed before the MLRS arrives in its assigned firing position. This allows the mission to be executed immediately so that the vehicle can be far away by the time the rounds begin to impact the target, a modern version of the classic 'hip-shoot' fire mission.

During a typical MLRS fire mission, the crew will get their order by secure SINGARS frequency-hopping radio, enter the data, make sure the vehicle is securely buttoned up with the crew inside and press a switch to execute. The mission can include just 1 rocket or a salvo of all 12 in the launcher, and each one of them tears out of the launcher with a deafening roar.

■BELOW: Upholding the Russian tradition of employing rockets for long-range bombardment is the *Smerch*. Its 300mm (11.8in) rockets can engage targets at 10–70km (6.2–43.4 miles).

The individual M26 rocket weighs 306kg (675lb), is just under 4m (13.1ft) long and has an external diameter of 227mm (8.94in). It is fired from its shipping container, supported by sabots and spin lugs. At launch, tracks inside the launch tube rotate the rocket. As it emerges from the tube, small explosives deploy spring-loaded fins canted at 1.25 degrees; after a short delay, these fins pop into place and maintain rotation during flight, stabilizing it and ensuring that the rocket maintains excellent accuracy.

The rocket uses a simple solid-fuel motor that accounts for about half its length. The rest of the standard M26 rocket is stuffed with DPICM, right up to the nose where a remotely settable time fuse is placed. Just behind the nose of the missile is a connector for the wiring harness; at launch, the umbilical disconnects as the rocket itself is propelled out of the tube.

As the rocket approaches its pre-programmed target, the fuse fires a very small charge that pops the canister holding the warheads open. In flight, each of these 644 munitions is held securely in styrofoam blocks; however, when the warhead opens, all of this shreds, and the munitions begin to scatter several hundred metres over the intended target area.

Each DPICM has a drag ribbon, a small loop of material that serves as a drogue parachute, slowing the submunitions and pointing it downwards. From the ground, an observer might see the rocket streaking silently down at the end of its trajectory, its flight motor spent. There is a rather quiet popping sound as the DPICM pod breaks open, then a cloud of small objects and shredded styrofoam begins falling from the sky. Within a few seconds, the first hit the ground and detonate.

Each M77 submunition is small, only 38mm (1.5in) across and 81mm (3.2in) high, a steel cylinder filled with a shaped-charge explosive and topped with a tiny M223 fuse. When this little device lands on a vehicle, the fuse fires and the shaped charge blasts a small, intense jet that burns through up to 102mm (4in) of armour. At the same time, the steel shell fragments, scattering material at high velocity in all directions. This secondary effect will kill or wound personnel within about 15m (49ft). Individually, these M77s are not especially impressive weapons. When 644 of them drop in on an area 200m (220yd) by 100m (110yd), however, those circles of destruction overlap and there is no escape. When all 12 saturate an area, a tremendous amount of damage can be created.

Brilliant Anti-Armour Submunition
Besides the standard unguided warhead, MLRS fires some specialized precision weapons. One of these is called the BAT, the Brilliant Anti-Armour Submunition, 13 of which are delivered by the Army Tactical Missile System (ATACMS) Block II missile fired from the MLRS launcher. Each strange-looking BAT has its own sensors and flight controls to identify then attack enemy armour from

overhead. Two variants are currently being developed: one using the heat signature of the target, the other its sound signature; an infrared sensor provides terminal guidance data.

This programme is currently developing even more sophisticated and complex weapons that can track, engage and destroy all kinds of enemy combat vehicles. The ATACMS Block II has tremendous range: out to 140km (87 miles). Once perfected and fielded, this system will give a ground force commander a very deep and powerful punch against enemy armour, self-propelled artillery, mobile missile systems and vehicles of all kinds.

ATACMS

Two basic rockets are used with MLRS launchers, the M26 and the Army Tactical Missile System (ATACMS), the latter being much larger and with substantially greater range and payload. Good to more than 165km (102 miles), ATACMS in its Block I configuration delivers 950 M74 submunitions to the target. A newer version, Block II, has on-board GPS navigation and a range of

more than 300km (186 miles), although carrying a smaller payload.

Although three men are assigned to the MLRS, two or even one can perform all its mission, including re-loading and firing. It has been a tremendously successful system, in and out of combat. During Operation Desert Storm, the MLRS executed many fire missions and was devastating to Iraqi infantry, artillery and armour units. The Iraqis who survived its submunitions had an expression for these MLRS attacks: they called them 'steel rain'.

Russian BM 9A52 300mm *Smerch*

Given the long and successful tradition of Russian rocketry, it should be no surprise that a large part of its current systems are based on this technology. The most advanced – and a competitor of the US M270 MLRS – is the Russian *Smerch*, or 'Sandstorm', system. Developed in the late 1970s and first fielded in 1987, the 9A52 *Smerch* is an extremely capable system that uses guided 300mm (11.81in) rockets with ranges which are far in excess of the standard 220mm (8.7in) free-flight rockets fired by the M270.

The system is based on a large 43,690kg (43 ton) wheeled combat all-terrain vehicle, which is designated the MAZ-543M. On this foundation is a 12-tube launcher system which is controlled from the vehicle's cab. Power to the vehicle is supplied V-12 diesel engine, generating 386kW (518hp). Maximum road speed is 60km/h (37mph), and road range is a very impressive top distance of 850km (528 miles).

The launcher elevates from an angle of 0 to 55 degrees, and is able to traverse 30 degrees from the centreline. Before firing, two stabilizing jacks are lowered from between the third and fourth road wheels. Each vehicle is capable of rolling into a firing position and then sending the first rocket downrange in only three minutes. Each vehicle takes only three minutes to move out of the position before the enemy has retaliated.

Four men crew each system, but many more help execute each battery's fire missions. Part of the battery includes a fire-direction centre with secure communications and a data link to the Vivarly fire-control system which is used with the rockets.

Accuracy for the 9M55K rockets is phenomenal, if true. According to its manufacturers, deviation at 7km (4.3 miles) is just 150m (164yd). When one vehicle salvos all 12 rockets with one of the several submunition projectiles, an area of about 672,000sq m (736,200sq yd) will be saturated with bomblets, an area larger than approximately half a square kilometre.

In Russian service, there are 23 Smerch systems authorized for each battalion, and four battalions form a brigade, a tremendous amount of potential long-range area firepower.

Primary missions for the Smerch are deep-area suppression targets: enemy artillery batteries, tactical operations centres, refuelling and rearming points, established or hasty airfields and aviation-support facilities, troop concentrations and combat vehicles of all kinds, especially in convoys or in tactical formations. In addition, the system can conduct 'area denial' missions by distributing anti-tank and anti-personnel mines over wide areas.

Three warheads were in common recent issue. The 9M55K dispenses 72 submunitions, each built around a 1.8kg (4lb) charge and a fragmentation case designed to be effective against personnel and thin-skinned vehicles. Another warhead uses a 92.5kg (204lb) high-explosive charge to defeat light armour, soldiers and field fortifications. Yet another, the 9M55K1, includes five

BM-21 *Grad* (Hail) Multiple Rocket Launcher

Calibre: 122mm (4.8in)
Rocket weight: 77.5kg (170.85lb)
Rocket length: 3.2m (10.5ft):

Effective range: 20.4km (12.7 miles)
Elevation: 0° to 55°

Traverse: 172°
Maximum velocity: 690m/s (2264ft/s)
Country of origin: Russia

MOTIV-3M 'smart' anti-armour submunitions that seek and destroy tanks and similar vehicles by sensing their infrared signature and homing on the target for a top attack. The anti-personnel and anti-tank versions have a self-destruct feature that detonates the submunition two minutes after impact if the normal fuse fails to function.

Early versions of the rocket used with this system had a minimum engagement range of 20km (12.4 miles) and a maximum of 70km (43.5 miles). Current versions will reach out to 94km (58.4 miles), and a projected model is planned to possess a maximum range of no less than 124km (77 miles).

Kuwait purchased 27 SA52s in 1995, and the United Arab Emirates, Algeria and India all have some as well.

Russian BM 9P140 *Uragen* MRS

A simpler, more economical and shorter-range rocket system than the Smerch, called the BM9P140 *Uragen*, or 'Hurricane', entered Soviet service in 1977. The *Uragen* is another option for a commander who needs an area weapon for suppressing deep enemy targets such as troop and vehicle concentrations, command and control facilities, convoys and fortified positions.

In Russian service, these rocket systems are assigned to military districts in rocket regiments or brigades. Each *Uragen* brigade is authorized four battalions, each of which fields 12 launchers and 12 'transloader' re-supply vehicles during peacetime and 18 launchers and transloaders during combat operations. The *Uragen* was, until the Smerch took over the role, the Russian 'front' or artillery regiment commander's long-range punch. Each salvo from each launcher was the equivalent of a whole battery of heavy tube artillery firing a time-on-target (TOT) mission – more so, actually, because of the huge warhead fitted on each of the rockets.

Sixteen 220mm (8.66in) rockets are carried in each vehicle's launcher and can be fired individually or at about one-second intervals in a massive barrage. They have a maximum published range of 40km (24.85 miles) and are both spin- and fin-stabilized. When first introduced, this performance was substantially better than the then-current 122mm (4.8in) BM-21 Warsaw Pact rocket artillery performance, relegating this latter system to use at division level.

Valkyr Rocket Launcher

Calibre: 127mm (5in)
Rocket weight: 53.5kg (118lb)
Rocket length: 2.68m (8.79ft)
Effective range: 22,700m (14.1 miles)

Elevation: n/a
Traverse: n/a
Maximum velocity: 250m/s (820ft/s)
Country of origin: South Africa

Bandkanon

Calibre: 155mm (6.1in)
Weight: 53,000kg (11,6600lb)
Length: 11m (36ft 1in)
Effective range: 26km (16 miles)
Elevation: -3° to 40°

Traverse: 30°
Muzzle velocity: n/a
Country of origin: Sweden

The launcher part of the system traverses left and right 30 degrees and elevates to 50 degrees, operated by electric motors rather than hydraulics. The rockets, each about 5m (16ft) long, are rotated by rails as they leave the tubes, imparting their initial spin. Each has an electrical fuse system that will detonate the 90–100kg (198–220lb) warhead over the target. Warhead options include a simple, large, high-explosive version plus chemical, fuel-air explosives (FAE) and several versions that dispense anti-personnel and anti-tank submunitions. The anti-personnel round delivers 312 tiny mines, each designed to incapacitate a soldier. The anti-tank warhead can scatter 24 large mines, each of which can destroy a main battle tank. A single vehicle delivering a full 16-rocket salvo has an effective reported footprint of a little less than 0.5sq km, an area equivalent to 100m (330ft) by 426m (1398ft). Minimum range is 10km (6.2 miles), while maximum reported range is 50km (31 miles). Re-loading takes 15 minutes and is assisted by a hydraulic crane on the transloader vehicle.

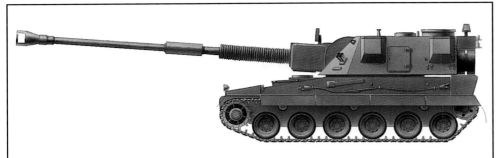

AS90 Self-Propelled Howitzer

Calibre: 155mm (6.1in)
Weight: 45,000kg (99,208lb)
Length: 7.2m (23ft 8in)
Barrel length: 52 calibres
Effective range: 40km (24.8

miles)
Elevation: -5° to 70°
Traverse: 360°
Country of origin: Great Britain

Underneath the 16-tube launcher is a very interesting vehicle, the ZIL-135LM, an 8 x 8 wheeled truck with two engines – one for driving the wheels on the right-hand side, the other the ones on the left! Despite the novel power train, this vehicle is supposed to have excellent off-road performance and will do 65km/h (40mph) on the highway. Four men serve

■LEFT: An example of the trend toward more complex and capable artillery systems is the AS90 from BAE Systems. Its automated systems permit extremely rapid and accurate fire.

on the crew, and they can emplace the vehicle and get a shot off in just three minutes, then be gone three minutes later, when the counterbattery fires start falling. The whole vehicle is unarmoured and has no NBC protection, only a simple R-123M radio, and no fire-control computer or GPS navigation system.

However, it does have a PG-1M panoramic sight and K-1 collimator, but not much more. It is a typical Russian system: plain, solid, almost 'soldier-proof', designed for austere combat conditions and without any frills, reliable and effective at its intended missions.

Russian BM-21 122mm MLRS
Although this multiple-launch rocket system, the *Grad*, or Hail, has been around for 40 years, it has been successful in both combat – against China in 1969 and in Afghanistan in the 1980s – and export marketing. The BM-21 has been issued to artillery units of 50 nations, most either members of the former Soviet Union or their clients: Cuba, Hungary, China, Pakistan, India and many others. Despite its age and simplicity, the BM-21 was still in production with as many as 12 nations in the late 1990s.

Part of that durability may have to do with the system's tremendous effectiveness. In Afghanistan, the Soviets used it on Mujahedeen positions that were resistant to tube artillery. First, an air strike would be sent in to keep the heads of the enemy soldiers down while the BM-21s dashed up into their firing positions; without any armour, and with all that solid rocket fuel in the launch tubes, they were juicy targets, and they were easily defeated.

As soon as the helicopter gunships or Su-25 CAS fighters pulled out of their runs, the BM-21s salvoed their 40 rockets, then quickly turned around and made a dash for safety. Each BM-21 salvo can pulverize 190,000sq m (227,238sq yd) with 122mm (4.8in) high-explosive or

155/45 NORINCO SP Gun

Calibre: 155mm (6.1in)
Weight: 32,000kg (70,548lb)
Length: 6.1m (20ft)

Barrel length: 45 calibres
Elevation: -5° to 70° (est)
Traverse: 360°

Muzzle velocity: n/a
Country of origin: China

ICM, leaving anybody still alive on the ground either stunned or wounded. The Soviets had their problems in Afghanistan, but they learned to solve some of them with the BM-21.

A standard Ural 375D truck provides the foundation for the system. This six-wheeled truck is used for all sorts of applications in the Russian Army and is simple, strong and reliable. It is powered by a six-cylinder, 134kW (180hp) diesel engine and has very good performance both on and off the road. Maximum speed is 80km/h (50mph) and the truck's range is 1000km (621 miles).

Six men crew the BM-21, and they can have it ready to fire in three minutes. The launcher elevates to 55 degrees and

traverses 120 degrees to the left and 60 degrees to the right. All 40 rockets can be fired in one 20-second salvo, and the launcher restowed and the vehicle back on the road in about half a minute. Re-loading the launcher takes no longer than eight minutes.

Maximum range for the standard-issue rockets is 20km (12.4 miles), with a minimum engagement range of 5km (3 miles). The original warhead was a large high-explosive version, but the system has been so popular that a family of others has been developed for it and the entire system upgraded. A white phosphorus incendiary warhead was issued in 1971, followed by smoke, chemical and anti-personnel

submunitions. In 1998, an improved rocket motor was demonstrated with double the range of the earlier type, now ranging to 40km (24.9 miles). At the same time, a whole new range of 122mm (4.8in) warheads were unveiled, including anti-personnel mines, anti-tank mines, improved high-explosive, improved smoke and a range of electronic warfare (EW) devices. These latter munitions are small jamming transmitters that work for about an hour.

SELF-PROPELLED SYSTEMS
Back in the 1950s, when NATO and the Warsaw Pact nations were fielding simple howitzers bolted to simple tracked combat vehicles or depending on towed

Mk F3 155mm Self-Propelled Gun

Calibre: 155mm (6.1in)
Weight: 17,410kg (38,040lb)
Length: 6.22m (20ft 5in)
Effective range: 20,000m (21,875yd)

Elevation: 0° to 67°
Traverse: 46° or 50° depending on elevation
Muzzle velocity: n/a
Country of origin: France

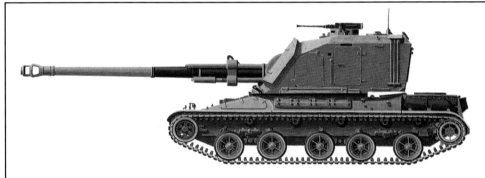

GCT 155mm SP Gun

Calibre: 155mm (6.1in)
Weight: 42,000kg (92,595lb)
Length: 10.25m (33ft 7in)
Effective range: 23,300m (25,480yd)

Elevation: -4° to 66°
Traverse: 360°
Muzzle velocity: n/a
Country of origin: France

■ **ABOVE: A French detachment of the Mk F3 155mm (6.1in) gun. Designed around the French AMX-13 tank drive train and hull, the F3 saw service with France from the 1960s till the 1980s.**

guns entirely, the Swedes were designing something unique. That system, the Bofors Bandkanon 1A, evolved during the late 1950s, appeared in 1960 and is still very much in service. Its designers tossed out almost all the rules and conventional wisdom. Bofors designed many excellent automatic anti-aircraft guns of large calibre during World War II, so it was natural that they would produce the first fully automatic self-propelled artillery system, with a turret and loading

mechanism which had been inspired by the 'pom-pom' guns of that era.

While other systems of the time were depending on manpower to fuse and load projectiles in the breech, the Bofors 155mm (6.1in) gun is loaded from a 14-round magazine attached to a loading mechanism installed over the breech. This device allows the gunner to select, load, arm fuses and fire one or all the fixed rounds individually or, as Ian Hogg observes, in a burst from the world's largest machine gun. Elevation is done by electrical drive, but traverse is manual. Both elevation and traverse are quite limited by modern standards: minus 3 to 40 degrees vertically and 15 degrees left or right of centre.

Such ammunition handling requires fixed ammunition, though, and that limits the Bandkanon's flexibility. It is also a very slow self-propelled vehicle, with a top speed of just 28km/h (17mph) on the road, and a 9km/h (5.6mph) crawl across open ground.

The crew is entirely isolated from the cannon in two separate mini-turrets, one on each side of the breech. On the left side are stations for the commander, gunner and radio operator. On the right are seats for the ammunition handler and an anti-aircraft machine-gunner. The driver sits near the centreline of the hull, forward of the gun, with the engine and transmission mounted transversely at the front of the vehicle.

That power pack is another usual one: a 179kW (240hp) Rolls-Royce diesel and a 224kW (300hp) Boeing gas turbine, both geared to a common transmission. The gas turbine is used for off-road operations and the diesel for normal road marches.

Twenty-six Bandkanons have been issued to Swedish forces, and they have recently been upgraded with new engines and transmissions, better navigation equipment and modern gun-laying components. It remains, 40 years after its introduction, the fastest gun in the world, on the slowest chassis.

British 155 SP AS90

The AS90 is Britain's answer to the M109, based on Vickers 155mm (6.10in), 39 calibre cannon. It is a recent design, as military systems go, having been designed in the 1980s and issued to field units in 1992. British Army units have 179 of these advanced self-propelled howitzers, and export models are also being used by such formerly unlikely nations as Poland.

The basic cannon fires NATO-standard ammunition with a maximum range of 24,700m (27,012yd) with normal projectiles and about a further 6km (6562yd) with rocket-assisted projectiles. Advanced navigation and communications systems permit the AS90 crew to execute fire missions without conventional gun-laying procedures; a dynamic reference unit (DRU) and automatic gun-laying system (AGLS) orient the gun for indirect fires with one-mil precision and great speed. AS90 gunners have a direct fire capability, too, and can engage moving targets.

An automatic loader speeds up engagements. Although the loaders in the British Army are a sturdy lot, those 45kg (99lb) projectiles will tire anybody out after a while. The loader makes possible a very intense burst rate. When the AS90 was going through its test programme, 2 of them were able to saturate a target with 6 high-explosive rounds in 10 seconds, or about 225kg (500lb) of steel and high explosive shredding the impact area. The gun's three-shot burst cannot be sustained long, but it can fire 1 round every 10 seconds for 3 minutes, then 1 every 30 seconds after that. BAE

■LEFT: First delivered in the late 1970s, the GCT has become an excellent replacement for the F3. There is an automatic loading system that will help put 8 rounds downrange in 60 seconds.

157

Systems, the present manufacturer, is testing barrel-cooling devices that will allow it to increase that rate, one of several planned enhancements.

Some AS90s will be upgraded with a much longer 52 calibre barrel that will increase maximum range to more than 40,000m (43,745yd). The upgrade will also automate more of the ammunition loading subsystems with a modular charge system built by a South African company. Another upgrade programme modifies the AS90 to operate in Middle Eastern climates and terrain, with protection against blowing dust and dirt, a model known as the Desert AS90. A variant uses a chassis designed and built in Poland, the AS90 Braveheart.

The hull and drive train were designed specifically for this self-propelled system, rather than being converted from another armoured vehicle, as has been the case with other systems. Steel is used for the hull; while not protected against anti-armour rounds, the turret and hull will be capable of withstanding impacts by small-arms fire and medium machine guns, as well as shell splinters.

Power comes from a 492kW (660hp) Cummins diesel engine and automatic transmission. The Desert AS90's drive train has additional cooling and traction features, including a specialized track, for the hot, sandy operating conditions. This version also has a thermal cover for the turret that helps mitigate solar heating. Five men normally crew the AS90: the driver, the commander, the gunner and two loaders.

Chinese 152mm SP Howitzer

China's NORINCO (China North Industries Corporation) makes an amazing range of weapons and ammunition types, and it sells them all to a large number of clients. Among their products are several self-propelled guns designed for export, including this M109 152mm (6.1in) howitzer lookalike.

The turret of this self-propelled gun encloses the breech of a very large cannon, which is a variant on a towed 155mm (6.1in) system offered for sale by the same company, and which is described in the towed artillery section later in this book.

■ LEFT: The *Panzerhaubitze* 2000 combines cutting edge technologies to improve navigation, range, rate of fire, and accuracy. Like similar models, it is extremely expensive.

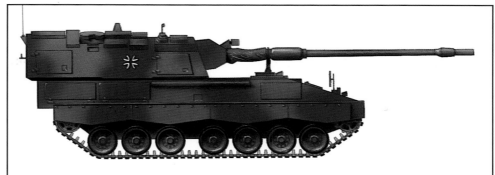

Panzerhaubitze (PzH 2000) 2000

Calibre: 155mm (6.1in)
Weight: 55,000kg (121,254lb)
Length: 7.87m (25ft 10in)
Barrel length: 55 calibres
Effective range: 36.5+km (22 miles)

Elevation: -2.5° to 65°
Traverse: 360°
Muzzle velocity: n/a
Country of origin: Germany

Soltam Rascal Light 155mm SP Howitzer

Calibre: 155mm (6.1in)
Weight: 19,500kg (10.19 tons)
Length: 7.5m (24ft 7in)
Barrel length: 39 or 52 calibres
Elevation: 0° to 65°

Traverse: 30°
Muzzle velocity: n/a
Country of origin: Israel

A power loading system feeds the projectiles and propellant semi-automatically, at all angles of elevation. These projectiles include an extremely wide range of options, including any of NATO's types and NORINCO's own designs. Among these are several types of extended-range projectiles, including a base-bleed version that can hit targets 39km (24 miles) away.

Turret and hull are made of steel rather than aluminum, adding considerably to the system's overall weight. Along with the long, 45 calibre tube, the whole vehicle weighs 32,000kg (70,548lb), about 7000kg (15,400lb) more than the M109. With the tube forward, the NORINCO 152mm (6.1in) self-

propelled gun is a little more than 10m (33ft) long. Like others of its breed, it is also wide: 3.2m (10.5ft). It is about 3.5m (11.5ft) high with the 12.5mm (0.49in) machine gun installed, and about 2.6m (8.5ft) high to the roof of the turret.

The turret will traverse through 360 degrees, but firing is normally done with the tube orientated fairly close to the centreline of the vehicle. Stabilizers at the rear of the hull help manage recoil; however, with the heavy tube at right angles to the hull and with Charge Nine propellant bags loaded, even this heavy vehicle would have problems.

The drive train uses torsion-bar suspension and five road wheels, each with a shock absorber. The tracks are

powered by a drive sprocket at the front and supported by three return rollers, all connected through a manual transmission to a 391kW (525hp) air-cooled diesel engine. NORINCO's published maximum speed for the vehicle is 56km/h (35mph). The fighting compartment is pressurized, and an NBC overpressure system is offered. Also offered is a muzzle velocity sensor that provides the fire direction centre with data on each round fired.

NORINCO would like to sell this system as part of a whole mobile artillery battery package, complete with all the vehicles normally associated with a self-propelled unit: ammunition supply, command post, forward observers and fire direction centre (FDC). The FDC offered includes laser range-finding and communications systems, GPS and computerized data processing equipment.

French Giat 155mm SP Gun Mk F3
Like so many other European nations after World War II, France equipped her artillery formations with the cheap, slightly used US systems that had been declared surplus and were available at deep discount prices. Soon enough, however, tensions with the Warsaw Pact nations inspired France to re-equip with more powerful and modern systems. The French had been using US self-propelled M41s during the postwar years, as an interim measure, but began work on their own design in the 1950s; the mature system was issued to the artillery regiments in the 1960s.

Designated the *Canon de* 155mm (6.10in) *Mlle* F3 *Automoteur*, it was a simple, economical and effective weapon system, but with a few quirks. Ten men are needed to operate the Mk 3, but only two can actually be carried as crew for

■ABOVE: Another self-propelled gun system mounted on a truck chassis is France's *Caesar* 155mm (6.1in). It is designed to operate independently and remote from its fire-direction centre.

any distance. An additional two crewmembers can ride along when it is being repositioned, but most of the detachment must normally ride in another support vehicle.

Like some other self-propelled guns of that era, armour protection for the crew was omitted entirely, and with it any protection against nuclear, biological, or chemical threats as well. Unfortunately for the French, they discovered in Indochina, Algeria and elsewhere that this oversight was more of a problem than expected, and it was a design defect that was wisely not repeated with later self-propelled systems.

But the Mk F3 was quick, powerful and agile enough to provide direct support for armoured and mechanized infantry formations, and the 155mm (6.1in) round was a big improvement on the 105mm (4.13in) projectile. More than 600 have been made, and it has been a fairly popular export product for its current owner, Giat Industries.

The hull is welded steel and the basic layout and power train is quite conventional, based on the AMX-13 tank design; an eight-cylinder 335kW (250hp) gasoline engine propels the F3 to 60km/h (37mph) and a road range of 300km (186 miles). Stowage bins along the hull accommodate basic items of equipment, and a pair of spades at the rear stabilize the gun during fire missions. The driver sits at the left front of the hull and the commander directly behind him, both with a bit of armour protection: 20mm (0.79in) at the front and sides, and 10mm (0.39in) on the top and bottom of the hull.

Ammunition and most of the crew are transported on a VCA tracked vehicle or a 6 x 6 truck. Twenty-five rounds of separate-loading ammunition are normally available on this vehicle, with a mix of high-explosive, illumination, smoke and ER projectiles, propellant bags and fuses. Both French and NATO standard projectiles are used, including a base-bleed high-explosive projectile that can be fired to 25,330km (27,670yd). The cannon itself, designed by Atelier de Construction de Tarbes (ATS), is a bit stubby by modern standards, at only 33 calibres long, somewhat limiting its

range. It will elevate from 0 to 67 degrees and can traverse 30 degrees right, but only between 16 to 20 degrees left. When the US M107 high-explosive projectile is fired with US/NATO Charge Nine propellant, maximum range is just 14,700m (16.076yd); with French propellant, the same projectile reaches 18,000m (19,685yd).

During the 1990s, the F3 was offered with a longer 39 calibre gun and Detroit Diesel engine. Many nations have used it and its supporting ammunition vehicle, including Argentina (which built a dozen of the systems itself), Venezuela, Chile, Morocco, the United Arab Emirates, Iraq and Kuwait, among others.

French Giat 155mm SP Gun GCT

Along with the artillery formations of the United States and other European nations, France began adopting self-propelled artillery systems that provided better protection for the crew and all-round traverse for the gun in the late 1960s. The result was a 1969 requirement for a design to replace all 155mm (6.1in) and 105mm (4.13in) self-propelled cannon then in French service, and the result was the *Grande Cadence de Tir*, or GCT.

This vehicle is a very modern system with some typically French oddities. For one thing, the turret is amidships, rather than at the rear, where most other self-propelled gun designers place it. That is partly because the hull for the GCT is very nearly identical to the one used for France's AMX-30 tank, instead of one designed specifically for this application.

2S7 Self-Propelled Gun

Calibre: 203mm (7.9in)
Weight: 46,500kg (102,300lb)
Length: 13.12m (43.29ft)

Effective range: 30,000m (32,810yd)
Elevation: 0° to 60°

Traverse: 30°
Muzzle velocity: n/a
Country of origin: USSR

Then, too, the turret itself is huge in comparison to that of the competition at 3.25m (10.7ft) high; the M109 (another big turret) is only 2.8m (9.2ft) high at the turret roof. It is also spacious and protects the crew from the usual battlefield hazards, as well as isolating them from the breech and ammunition. The cannon is controlled and loaded automatically by the gunner, who uses a control panel in order to select and to load the rounds.

Forty-two separate-loading rounds are carried in racks at the rear of the turret, with each rack holding six projectiles or propellant cases of the same type. These racks are refilled from outside; armoured panels drop down at the rear of the turret forming work platforms for the crew. All four men can re-stock the racks in about 15 minutes, but two of them can accomplish the job if necessary. Forty additional propellant charges are stowed in a separate bin inside the turret.

The gun itself uses a 40 calibre tube and hydraulically operated breechblock with emergency manual controls. This breech is fed by a fully automatic loading system controlled by the gunner. He can select from one to six rounds of the same or of different types and programme the fire mission to be executed automatically. Once initiated, the system can fire all 6 rounds in just 45 seconds.

The GCT first appeared in Saudi artillery regiments in 1978 and with French units two years later, with five guns to a battery and four GCT batteries forming a regiment. More than 400 have been built, mostly for the French Army, but with large numbers sold to Iraq, Kuwait and Saudi Arabia.

The Indian Army, another set of independent thinkers, requested a design for a self-propelled gun system that would be installed on the Russian T-72 tank hull already built in that nation under licence. The GCT was adapted to this requirement, as were three other gun and turret systems: Vickers AS90, South Africa's LIW T6 and one from Slovakia, the Zuzana. All were 155mm (6.1in) guns and all, it turned out, were too heavy for the T-72 hull and drive train.

German 155mm PzH 2000

The trend towards extremely advanced weapons technology finds a good example in Germany's *Panzerhaubitze* 2000 self-propelled gun system, one of the most advanced and expensive artillery systems available today. The PzH 2000 is the outgrowth of a failed attempt by Italy, the United Kingdom and Germany to share development costs for a new self-propelled gun, the AS70, which collapsed in 1986. Germany then went on to develop its own system, which finally entered service with the German Army; the PzH 2000 has also been accepted by the Dutch and Italian armies. The Greek Army has tested it, too.

The requirements for this system were quite a challenge: fully automatic loading, a high capacity for on-board ammunition storage, advanced navigation technology for autonomous operations, superior ballistic protection against conventional and unconventional battlefield threats and 30km (18.6 mile) range with conventional 155mm (6.1in) high-explosive projectiles. Krauss-Maffei Wegmann (KMW) and Rheinmetall Landsysteme produced the winning design, with the first production contract for 185 systems approved in 1996.

This vehicle is the BMW or Mercedes of the battlefield, with every custom feature and creature comfort. Each PzH 2000 can function as a kind of rapid-response, one-gun battery. Its GPS and related navigation subsystems provide continuous, highly precise position data to the on-board fire-control computer.

The computer, produced by EADS (previously DaimlerChrysler Aerospace) integrates extremely detailed information on the gun elevation, cant angle, meteorological data, propellant temperature, bore-wear, and other variables with position information and target location to compute the fire-mission gun data.

A small radar system measures true muzzle velocity of each round and that data is fed to the computer. The computer can automatically select the ammunition, load it, aim and fire the mission, based on data sent from the fire direction centre by secure radio data link. The commander can monitor the gunner's engagements or take control himself, a handy feature when an enemy tank suddenly appears on the battlefield and a direct-fire mission is required.

Although the 155mm (6.1in) gun meets all NATO standards and can fire projectiles produced by dozens of

■ **RIGHT: Russia manufactures some giant weapons, like the 240mm (9.45in) self-propelled mortar, designated 2S4. It fires just about any kind of round, including nuclear shells.**

suppliers, the PzH 2000 is based on a Rheinmetall cannon and auto-loader with some non-standard features. The tube is 52 calibres long and chrome-plated, and it uses a hydraulically operated breech assembly with manual emergency backup. Chamber temperature is automatically monitored. Each round is fired by a percussion fuse resembling a standard rifle cartridge case; these are loaded automatically from a magazine on the back of the breech containing a total of 32 primers.

One of the key features of the gun is a modular propellant management system based on charge increments, each stored in magazines at the rear of the vehicle where they can be removed by the autoloader. While there is nothing new about variable-charge modules in artillery, the ways in which they are integrated into this weapon are somewhat novel, and the manufacturer and German Army claim improved range and bore life, and faster loading. With a maximum Charge Six, the cannon will range standard projectiles out to a distance of 40km (25 miles).

Five men form the normal detachment: a commander, driver, gunner and two ammunition handlers. Together, the German Army claims they can replace three M109A3G self-propelled howitzers, the system being superseded, because of the speed and efficiency with which the PzH 2000 can put steel on target. That rate is indeed quite impressive; during trials, the system fired 3 rounds in less than 10 seconds and 12 in less than 1 minute. Sustained fire missions can be performed at as many as nine rounds per minute.

At that kind of rate, the ammunition storage bins will quickly be empty, so the PzH 2000 has its own elegant ammunition handling system. Projectiles are loaded in racks at the rear of the turret and are fed mechanically to the power loader. Two crewmen can re-supply the vehicle in about 12 minutes, loading 60 projectiles and 288 propellant modules with a power system that speeds the process compared to other, older self-propelled guns.

The chassis is welded steel plate and is powered by a 745kW (1000hp) diesel

G6 155mm Self-Propelled Gun

Calibre: 155mm (6.1in)
Weight: 47,000kg (103,617lb)
Length: 9.2m (30ft 2in)
Elevation: -5° to 75°
Traverse: 80°
Effective range: 50km (31 miles)
Muzzle velocity: n/a
Country of origin: South Africa

LEFT: This is South Africa's G6 155mm (6.1in) self-propelled gun. It has a range of 50km (31 miles), and can fire its first round under a minute after the vehicle comes to a halt.

engine. Full of fuel, ammunition and crew, the PzH 2000 weighs 55,883kg (55 tons), approximately twice the weight of a M109. Rated speed is 60km/h (37mph) on roads and 45km/h (28mph) cross-country.

Israeli 155mm SP Howitzer

Soltam makes several self-propelled howitzers, but the Rascal is the lightest. At only 10,160kg (10 tons), it will easily cross small bridges that would collapse under heavier self-propelled artillery vehicles, most of which are more than twice as heavy. It is one of the very few such vehicles that can be carried by helicopter and is easily transported by the C-130.

The hull and drive train are welded steel and of unique design, rather than based on an existing tank chassis. One novel feature of the hull is a driver's station that is higher on the tank than normal, with much better visibility. Four men are the normal detachment, with the other three working in a fighting compartment in the middle of the hull. As it is such a light vehicle for such a powerful cannon, the Rascal deploys two spades at the chassis rear when firing.

At the rear is mounted the very light cannon, either 39 or 52 calibres in length. This weapon has its trunnions at the very extreme end on the breech itself and is mounted on a powered turntable that can rotate the gun 30 degrees left or right. Thirty-eight projectiles are carried in exposed racks at the rear of the vehicle, and the propellant increments are stored in an armoured bin positioned just forward of the gun.

The normal range of 155mm (6.1in) rounds are fired, and, with the 52 calibre barrel, Soltam claims a better than 40km (25 mile) maximum range. A 261kW (350hp) diesel engine and automatic transmission will move the Rascal along at good speed for a tracked vehicle, but Soltam is not saying just how fast. A wheeled version has been offered for export customers such as India that are in the market for such systems.

This vehicle is optimized for highly mobile, rapid-reaction operations, not for sustained-fire missions. Loading is manual with powered assistance of a crane and a rammer, but autoloaders are heavier than crewmen, and the projectiles and propellant are delivered to

the breech in the traditional way, with manpower. Modern navigation and communication systems are installed and the Rascal is capable of autonomous operations, linked to its battery fire direction centre by secure digital radio.

Russian 120mm SP Howitzer-Mortar
Based on the BMP-3 hull and drive train, this compact and lightweight self-propelled artillery system is designed for use with light forces. The BMP has been a very successful armoured personnel

carrier in many variations. It is very low, very fast and quite reliable. The common BMP-2 mounts a 76mm (3in) gun in a two-man turret, while the BMP-3 uses a 20mm (0.78in) cannon. Both are infantry fighting vehicles with a primary mission of delivering soldiers close to their objectives under cover of armour. The 120mm (4.7in) Howitzer-Mortar Vena, delivers only artillery rounds.

The cannon is fully automated and can be programmed for elevation and traverse. It will fire both Russian and

some 120mm (4.72in) NATO projectiles to 13km (8 miles) for high-explosive rounds and 7.2km (4.5 miles) for mine dispensers. The tube will elevate to 80 degrees and depress to minus 4 degrees, with full 360-degree traverse. It is a light system – only about 19.305kg (19 tons) – and can easily be transported by aircraft and delivered by parachute.

Russian 125mm 2S25 SPRUT-SD
Another new lightweight Russian self-propelled artillery system is the 2S25.

machine gun. Although the main gun has all-round traverse, its elevation is restricted to a fairly narrow range: minus 5 to 15 degrees to the front.

It is a fast and mobile little package, good for 70km/h (43mph) on paved roads. It is fully amphibious, with waterjet propulsion to 10km/h (6.2mph) afloat. It can even fire its main gun while afloat. Road range is supposed to be 500km (311 miles). Power is supplied by a 380kW (510hp) diesel engine. That light weight and agility comes at a price, however; the 2S25 is very lightly armoured and only protects against 12.5mm (0.49in) heavy machine-gun fire from the front.

French 155mm *Caesar* SP Gun

France has produced another entry in the wheeled self-propelled gun marketplace, a 155mm (6.1in) gun on a standard Unimog 6 x 6 chassis called the *Caesar*. Another speculative design, the *Caesar* has been developed by Giat Industries and Lohr Industrie. As of the time of writing, the French Army has ordered five for evaluation, and Malaysia has also tested the system. It is optimized for solo operations as part of a light rapid-reaction force.

Caesar uses a six-man crew to operate the vehicle and its rapid-fire, auto-loading cannon. The gun system has a cycle time of 5 seconds per round and may fire a 3-round burst in 15 seconds, but its sustained fire rate is 6–8 rounds per minute. A total of 16 rounds are stowed on the vehicle, and consequently the *Caesar* requires the services of a dedicated support vehicle with a large capacity for ammunition stowage.

This system includes all the luxury options: radar-based muzzle-velocity detector, inertial and GPS navigation, an advanced EADS CS2002 ballistic computer and hydraulic gun-laying controls. With these systems, *Caesar* can be in action 60 seconds after arrival at the firing position and it can be gone again in 30 seconds.

One of its primary rounds is the Ogre cargo shell that ejects 63 submunitions for use against enemy armour, artillery and command centres. Six Ogre rounds will saturate a 3 hectare (7.4 acre) area with 378 submunitions, each of which can defeat up to 90mm (3.54in) of overhead armour. It will also fire the Bonus munition with two smart armour-seeking submunitions. Bonus rounds can be fired to 34km (21.1 miles), are dispensed over a target area and use sensors to identify

This light vehicle mounts a smoothbore 125mm (4.92in) gun designed to fire anti-armour sabot rounds, shaped charge HEAT, high-explosive fragmentation and precision munitions. It only weighs 18,289kg (18 tons) and can be delivered by parachute, a skill which the Russians have perfected over many years. Its builders, however, claim that the SPRUT-SD can be air-dropped with the crew inside, but this is something not even the bravest of the US Airborne troopers would want to do!

ABOVE: The Paladin shares the same hull and suspension as the M109, but everything else has been uprated and improved, with better armour and a 39-calibre M284 howitzer.

Three men crew the 2S25: a driver, commander and gunner. The cannon, designated 2A75, has an auto-loading system that eliminates the loader and permits up to eight rounds per minute. Forty rounds are carried for the main gun, plus 2000 more for the 7.62mm (3in)

then attack tanks and similar vehicles from the top with an explosive-formed molten penetrator.

The basic Unimog vehicle has been in widespread use for years and is built around a six-cylinder diesel engine of 179kW (240hp). With the *Caesar* modification, it can attain 100km/h (62mph) and a road range of 600km (373 miles) without refuelling.

Russian 203mm SP Gun M1975

Self-propelled guns do not get any bigger than the S203, So-203 or 2S7, the world's largest. It has been a very successful design, and more than 1000 are reported by Janes' Information Services to have been manufactured. Originally issued to Soviet Front artillery units during the mid–1970s, this gun is yet another option for deep-fire missions.

Everything about the S203 is large. The hull is immense inside and out. Commander and driver sit at the front, with seats and stowage space behind them for the other five men on the gun crew. Hull and drive train are designed specifically for this vehicle and are not conversions from other systems. Shutters can be deployed to cover the windscreen, and the cab's 10mm (0.39in) steel plate provides some protection for the crew against oncoming small-arms fire and artillery fragments.

The tube seems like something left over from a battleship. Official model number for the cannon is 2A44. It is 203mm (8in) in diameter and is 56 calibres long, or almost 13m (43ft) from breech to muzzle. Only four separate-loading rounds are carried on the vehicle itself; another 36 are provided by the

S203's dedicated ammunition re-supply vehicle. The cannon is aimed with the same sights used on so many other Russian cannon, the PG-1M panoramic sight and the OP4M-87 telescope for engaging targets directly. The gunner operates the gun from the left side of the breech using powered controls with manual emergency alternates.

Before firing, the crew deploys a large spade at the rear of the vehicle and makes sure it is well dug in, controlling some of the gun's recoil. Loading is, of course, done with powered equipment that moves the projectile into the breech and rams it home, followed by the cartridge. The propellant charges are typically oversize. The primary zone weighs nearly 45kg (100lb), with additional increments from about 12–25kg (26–55lb).

Only 450 rounds may be fired before the bore has eroded so much that it must be relined, evidence of the extreme power of the weapon's ammunition. Muzzle velocity is 960m/s (3150ft/s), and maximum range with conventional, unassisted rounds is 37.5km (23.3 miles).

Russian 240mm SP Mortar

There are not very many mortars capable of delivering a nuclear projectile, but the Russian M1975 2S4 is one of them. By NATO standards, it is more like a big howitzer than a mortar, and not even the huskiest Russian crewman can 'drop fire' rounds from this hulking weapon. The tube and base-plate are so large that they are mounted to the exterior of the vehicle and operated by hydraulic controls. Even the ammunition (the high-explosive round weighs about 130kg/287lb) is too

heavy to be managed manually, and so is loaded by powered equipment.

The vehicle is based on a modified hull and drive train designed originally for the SA-4 surface-to-air missile system. This hull is fabricated of steel and provides protection against small arms fire and artillery fragments. The drive train includes a 387kW (520hp) V-12 diesel engine, and the 2S4 can operate at up to 60km/h (37mph) on paved roads. Road range is 500km (310 miles) on a full tank of 850 litres (187 gallons) of fuel.

As to be expected, the system has all the agility required for off-road operations in a combat environment. The driver is in the normal spot on the left front, with the detachment commander behind him in a cupola with all-round visibility. At the rear of the vehicle are the crew compartment and ammunition storage bins. Nine men crew the 2S4 when firing, four operating the mortar and another five feeding them with the prepared ammunition.

The heart of the system is the 240mm (9.45in) mortar Model 2B8. This weapon is loaded and operated by the crew from inside the vehicle. Two magazines, each holding 20 rounds, feed the mortar through a hatch in the hull. Loading is accomplished by hydraulically raising the tube up and over the hull where it lines up with the hatch. The selected round is mechanically delivered to the breech and inserted, then the breech closed and the tube returns to its firing position.

When set up for firing, the mortar points away from the vehicle, and the crew aim the tube with their powered controls, from 50 to 80 degrees vertically and 10 degrees left or right of centre. Rate of fire is a minimum of 60 seconds per round.

The basic round for the 2S4 is the 130kg (287lb) 3OF-864 high-explosive fragmentation projectile, with a maximum reported range of almost 10,000m (11,000yd). A larger rocket-assisted high-explosive round nearly doubles both the range and weight of metal on target; it weighs 228kg (503lb) and will reach out to 18,000m (19,685yd). Also fired are chemical, bunker-busting and tactical nuclear weapons, plus a very effective precision-guided munition.

The Russians found this mortar to be extremely useful against the Afghans and the Mujahedeen, particularly when used with the laser-guided *Smel'chak* ('Daredevil') projectile. In June 1985, a Soviet force attempted to engage

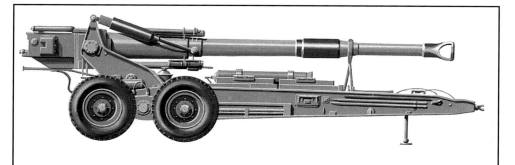

Soltam 155mm Towed Howitzer

Calibre: 155mm (6.1in)
Weight: 9500kg (20,944lb)
Length: 5.18m (17ft)
Barrel length: 32 calibres
Effective range: 23,500m

(25,700yd)
Elevation: -10° to 52°
Traverse: 90°
Muzzle velocity: 820m/s (2690ft/s)
Country of origin: Israel/Finland

Mujahadeen irregulars in the Pandshir Valley and located a fortified enemy position that was, because of the rugged terrain, protected from tube artillery fire. A 2S4 battery commanded by Senior Lieutenant A. Beletskiy was ordered to destroy the stronghold. The unit had both laser range-finders and the then newly-introduced *Smel'chak* round.

Beletskiy 'lased' the target and got a return of 2350m (2570yd). His fire direction centre then computed the solution. One spotting round was fired and the data adjusted, then the *Smel'chak* round was fired. It homed perfectly on the ground laser designator's reflected energy and hit directly on the position. The battery destroyed the target with 12 rounds.

M109A6 155mm Self-Propelled Gun Paladin

Calibre: 155mm (6.1in)
Weight: 28,738kg (63,356lb)
Length: 6.19m (20ft 4in)
Effective range: 30km (18.75 miles)

Elevation: -3° to 75°
Traverse: 360°
Muzzle velocity: n/a
Country of origin: USA

South African 155mm SP Howitzer

In 2000, US Army Chief of Staff General Eric Shinseki astounded the armour and artillery branches of his service with comments suggesting that tracked vehicles would soon be a technology of the past and that they could someday be replaced by wheeled tanks and self-propelled artillery instead. The idea of heavy guns fighting from wheeled chassis is a novel one in the United States, but well established elsewhere, and General Shinseki may well have had something like the South African LIW G-6 in mind.

Wheeled combat vehicles with powerful high-velocity guns have some problems to confront. For one thing, the recoil forces are tremendous, and the simple dead weight of a heavily armoured vehicle helps with stability. So does the huge footprint of a tracked vehicle. It is possible to roll a tracked vehicle on a slope, but it is a challenge.

Not so with a wheeled vehicle, and especially with one the centre of gravity of which is somewhat top-heavy because of a large cannon with its massive breech and mount. During trials of wheeled combat vehicles, the US Army has had several such incidents. Its gunners have also discovered that it is possible to roll such a vehicle right over on to its side when they are engaged in firing at right angles to the hull.

Despite these problems, Shinseki was thinking about the virtues of such systems. They are easier to build, much faster on the road and almost as fast over broken ground, easier to deploy and less complex. That means they are less expensive than a conventional tracked system such as the Abrams. The Russians

have employed a lot of them, although primarily as personnel carriers, and not tanks or self-propelled guns.

These virtues were all incorporated in the South African G-6, a 155mm (6.1in) cannon system that will get up to 90km/h (56mph) on the road and has a range of 700km (435 miles) on the highway. It is a spacious, heavy vehicle with plenty of working room for the crew of six. It weighs 47,000kg (46.25 tons), a bit more than the AS90 and far more than the M109 or GCT. It has all the limitations and virtues of wheeled combat vehicles and can only fire across an 80-degree frontal arc. Its cross-country performance is somewhat more restricted than that of a tracked vehicle, but that does not seem to have been a problem for the South African forces.

The cannon and its associated components are built by South Africa's government-owned corporation, Denel. Vickers manufactures the hull and drive train. Power for the vehicle is supplied by an air-cooled 391kW (525hp) diesel and a manual transmission. Published range is 700km (435 miles) for 700 litres (154 gallons) of fuel, far better economy than a tracked vehicle. South Africa has a reputation for cutting-edge military technology, and that has certainly been the case with its artillery. Their version of the 155mm (6.1in) family of projectiles includes a rocket-assisted design that can engage targets at the amazing distance of 50km (31 miles).

Six men crew the G-6: commander, driver, gunner, loader, breech operator and ammunition handler. They can get their first shot off within 60 seconds of arrival at the firing position and be gone

in just 30 seconds, long before the counterbattery fire begins to impact. The vehicle is well protected against heavy machine-gun and 20mm (0.79in) cannon fire and artillery fragments, far better protected, indeed, than many other self-propelled guns.

Although the G-6 seems to have been quite successful with the South African armed forces, who have ordered 43 of them, the only other nations to employ them are Oman (24 systems) and the United Arab Emirates (78 systems).

US 155mm Crusader M2001

Currently undergoing initial firing trials, the US M2001 Crusader continues the trend towards extremely expensive, complex and automated self-propelled gun systems that are expected to do the work of several traditional self-propelled guns. When the first production systems are delivered in 2006, the US Army will have a reasonably lightweight and deployable howitzer that can put 10 or more rounds downrange in 60 seconds. It will also be able to be refuelled and re-armed in 12 minutes, and, in batteries of six, can put 15.241kg (15 tons) of steel on target in five minutes.

The trend to dedicated support vehicles has been taken to a new level with Crusader. Teamed with an ammunition re-supply vehicle designated M2002, the whole system is intended to be highly automated and autonomous. All ammunition handling is done by powered equipment, with the projectiles and propellant fed to horizontal magazines at the rear of the turret. The M2002 carries 110 rounds and can be re-loaded in approximately an hour.

Only three crewmen are assigned to
serve the M2001 and M2002, and they
control loading and firing operations from
under full ballistic and NBC (nuclear/
biological/chemical) protection. The whole
rearm and refuel process can be done
while under fire or in a contaminated
environment, something previously
impossible for SP guns.

The M2001 carries 48 rounds and can
have the first one in flight within 15
seconds of arrival at its firing position.
Automating the gun-laying process
enables the Crusader to fire an incredible
eight-round TOT mission thanks to a
specialized fire control computer that
generates solutions for each round, then
automatically aims and fires the gun in
sequence. The bore is chrome lined and
has the unusual feature of a liquid-
cooling system, two of the reasons for the
high rate of fire possible.

Both vehicles can be carried as a
single load aboard a C-17 or C-5 cargo
aircraft, but the US Army is going to try
replacing the existing diesel engine with
the same gas turbine LV100-5 to be used
on the M1A2 Abrams main battle tank.
This will have some advantages for the
Crusader, particularly lighter weight and
better acceleration, but at the cost of
lower fuel economy.

US M109A6 Paladin SP 155

The latest version of the M109, the A6, is
the fourth major improvement of the
design, but it is a substantial one and is
essentially a new system. Like other
modern self-propelled howitzers, it is
intended to be able to operate
independently, receiving fire missions
while on the move and executing them
quickly through the aid of computers
linked to the loading and aiming
components of the cannon.

Along with many of the combat
vehicles in the US Army, the A6 is
equipped with digital communication and
navigation systems. The frequency-
hopping SINCGARS radio on the A6
provides greater security than previous
systems, and a new fire-control system
permits almost instantaneous 'hip
shoots'. Within 60 seconds of receiving a
fire mission while on the move, the A6's
systems can automatically point the gun

using position data provided by GPS and
an inertial navigation system. The gun
tube is longer – 52 calibres long – and
can fire more powerful charges than
previous models. The entire turret is
larger and has a Kevlar spall liner to
provide protection against the effects of

enemy fire. It also protects the crew with
an overpressure NBC system that
includes an air-conditioning subsystem
for the four-man crew.

Although not accepted by the US
Army, an Israeli version with a flick-
rammer can fire 3 rounds in 13 seconds.

Israeli 155mm Howitzer TIG 2052

Israel's existence, more than virtually any other nation on the globe, is based on a highly efficient, effective army, with weapons to match. After using surplus World War II artillery for many years, the Israelis have been very successful at developing their own designs, including excellent towed and self-propelled systems produced by Soltam, a private company from Israel which specializes in artillery design.

Beginning in 1980, Soltam developed a lightweight, highly mobile 155mm (6.1in) gun based on NATO standards, but with innovative features then just being demonstrated on Finnish and South African towed cannon systems. One of these was the addition of an engine to provide power to move the howitzer short distances without having to hitch up a

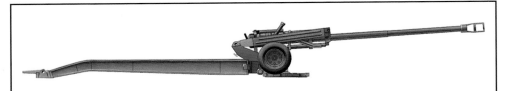

Royal Ordnance Light Towed Howitzer

Calibre: 155mm (6.1in)
Weight: 3810kg (8400lb)
Length: 6.045m (19.83ft)
Barrel length: 39 calibres
Effective range: 24,000m (26,685yd)

Elevation: -5° to 70°
Traverse: 45°
Muzzle velocity: n/a
Country of origin: United Kingdom

towing vehicle, for setting up the gun at its firing position and to energize an auto-loader. Soltam was not the first with an auxiliary engine on a towed howitzer, but it was among the first, and has helped prove the concept. Without such an engine and its associated features, eight men would be required to crew such a cannon. With the engine, only four typically serve the piece, a notable saving in manpower. The current version of this system is called the Towed Independent Gun 2052. It is available in 39- 45- or 52-calibre length barrels and can deliver fire to targets up to 41km (25.5 miles) away.

Power for the gun is supplied by an 59kW (80hp) air-cooled diesel engine attached to the left trail and controlled by a driver with very simple controls. A hydraulic pump drives motors on two wheels, controlled by a joystick. This same pump can actuate a cylinder that spreads the trails and elevates the carriage on its platform. Once the gun is positioned properly for firing, the engine powers the automatic loader, feeding projectiles and propellant at any angle of elevation.

One of the other features that surprised the artillery community when the gun was first introduced is its ability to be 'folded up' for transport. The tube and cradle can be unlocked and then rotated 180 degrees so that the muzzle is pointed back along the trails, making for a much more compact load when the weapon is moved either by air or road. Although Soltam did not introduce this feature, it and several other design firms adopted it very soon after it first appeared. It makes the gun very easy to stow aboard a transport aircraft or to tow in confined areas, where the long tube of a conventional howitzer would not be able to fit.

Under its own power, the TIG 2052 can move along at up to 17km/h (10.6mph) and as far as 120km (75 miles), but such long-range excursions are unlikely. Instead, the gun team can move the gun into its assigned firing position without reliance on other vehicles that might be busy collecting ammunition from a re-supply point or with some other chore.

That long, 52 calibre barrel permits fire missions at extreme ranges, up to 41km (25.5km) with base-bleed high-explosive projectiles. It will elevate to 70 degrees and depress to minus 3, and is equipped with day- and night sights for direct- and indirect-fire missions. Traverse is 39 degrees left or right, although the whole gun can be rapidly pivoted on its pedestal to obtain a full 360-degree field of fire.

British 155mm ULW Field Howitzer

During the 1980s, Vickers Shipbuilding and Defence foresaw a need within both British and US military forces for a lighter version of the 155mm (6.1in) towed gun. Both the US Army and US Marine Corps are huge markets, and the latter has always been tasked with a rapid-reaction mission that put special emphasis on mobility and firepower. The M198 is a hugely successful cannon, but weighs more than 7000kg (15,400lb). While it is air-mobile, only the CH-47 and CH-53 helicopters can move it around the battlefield; it is much too heavy for the UH-60 Black Hawk that provides much of the US Army's lift capability.

Although designed in Britain, the tube and breech components used for tests in the United States have been constructed in the ancient US Army arsenal at Watervliet, New York, with the carriage and mounts built in the United Kingdom. With a promise from the US Army to

consider anything the company developed on its own, Vickers designed in 1987 and built in 1989 a very slender 155mm (6.1in) cannon system.

The new system had been based around standard NATO ammunition and certain criteria. It had to be light enough to be carried as a single external load under the Black Hawk, i.e. less than 4000kg (8800lb); it had to be capable of quick disassembly into components suitable for smaller helicopters; it had to have a range in excess of 24km (14.9 miles); and it had to be extremely stable. Two Vickers prototypes were constructed and tested by both US services, along with lightweight 155mm (6.1in) cannon offered by other vendors.

Essentially, what the US services were looking for was a cannon that had all the performance of the 25-year-old M198, but at about half the weight. Extensive firing trials were held at the Yuma, Arizona, Proving Grounds, then the system was put through all its operational paces with the Marines at Camp Pendleton and Twenty-Nine Palms, California. The Vickers design was selected in 2000 by a joint panel of US Army and Marine Corps officers for adoption, and the UFH will replace all USMC 105mm (4.13in) and 155mm (6.1in) towed cannon during the next few years. US light forces, including airborne and air assault divisions, will use it for general fire-support missions.

The tube and breech are essentially the same as those on the M109A6 Paladin Self-propelled 155mm (6.1in) system, but without the bore evacuator. The tube is 39 calibres, or slightly more than 6m (19.7ft) long, and it is equipped with a large two-baffle muzzle brake. The UFH uses a hydraulically operated screw breech and advanced composite materials, among other novel features.

Much of the cannon is constructed from aluminum and titanium alloys, and this has lightened the system considerably. The whole package weighs about 3700kg (8160lb), light enough that the gun and its entire detachment of seven men can be carried by a single Black Hawk. It has also been carried as an external load by the V-22 Osprey tilt-rotor aircraft and as an internal load by all the US Air Force's cargo aircraft.

■**RIGHT: The British L118 105mm (4.13in) Light Gun is very light, easily transported by medium-lift helicopters like this Puma, which made it a useful weapon during the Falklands War.**

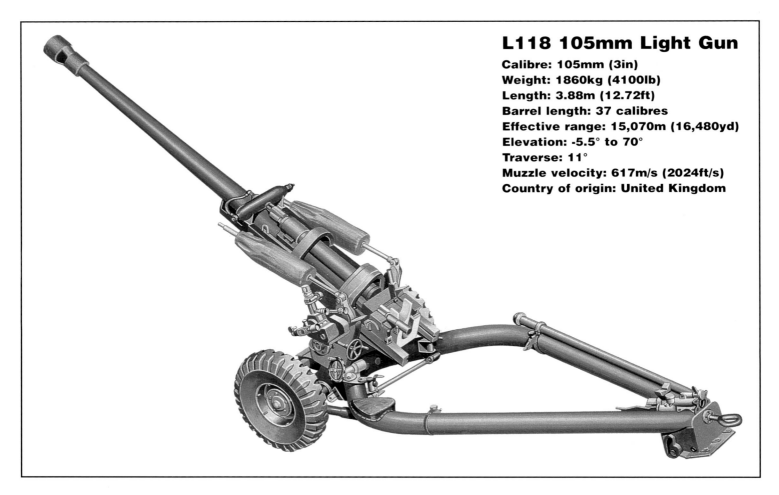

L118 105mm Light Gun
Calibre: 105mm (3in)
Weight: 1860kg (4100lb)
Length: 3.88m (12.72ft)
Barrel length: 37 calibres
Effective range: 15,070m (16,480yd)
Elevation: -5.5° to 70°
Traverse: 11°
Muzzle velocity: 617m/s (2024ft/s)
Country of origin: United Kingdom

This detachment can have the gun in operation in two minutes, and they can pack it all up again just as fast. When the gun needs to be disassembled for transport by smaller helicopters, the detachment can break it down in about 20 minutes. Four outriggers made from lightweight alloy stabilize the cannon; they can be quickly unfolded and the wheels elevated as soon as the gun is brought into action.

The UFH elevates from minus 5 to 70 degrees, and it will traverse 22.5 degrees from the centreline. An automatic feed tray helps the crew put up to four rounds downrange in 60 seconds, out to a range of 30km (18.6 miles) with the rocket-assisted projectile or 24.7km (15.3 miles) with standard rounds. This design folds up in a similar way to the Russian D-30, with a towing eye attached below the muzzle brake, and can be moved by almost any vehicle on the battlefield.

As part of the US Army and US Marine Corps' incorporation of digital information technology, it is planned to give the UFS its own digital fire-control link to the Advanced Field Artillery Tactical Data System (AFATDS). It will also have a powered rammer, a laser range-finder, super-elevation computer

and night sight for direct engagements, as well as its own on-board inertial navigation device to provide precision location data and its own generator. Additionally, it will incorporate a device to measure actual muzzle velocity of each round and the systems to transmit that data to the fire direction centre.

British 105mm Light Gun/US M119
The US armed forces are normally at least as parochial about equipment as any other nation and avoid buying weapons designed elsewhere if there is any alternative. But the US Army has enthusiastically taken to the British L118 105mm (4.13in) Light Gun, which is slightly modified and designated the M119 in US service.

The Light Gun is a product of Royal Ordnance, Nottingham, England, and it was issued to the artillery regiments of the commando and parachute regiments during the early 1970s. The L118 served with distinction during the Falklands War with Argentina, sometimes firing 400 rounds per gun per day. Its light weight – 1858kg (4096lb) – allowed the gun to be moved about by helicopter as an external load, with crew and ammunition inside.

One of the novel features of the Light Gun is its trail, a variation on the old 'box' trail layout which was used and discarded by weapons designers many years ago. The difference this time is that the L118/M119's trail uses thin tubular steel as curved components that provide clearance for the breech during high-angle fire and support during operations, without the weight penalty of conventional trails.

Normally, almost any tactical vehicle, including the HMWWV Hummer, can tow the weapon. When used by the British forces, the L118 is crewed by six men; American versions use seven men (section chief, ammunition team chief, gunner, assistant gunner, driver and two cannoneers, all with the Military Occupational Specialty 13 Bravo). It fires conventional projectiles (high-explosive, HEAT-FS, smoke, illumination, fleshette and many others) to 14km (8.7 miles) and rocket-assisted ones to 19.5km (12 miles).

In US service, as with British, the weapon is issued to light forces: airborne, ranger, air assault, mountain and similar agile units. Six M119s form one battery in the direct-support battalions of these divisions and mechanized infantry divisions of general support battalions.

GLOSSARY

Windage – the space between the outside of the projectile and the surface of the bore. A perfect seal is not practical and some leakage of propellant gasses past the driving band is inevitable.

Cannon, or Gun – the definition of these terms varies a bit. Both refer to a high-velocity, direct fire system. Some definitions require a cannon or gun to use a single propellant charge. This definition certainly fits for the cannons used in tanks like the M1 Abrams but doesn't (with a few oddball exceptions) really apply to most modern towed or SP artillery. Modern artillery systems normally include features of both the cannon and howitzer thanks to the use of semi-fixed (qv) ammunition that permits the same weapon to fire both direct and indirect missions.

Howitzer – an artillery system intended primarily for indirect fire at targets which are out of sight. Howitzers typically have lower velocities than proper cannon, an arcing trajectory, and use semi-fixed ammunition that can be modified to produce a range of velocities and ranges.

Mortar – typically a smoothbore muzzle-loading weapon that delivers indirect, plunging fire. Most mortars elevate from about 40° to about 80°, and a few can even drop rounds on themselves.

Obturation – the process of sealing the breech of a piece, either with a metallic cartridge case, or with a pad that expands under the pressure of propellant gasses.

Direct fire – engaging a visible target, the work of cannon and the direct fire sight

Indirect fire – engaging an invisible target, the work of howitzers and their baby brothers, the mortars

TOT – 'time on target', a method of delivering multiple projectiles to one target at the same moment

FO – 'forward observer', a person on the ground or in the air with direct sight of the target. The FO requests (USA) or orders (UK) fire missions and corrects the fire

FDC – 'fire direction centre', the battery nerve centre where targets are plotted and fire missions designed, the gun data computed and sent to the individual guns

Battery – an administrative term describing one or more guns/howitzers/mortars/rocket launchers functioning as a unit. Normally three or four guns, but as many as six and rarely (800mm 'Gustav' railway gun of World War II) just one. An artillery battery typically includes a headquarters section, fire direction section, forward observer teams, several gun detachments, and an ammunition handling section.

Hip Shoot – an American slang expression for a hasty engagement, particularly when a battery moving across the battlefield is ordered to execute an immediate fire mission

Charge – modern field and heavy artillery use small modules of propellant, normally in fabric bags, that allow each round's ballistics to be customized, from Charge One (low power) to Charge Six or Seven (maximum range and velocity). The FDC specifies the number of modules or increments when issuing fire orders along with type of projectile, fuse setting, elevation and traverse

Deviation – no gun is perfectly accurate and no two free-flight projectiles strike in exactly the same place, except by accident. Wind currents change, the tube warps as it heats up, minute variations from one bag of propellant to another, and many other factors, prevent perfect accuracy in the practical world of artillery. So some variation is expected from one shot to another, and is considered acceptable. The best modern guns claim accuracy of about .5 percent of range, or 50 metres (55yds) at 10km (6 miles).

Organic – refers to any asset 'owned' or permanently issued to an organization; 60mm mortars are typically the only organic indirect firepower available to an infantry company. Organic assets are important because they are readily available to the unit – anything else requires begging and pleading with other units with other priorities.

INDEX